CONTENTS:

Forward and Dedication	03
Herb & Spice blends, Sauces	05
Soups, Chowders & Consommé's	14
Salads & Dressings	56
Comfort Foods	78
Crockpottery	122
Old Fashioned Breads	140
Sandwitches	170
Teas & Special-teas	181
Stones and their vibrations	193
Homemade Happiness (desserts)	195
Celtic Astrology of the Woods	223
Pied Piper Pickles	236
Wine, Mead & Beer	243
Herb Craft - Potpourri, Sachets	252
Essential Oils, Vinegars & Waters	256
Soaps & Lotions	260
Herbal Bathes, Salts and Oils	267
Salves and Ointments	280

Mini Magickal Cookery 288
Recipes that require no cooking: edible play dough, refrigerator pickles, freezer jam/jelly, peanut butter, ice cream, pickles, watermelon soup, hummus, etc.

Comprehensive Herbal 307
Weights and Measures, Medicinal, Culinary, and Magickal uses; of herbs, spices, edible flowers, and other various useables & edibles

Tasseomancy (Tea Leaf Reading) 362
Grimoire (Book of Spells) 389
Sources (List of Magickal Authors) 417

Forward

This book is a compilation of recipes and knowledge sourced from hundreds of pieces of paper and life times of listening and watching my dear Sainted Great-Great Aunts and Grandmothers on down. For I now recognize that the knowledge I had considered common is not common knowledge at all! All Kitchen – Hedge Witches come from different backgrounds and religious beliefs, however we have all been taught to keep ourselves open to the knowledge that lives amongst us all. From the beginning of time we have been world renown as Herbalists, Priests, Spiritualists, Healers, and Wise Woman. We have been known for openly sharing our knowledge, potions, methods, salves, and skills with every needy person we came across. Recipes are only the beginning of our knowledge, for we are well known for our abilities to create everything from love spells and incantations to hexes and invocations; from healing salves and soaps to essential oils and teas! So herein lies bits of our wisdom, fortunetelling skills, and love spells, to enrich your own life with their fun and frolic. Most notably, however I wanted to honor these women that taught me my skills. Thus by composing this book I am in my turn, living my life the way they taught me to, by sharing the information I was born with and given as I was taught and grew, openly with you the reader. In this book the abilities, knowledge and spirits of my generations reside with you and as such will live forever therefore, I just want you to wrap your arms around my sweet dear ancestors and embrace them as deeply as you can.

Dedication:

To the wise woman that came before us, the wise woman we are today and those wise women that we are raising for tomorrow – regardless of our paths or whatever guise we come in - I dedicate this book.

Foreknowledge you will need:

gal   = galleon
4 quarts = 1 galleon
qrt   = quart
32 oz = 4 Cups = 2 pints = 1 quart
 pt   = pint
16oz = 2 Cups = 1 pint = 1 lb (pound)
C   = cup
8 oz = Cup = ½ lb
6 oz = 2/3 Cup
4 oz = 1/2 Cup = ¼ lb
2 oz = 1/4 cup
4 tsp = 1 Tbsp
Tbsp = Tablespoon
tsp   = teaspoon

Spice & Herbal Mixtures

Herbs De Provence

1 Tbsp Rosemary
3 tsp French Thyme
2 tsp Tarragon
1 tsp Basil
3/4 tsp Savory
¼ tsp each: Lavender, Marjoram, Fennel-cracked

Combine in a small glass jar and keep in a cool cupboard; for use on meats, vegetables, soups and stocks – especially great on eggplant, zucchini, poultry and wild meats.

Pot Herbes

3 tsp Parsley
2 tsp Chives
1 tsp Chervil
¾ tsp each: Thyme, Marjoram
3-4 Turkish Bay Leaves

Mix together all ingredients in a small jar and keep in a cool cupboard; flavorful soups, stocks, poultry, chicken fish and vegetables.

Fines Herbes

1 Tbsp French Chervil
3 tsp Parsley
2 tsp each: French Thyme , Tarragon

Combine in a small glass jar and keep in a cool cupboard; for use with egg and fish dishes.

Savor De Mexicano

2 Tbsp Chili pepper, ground
1 ½ tsp Paprika
1 tsp Onion powder
¾ tsp Garlic powder
¾ tsp Cumin seed
½ tsp Salt
¼ tsp each: oregano, coriander, allspice, cloves

Mix the ingredients together in a mortar and grind with a pestle. Add to taco meat, chili or any other dishes that call for a Mexican southwest flavour.

Seafood Transfusion

Cheesecloth
3 bay leaves
2 tsp dried ginger pieces
1 tsp each: brown mustard seed, black peppercorns, dill seed, coriander seed, whole cloves, whole allspice

Tie all ingredients together inside cheesecloth and beat soundly then add to any seafood dish. Take out the cheesecloth before serving.

Asian Five Spice

1 tsp each: cinnamon, cloves, fennel seed, ginger, black pepper

Beat soundly with a mortar and pestle and use for any oriental cuisine

African Curry Tincture

½ C each: coriander seeds, turmeric
¼ C each: fenugreek seeds, cinnamon
1/8 C each: ginger, mustard seeds
1/16 C each: cayenne pepper

Mix together and beat thoroughly with a mortar and pestle; store in a brown glass jar until needed, use to taste.

Italian Transfusion

1 Tbsp Oregano
3 tsp Basil
1 tsp each: Rosemary, Thyme
½ tsp each: Sage, Marjoram

Combine in a small dark jar and keep in a cool cupboard; best in red sauces, white sauces, pizza and squash.

Indian Algamation

1 Tbsp each: Turmeric, Coriander, Cumin
2 ½ tsp each: Fenugreek, Black Pepper
1 ¾ tsp each: Ginger, Mustard, Fennel
¾ tsp each: Allspice, Red Pepper

Combine all ingredients in a small dark jar and keep in a cool cupboard; best with shrimp, vegetables and Indian cuisine.

Cajun Harmony

¼ C Cayenne Pepper
3 Tbsp sugar
2 Tbsp each: Chili Powder, Garlic Salt, Onion Salt
1 Tbsp each: Paprika, Black Pepper, Celery Salt
3 tsp Red Pepper
5-7 Bay leaves

Combine all ingredients in a small dark jar and keep in a cool cupboard; best with seafood, fish, poultry.

Arabian Spice Fusion

1 Tbsp each: cardamom, cumin and coriander seeds
3 tsp each: black pepper, fennel seed
1 tsp each: saffron thread, pomegranate powder
2 dried limes

With a large mortar and pestle crush all seeds and dried limes then add pepper, saffron and pomegranate. Remove to a dark jar in a cool place and use as needed.

Moroccan Spice Blend

3 Tbsp cinnamon
1 Tbsp Caraway seed
1 tsp each: Cumin, Cardamom
1 pinch Cayenne Pepper

Crush seeds and mix together. Keep in a brown bottle in a cool cupboard until needed and use to taste.

English Pudding Spice

2 tsp each: allspice, ginger, nutmeg, clove
1 tsp each: cardamom, coriander
1 stick cinnamon

Grind all ingredients together (except cinnamon stick) and pour into a glass jar with the cinnamon stick and use as needed for dessert recipes. Keep in a cool place.

Guardian Angel Love Spell:

This is a very powerful love spell so make sure you use the right intent – to love and be loved – if done for possession then you will be the one possessed!
Sing or Chant:
Love within me, Love without, Love surround me all about, Love beneath me, Love above, Angels search for my great Love, Bring him here for me to adore, have him knock at my front door!

Repeat 3X whilst turning in a circle, imagine pure love building up inside you and being set free and led by the Angels to return in kind! Add your own touches – like vanilla bean and rose petals for incense, and dance with joy!.

Sauces

Chili Pepper Sauce

10 chili peppers – seeds and stems removed
1 tsp salt
3 garlic cloves - peeled, minced
2 medium onions – peeled, minced
1 Tbsp olive oil
2 1/2 C boiling water
2 to 3 Tbsp flour
2 Tbsp cold water

Split fresh peppers keeping hands away from eyes (or wear gloves for hot). In a medium sauce pan add oil, sauté garlic, peppers and onion 3-5 minutes then mash, add hot water and set to simmer for 10-12 minutes. Thicken like gravy with the flour, mixing to a smooth paste with cold water.

Green Chili Sauce

3 green tomatoes, peeled, seeded & chopped
½ C chopped green onions
1 garlic clove-peeled and crushed
2 Tbsp parsley-chopped
¼ C green chilies-chopped
2 each: jalapenos-pickled, peppers-seeded, minced
1 tsp ground coriander, soak in 1 tsp. water
1/2 tsp salt

Drain the water from the coriander and add it to all ingredients. Chill at least 1 hour before serving. This sauce keeps well in the refrigerator in a covered jar.

Sweet and Hot Chili Sauce

5 Tbsp white vinegar
1 Tbsp crushed red chili pepper
8 cloves garlic-peeled, crushed
Pinch of salt
16 oz whole canned tomatoes (with juice)
12 oz. Red Plum jam
9 oz pineapple juice
4 tbsp apple juice concentrate

Place all ingredients in a saucepan over medium heat. While stirring, let this mixture come to a boil. Reduce heat to simmer and cook for 20 more minutes.

Canned Spicy Chili Sauce

24 large tomatoes-peeled, cored, chopped
3 green peppers-seeded, cleaned-chopped
2 medium onions-peeled, diced
1 to 1 1/2 C red wine vinegar
1 1/2 C. sugar
1 Tbsp each: salt, celery seed
1 tsp each: ginger, cinnamon, allspice, cloves

Combine all ingredients in a medium saucepan over medium low heat and bring to boiling. Then lower heat and simmer until desired consistency, about 1 to 2 hours. Stir frequently to prevent sticking. Prepare home canning jars and lids according to manufacturer's instructions. Pour, hot, into jars, leaving 1/8 inch head space. Adjust caps. Process 15 minutes in a water bath canner. Yields about 8 pints. NOTE: Spicy Chili Sauce is not a bright red color because ground spices are used.

Canned Chili Sauce

6 1/4 lbs ripe tomatoes (peeled and cored)
2/3 cup white onions, chopped
1 1/2 cups sugar
1 teaspoon Tabasco sauce
2 cups cider vinegar
5 teaspoons salt
2 teaspoons ginger
1/2 teaspoon curry powder
2 cups vinegar
1 teaspoon cinnamon
1 teaspoon mustard

Choose fresh, ripe tomatoes without any blemishes. Wash tomatoes thoroughly.
Bring water to a boil and dip tomatoes into boiling water briefly, until skins break and are easily removed. Peel and core tomatoes. Measure out 6 1/4 lbs.
Coarsely chop tomatoes and onions. Combine all ingredients in a large stockpot and simmer for 2 hours. Stir frequently to prevent scorching.
Pour into clean, hot canning jars (pints). Adjust caps and process for 15 minutes in boiling water bath.

Fire Love Spell

Fire encircle my heart with your flame
As I whisper my true love's name
Encircle, encompass all about
Fill his heart within, without
Where upon he hears my voice
True love unselfish bears no choice
But to come unhindered here
Where I will hold forever dear!

Coney Island Style Sauce

1 lb extra lean ground round
1 large onion-peeled, chopped
2 cloves garlic-peeled, minced
6 oz tomato paste
1 C water
1 Tbsp each: sugar, mustard
2 tsp chili powder
1 tsp each: Worcestershire sauce, salt
½ tsp each: cumin, celery seed
¼ tsp black pepper-ground

Brown ground beef in a skillet, adding onions half way through. Add minced garlic when meat is nearly done. Add remaining ingredients; stir well to combine. Simmer over low heat 15 minutes.

Texas Style Hot Dog Sauce

1 lb extra lean ground beef
1 medium onion-peeled, diced
2 tsp each: paprika, curry powder
1 tsp each: oregano, chili powder
¼ tsp red pepper
8 oz tomato sauce
1 qt water

Combine in a large pot on medium heat until it begins to boil, then slow to a simmer for about an hour and mash to desired consistency.

Soups, Chowders and Consommés

Lemon Chicken Consommé

32 oz chicken broth
1 tsp minced parsley
½ tsp each: chervil, tarragon, chives
1 C heavy cream
2 eggs
¼ C lemon juice
1 Tbsp brandy
Serve with: cooked rice or vermicelli

In a large stock pot add the broth, parsley, chervil, tarragon and chives. Bring to a fast boil and then lower heat and simmer for 15 minutes. In a bowl combine the cream, eggs, lemon juice, and brandy – slowly add in 1 cup hot soup and then constantly stirring add it all back to the soup pot. Reheat but DO NOT LET IT BOIL again and serve over cooked rice or vermicelli.

Kiss and Tell (Mistletoe)

Oh Mistletoe, dear Kiss and Tell
Do not bring in 'fore Christmas bells
Every Kiss a berry pluck
To bring the lovers best of luck
But beware dear girl 'tis not a ruse
For under it a Kiss may not be refused!

Spicy Beef Consommé

16 oz beef broth
6 bay leaves
1 tsp crushed mint
2 Tbsp sugar
½ tsp each: cumin, ginger, chili powder, cardamom, lemon juice
Large pinch of saffron
1 C cooked rice
¼ C port wine
2-3 ribs of celery sliced very thinly

In a large pot combine the broth with the bay leaves and bring to a boil over a high heat, covered. Uncover, lower heat and simmer 10 minutes. Remove from heat and steep about 15 minutes then remove and discard bay leaves. Return to low heat uncovered and add mint, sugar, cumin, ginger, chili powder, cardamom, lemon juice, saffron and cooked rice then simmer for 10 minutes. Just before serving add wine and serve garnished with thin slices of celery.

Shhhhh – Ancient Knowledge Grows Here!

Always use cast iron for cooking meats, glass or earthenware for cooking herbs and copper for soups and sauces – Never use aluminum.

Always keep separate knives, pans, cutting boards etc. for vegetables and meat and never mix the two.

Always try and grown your own herbs and vegetables so you can concentrate on their purpose and make them and their magick grow stronger!

Mulligatawny Soup

1 lb chicken meat
¼ C butter
16 oz of each: chicken broth, vegetable broth, crushed tomatoes
1 C each: cleaned and diced onion, carrot and celery
1 green or red pepper cored, cleaned and diced
1 apple peeled and sliced
1/3 C flour
1 tsp curry powder
blade of mace
2 cloves
sprig of parsley
1 tsp each: salt, black pepper
Serve over long grain rice

In a stock pot cook vegetables and cubed chicken in the butter on medium heat until done (about 15-20 minutes) then add tomatoes and put in a blender until liquefied and return to kettle. Add the flour, spices, broths, and simmer 1 hour on low. Serve over boiled long grain rice.

To bring Success into your life

Make sure that the furniture in your home office or office corner is sturdy, steady, and kept clear and functioning. If your finances get stuck – clean your corner and bless it with incense to clear out any blockages. Always keep secret monies stashed inside your desk, a put a picture of yourself in a gold frame on your desk or wall and a bag of pecans to snack on for money and employment.

Imperial Court Soup

16 oz each: chicken broth, vegetable broth
2 C stale bread crumbs
1 C each: celery, carrots - cleaned and chopped
3 Tbsp butter
Sprig of parley
2 cloves
½ tsp peppercorns
½ bay leaf
Blade of mace
Cheesecloth
1 tsp salt
2 boiled chicken breasts, cubed
1/3 cup blanched almonds
1 C cream
½ C milk
2 Tbsp flour

In a stockpot cook the celery, carrot and onion in the butter for five minutes. Add parsley, cloves, peppercorns, bay leaf and mace tied in cheesecloth. Add broths, salt and bread crumbs and simmer one hour on low heat. Remove seasonings. Run the soup through a blender and pour back into pot. Chop the chicken meat and run through the blender and throw into pot. Put almonds into blender and make into a paste. Add to mixture and then slowly add the cream and milk. Reheat and bind with remaining flour and butter cooked together in a roux and serve.

**Hazel is a Holy Tree,
Put on earth for you and me;
Rods made from it uses be:
Water, Metal, and Divination three!**

Vegetable

Artichoke Soup

1 tbsp chicory leaves as garni
1 Tbsp olive oil
¾ lb artichoke hearts (fresh or canned)
1 lb leeks, sliced
1-2 fresh cloves garlic peeled and crushed
2 C each: vegetable broth, soy milk or cream

In a large 3-5 quart pot, sauté on medium heat the leeks with artichoke and garlic in the oil then add the broth and simmer for 10 minutes on low heat. Remove from heat and blend until smooth. Return to pan and continue cooking 10 minutes more and remove to soup bowls and garni with fresh chicory leaves. Serves 2-4 well.

What to Wear/ What it means (Bride & Groom)

Married in white, you have chosen right. Married in grey, you will go far away. Married in black, you will wish yourself back. Married in red, faithful in bed; Married in green, ashamed to be seen. Married in blue, you will always be true. Married in pearl, you will live in a whirl; Married in yellow, ashamed of your fellow. Married in brown, you will live in town. Married in pink, your spirits will sink. Married in gold, true love you'll behold!

Harvest Beet Soup

1 large white onion, peeled and coarsely cut
1 Tbsp butter
1 ½ C each: carrots, celery with leaves, diced
1 green pepper, cored, cleaned, cut small strips
1 small cabbage, shredded
14-16oz each: beets with juice, tomato puree
4 C broth (vegetable or beef) 32 oz
1 C cooked potatoes
Optional: 1 C of either: lima beans, cauliflower, peas, green beans or any leftover vegetable.
2 Tbsp each: red wine vinegar, sugar or molasses
¼ tsp ground cloves
1/2 tsp each: salt, black pepper
Optional: 2 Tbsp Marsala
4 oz of sour cream, as topping

In a large stock pot sauté the onion, carrots, celery, green pepper and cabbage in the butter on medium heat for 5 minutes. Add the beets, tomato puree, and broth and simmer for on low for 1 hour. Add potatoes and any other vegetables you want and simmer an additional 30 minutes. Add the vinegar, sugar, cloves, salt, pepper and simmer and additional 30 minutes. Add Marsala and simmer 15 minutes more and serve with sour cream on top. This soup is great as a main course and reheated the next day.

Shhhhh – Ancient Knowledge Grows Here!

All disease lives in the blood and fat of an animal, therefore it is necessary to trim all fat and soak all meat from 4-24 hours in salt water before using!

Autumn Cucumber Soup: Hot

1 Tbsp butter
½ onion, peeled and diced
1 large carrot, peeled and sliced
4 C chopped celery with leaves
3 cucumbers, peeled, seeded and diced
¼ tsp thyme
½ tsp tarragon
32 oz vegetable broth
2 eggs
1 C heavy cream
2 tbsp dry sherry
1/8 tsp lemon juice
Garnish with sweet paprika and sesame seed

In a double boiler (or two pans, one larger filled with water and one smaller set on top of the water) sauté the onion, carrot, celery in the butter. Add the cucumbers, thyme, tarragon, and broth and cook until all the vegetables are soft. Remove from heat and puree in a blender then put back in the double boiler over the heated water. In a medium mixing bowl beat the eggs with the cream, sherry and lemon juice, gradually add 1 cup hot soup stirring until well blended then add back to the soup continuing stirring until creamy. Serve in bowls sprinkled with sweet paprika and sesame seed.

Shhhhh – Ancient Knowledge Grows Here!

Keep a pot of basil growing in your kitchen as it keeps away all negative spirits. As well stir every thing in a clockwise motion to keep adding your love and devotion to every meal!

Thanksgiving Chowder

1 ½ cups fresh sweet corn or canned
4 C water
4 C of potatoes, peeled and cubed
1 white onion, peeled and diced
1 C cored, cleaned, diced red pepper
4 C scalded milk
8 common crackers
3 Tbsp butter
1/2 tsp each: salt, black pepper
1 small can diced green chilies or ½ cup fresh

In a stock pot sauté onion, red pepper, and corn for 5 minutes on medium heat. Add potatoes and water and bring to a boil. Boil until potatoes are soft and add the rest of the ingredients. And simmer for 20 minutes. Serve hot.

Dear Chicory

Dear Chicory, I gather thee,
In silence for I fear,
I will die soon, before the next moon,
If you are not heeded when near,
I'll cut you, before I am through,
With a knife of pure gold.
Gathered at noon, on July's moon,
Of the 25th, I am told.
For you'll give me, Invisibility,
And every box and door unlock,
And if I need to flee,
From the powers that be,
You'll open for me a rock!

Her Highness' Watercress Soup

32 oz vegetable broth
2 bunches of watercress, cleaned and finely chopped
3 Tbsp each: butter, flour
½ cup milk
1 tsp salt
Garnish: ½ C nasturtium flower petals

In a large stock pot add the butter and wilt the watercress. Add the vegetable broth and stir together the flour, salt and milk and add that in as well. Just before serving float the flower petals on top and serve.

The Wedding Box

Find a large to medium wooden box and begin filling it: to keep each other faithful, tie together the underwear that you both wore on your wedding night; to make sure neither of you ever leaves the other, tie together your socks; to make sure you find each other as becoming as that day your wedding day, include a picture of you both that each of you find beautiful; to ensure sexual prowess – add two acorns, 1 may apple and a container of jasmine; to bind the spell well include three things from each of you. Cross the box 3x singing the spell to each other: Forever our love will ever be; me to you, you to me! And seal it with a kiss! – This spell is very very strong but can be undone in an emergency, uncross everything, cut it all to pieces, burn and bury the remains.

Bavarian Cabbage Soup

1 onion, peeled and sliced
½ shredded cabbage
1 Tbsp butter
¼ C sugar
32 oz vegetable broth
4 oz egg noodles
1 tsp salt
½ tsp each: white pepper, celery seed
1 pinch each: dill, rosemary
¼ C lemon juice
3-4 dashes Tabasco
½ C dry sherry
Garnish with poppy seed

In a stock pot on low heat sauté the onion and cabbage for 30 minutes while stirring occasionally. Turn heat to high until all moisture has evaporated, stirring occasionally, add the sugar and continue heating until it looks glazed or caramelized. Add the broth and lower the flame to simmer for 30-45 minutes. Meanwhile in a separate pot, boil the noodles in salted water and drain. To the soup the salt, pepper, celery seed, dill weed, rosemary, lemon juice and Tabasco and simmer uncovered for 15 minutes. Add the cooked noodles and dry sherry (try ¼ and add an additional ¼ if you find it necessary). Serve hot sprinkled with poppy seed.

To Prevent Poverty

Make a wreath of alfalfa and hang in your kitchen!

Wood Wife Soup

4 large onions, peeled and sliced thin
¼ C butter, 1 tsp dark molasses, 2 Tbsp flour
6 C (48 oz) beef broth
1 C either, cognac, sherry or brandy
Tied together: 1 sprig each: parsley, thyme, bay leaf
6 thick slices French bread
6 oz Gruyere or parmesan or Swiss cheese grated

Cook onions in butter on low heat with molasses until brown and caramelized, about 30-40 minutes. Add flour slowly until thick. Blend in broth and ties herbs then simmer additional 30 minutes.
Meanwhile toast bread slices in the oven on 350 for 10 minutes. Remove soup to 6 individual stoneware bowls, top with 1 slice toasted bread and 1 oz of cheese and bake at 350 for 10 minutes or until browned on top.

Parsley, Sage, Rosemary and Thyme

Parsley dear parsley, grow for me.
For I am as strong as a woman can be;
Sage dear sage, in my garden divine,
I rule my household, keep my husband from wine.
Rosemary, dear rosemary, beside my house,
for I rule it well, not like a mouse;
Thyme dear thyme, by my garden gate,
will ease my discomforts, give courage to my mate!

Old Celt Soup

8 Idaho russet potatoes, peeled and cubed
1 celery stalk, cleaned and diced
1 large yellow onion, peeled and diced
1 C cleaned chopped carrots
32 oz vegetable stock
2 C milk
½ C butter
1/3 C flour
1/2 tsp each: salt, black pepper, parsley and dill

In a large pot (3-5 qrts) put in potatoes, celery, onion, carrots and vegetable stock and bring to a boil on medium heat. Once it is at a boil lower the heat and simmer for 20-40 minutes. Then add the herbs and seasonings and the butter as well. Mix the milk with the flour and add that to the pot and continue cooking for 10 minutes and serve.

A Sneeze Portends

Sneeze on Monday, sneeze for danger
Sneeze on Tuesday, kiss a stranger
Sneeze on Wednesday, for a letter
Sneeze on Thursday, something better
Sneeze on Friday, sneeze for sorrow
Sneeze on Saturday, see your sweetheart tomorrow
Sneeze on Sunday, is terrible and bleak
For the devil will have domination
Over your life for a week!

New Druid Potato Soup

8 large Yukon gold potatoes, cleaned and cubed
1 each: red pepper, yellow pepper, cleaned and diced
1 C cleaned and diced carrots
1 large leek, cleaned and diced
32 oz vegetable stock
2 C of milk
½ C butter
1/3 C flour
1/2 tsp each: salt, crushed red pepper, parsley

In a large pot (3-5 qrts) put in potatoes, peppers, leek, carrots and vegetable broth and bring to a boil on medium heat. Once at a boil, lower the heat and simmer on low for 20-40 minutes or until potatoes are soft. Add the herbs and seasonings and the butter as well. Mix the flour with the milk and add that as well. Continue cooking for 10 minutes and serve hot.

How Many (Sneezes)?

Once for sorrow, twice for joy,
Three times for a letter, four times for a boy,
Five for silver, six for gold,
Seven for a secret never to be told!

Charm for palpitations and hide-bounds

Palpitation and hide-bound, be off (*name*) ribs,
Since Christ, our Lord, spoke truth with his lips.

Cream of Cauliflower Soup

32 oz vegetable broth
1 cauliflower, cored, cleaned and chopped
¼ C each: butter, flour
1 yellow onion, peeled and diced
1 stalk (not rib) celery, cleaned and diced
½ tsp each: bay leaf, salt, pepper
2 cups milk

In a large stock pot on low heat sauté onion, celery and cauliflower in butter until soft. Add vegetable broth, bay leaf and bring to a boil. Combine flour milk, salt and pepper and add to soup. Continue cooking for 10 minutes then remove from heat and take out the bay leaf. Mash soup into a pulp or blend and serve.

Cell Phone Magick

To make someone leave: Joseph Josep Jose Jos Jo J. Or want your kids to call? Try Rob call home. Or add a "Come to Me, Want me Now, or Love me More. How about advancing someone's career? For instance: Brenda's Sign Service. The more they call the better the magick will work – however if they don't call the magick is too strong for them and you need to revise your wording and make the leap of faith easier – especially with the love charms as they can only increase their own feelings.

Forest Mushroom Soup

2 C chicken broths
4 Tbsp butter
1 small onion-peeled, diced
8 oz fresh mushrooms-cleaned, sliced
2 tsp flour
1 C each: whole milk, heavy cream
1 Tbsp dry sherry
½ tsp each: salt, black pepper, nutmeg-ground

In a large sauce pan or Dutch oven, melt butter on medium low heat and add the onion and mushroom, cooking until softened. Add the broth and bring to a slow boil, stir in flour slowly and maintain a slow simmer for about 1 hour. Stir in milk, cream and sherry but do not let boil. Add seasonings and adjust to fit your taste. Cool and refrigerate in a closed jar for 1 day to help flavour to develop. Gently rewarm before serving – can be used as a flavouring or sauce as well.

Charm for Sickness

Let the sick person, without having conversed with anyone, put water in a bottle before sunrise, close it up tight, and put it immediately in some box or chest. lock it and stop up the keyhole; the key must be carried one of the pockets for three days, as nobody dare have it except the person who puts the bottle with water in the chest or box.

Devonshire's Best Chestnut Soup:

50 large chestnuts, scalded, peeled and scraped (or boiled and mashed)
1 medium yellow onion, peeled and minced
1 Tbsp sugar
1 tsp each celery salt, white pepper
2 C milk
¼ C butter
¼ C flour
1 tsp each: salt, black pepper

With a mortar, bruise the chestnuts and place the pulp in a large pot with the butter and onion and simmer for 15 minutes. Add the sugar, seasonings, milk, and flour mixed and simmer an additional 30 minutes and serve hot in bowls.

Fortunetelling

Spring: The day in which you find the first spring flower portends how you will spend the rest of your year – for instance:

Monday is good fortune,
Tuesday your endeavors will succeed,
Wednesday is for marriage,
Or a baby if you please,
Thursday warns small profits,
Friday is for wealth,
Saturday warns misfortune,
To others warns poor health,
Sunday is the day you seek,
For it portends excellent work for weeks!

Poor Man's Stew

2 Tbsp butter
1 medium yellow onion, peeled and chopped
1 bunch of celery, with leaves, cleaned and diced
32 oz vegetable broth or chicken broth
3 C soft peanut butter
1 C heavy cream
1 tsp cinnamon
2 Tbsp tomato puree
3 drops of lemon juice
Dash of thyme
¼ C dry sherry
Pinch or two of sugar
Garnish sparingly with fresh tarragon or parsley

In a large cooking pot sauté butter with the onion and celery for 8-10 minutes or until soft then add the broth and remove from heat. Puree in a blender with the peanut butter and return to the saucepan. In a medium mixing bowl whip together the cream, cinnamon, tomato puree, lemon, and thyme and simmer on a low flame until the soup is thick and hot stirring often. Add the sherry and a pinch or two of sugar and serve with tarragon or parsley sprinkled sparingly on top.

To Season Cast Iron

Make a rub of olive oil, garlic and salt and rub your cast iron thoroughly. Then bake at 325 for 5 hours or burn it in a bon fire. Keep handy this mixture so when you must clean you cast iron you can rub it inside again and fire it dry on the stove – never towel dry. Be careful to never put the mix on the outside after the first time as the pan will catch fire!

Mashed Jack Soup: Cold

6 C fresh pumpkin, peeled and cut in cubes
1 C carrots, peeled and shredded
1 tsp molasses
6 shallots, peeled and diced
3 cloves garlic
4-5 C apple juice
2 sprigs thyme
1 tsp ginger
½ tsp each: nutmeg, cinnamon
¼ tsp each: cloves, cardamom, lemongrass
4 oz gruyere cheese, shredded
3 C cream

In a large pot add pumpkin, molasses, carrots, shallots and garlic with the apple juice and bring to boil on medium heat then turn to low and simmer 20 minutes. Remove from stove and puree in the blender. Put in a large serving bowl and mix cream and gruyere and let set 10 minutes then refrigerate until cooled and serve.

To Bring Prosperity

Attach a string to a lemon, and begin sticking it with colored (not black) stick pins in a circular pattern ending with a lucky star or sacred triangle or golden rectangle on the bottom to catch it all. Singing: Pretty golden lemon of mine, bring good fortune of every kind, as I decorate your rind, let this spell be cast and bind. Hang it in your kitchen in the eastern most corner to catch the morning sun.

Spicey Duergar Gazpacho: Cold

40 oz tomato juice
4 Tbsp balsamic or apple cider vinegar
1 Tbsp Worcestershire sauce
5 drops Tabasco sauce
3 Tbsp lime juice
1 tsp each: celery salt, black pepper, red pepper
1 C diced each fresh raw hard vegetables: yellow pepper, green pepper, baby carrots, baby zucchini, baby yellow squash and 1 bunch green onions OR 3 shallots OR 1 leek
1 C diced each: fresh raw soft vegetables: tomatoes, Persian cucumbers
1 can 15 oz sliced black or green olives, sliced
1 C dry roasted peanuts OR 1 can 15 oz garbanzo beans, drained
1 C sour cream, Optional

In a 3-5 quart pot over medium heat; add the tomato juice, balsamic vinegar, Worcestershire, Tabasco sauces and the hard vegetables and bring to a boil for 10-12 minutes and turn off. Meanwhile clean and dice all soft vegetables, olives and nuts/bean and place in a large 5 quart serving bowl. Add lime juice, salt, to the vegetables and stir. Pour the hot broth mixture over the vegetables while still hot and stir. Place in the refrigerator until cold, about 4 hours. May be served with a spoonful of sour cream per bowl. This makes a great diet soup and cures any bowel dysfunction as well. Serves 6

Positive energies are created with meditation and prayer, a kitchen witch uses them often and with great devotion and care!

Midsummer Soup

5 Persian cucumbers, peeled and shredded
8 small radishes, cleaned and shredded
3 scallions, tops cut off, sliced
2 Tbsp olive oil
1 clove garlic, minced
3 Tbsp each: fresh mint, dill
1 C cold plain yoghurt
1 C buttermilk
½ C sour cream
½ C whipping creams
2 Tbsp lemon juice
½ tsp salt, white pepper

In a saucepan on low heat sauté cucumbers, radishes and scallions in oil until soft with garlic and set aside and cool. When cooled, combine in a stoneware bowl all ingredients and blend well. Chill at least 1 hour or over night and serve.

S D P N Q C N
D P N Q C N
P N Q C N
N Q C N
Q C N
C N
N

Written on a piece of parchment and carried makes evil lose its way, keeps all ghosts and spirits at bay, breaks all spells of both Wizard and Faye, and sends all attachments on their way!

Winter Broccoli Soup:

1 large celery rib, thinly sliced
1 medium bunch broccoli, florets only, coarsely chopped
1 medium onion diced
2 small parsnips, peeled and sliced
4 C chicken broth or vegetable broth
Salt and pepper to taste
2-3 tsp lemon juice
Garni: fresh parsley

In a deep saucepan, place celery, broccoli, onion, parsnips, broth and pepper. Bring to boil over medium heat. Reduce heat and simmer until vegetables are very tender, about 20 minutes. Uncover and let cool 10 minutes. Mash or puree in a blender until velvety smooth. Reheat when ready to eat.

Winter Solstice Stew

4 C cauliflower pieces
2 C water
8 oz cream cheese cubed
5 oz American cheese spread
½ C potato flakes or buds

Combine cauliflower and water in a saucepan and bring to a boil. Drain, flake and set aside. Heat cream cheese and cheese spread in a large pot on low until almost melted. Add cauliflower and stir until dissolved or use a potato masher. Add potato flakes and simmer for 10 minutes and serve.

Seafood

Enchanted Siren Chowder:

3 ½ C shucked clams, drained
2 C peeled, diced shallots
5 Potatoes, peeled and cubed
1 C celery, cleaned with leaves and chopped
2 Tbsp flour
1 1/2 C milk
1 ½ C whipping cream
3 Tbsp butter
3 slices Apple smoked turkey bacon, chopped
4 8oz bottles of clam juice
1/2 tsp each: salt, white pepper, parsley

In the bottom of a pot, sauté on medium heat, the shallots and celery with the bacon until bacon is crisp. Add the flour, clam juice and potatoes and simmer for 20 minutes. Stir in seasonings, clams, milk and cream and bring just to a boil and turn off heat – do not let boil. Garnish with parsley and serve hot.

Counting Crows

One is a bad omen,
Two and your luck will tend
Three and your health will mend,
Four you will find wealth again,
Five and sickness will not end,
Beware six for a death portends!

Black Water Gumbo

2 C peanut oil
3 C flour
2 large onions, peeled, diced
3 C okra, cleaned, chopped
2 Tbsp butter
16 oz stewed tomatoes
3 cloves garlic, peeled, crushed
32 oz each: water, clam juice
1 lb each: sausage, no casing, shrimp, medium, cleaned, deveined, no tails
1 lb each: scallops, crab meat, catfish
1 tsp each: thyme, basil, cayenne, sage, celery seed, paprika
1 bay leaf
Garnish: 6-8 green onions, ½ C chopped parsley

Serve with hot cooked long grain rice

Make a roux by cooking on medium heat a roux of the flour and peanut oil until browned to your desire (5-50 minutes). Meanwhile cook okra and onions in butter until soft. In a large pot mix the roux with the okra mixture and add all the other ingredients and simmer 15 minutes, add garnish and stir and then simmer an additional 15-20 minutes and serve hot with rice.

To see if your soul mate is near to you, listen for the doves coo, surely it will be the next person to stop by or speak to you!

Kobold Stew

1 C each: carrot and onion, peeled and chopped
½ C Olive oil
2 lb each: New England Bay Scallops, lobster tail cleaned with shell off
2 lb medium shrimp cleaned, deveined, shell off
16 oz Crushed tomatoes
2 bay leaves
3 cloves garlic, peeled and crushed
½ C pimiento
¼ C snipped parsley tops
1 Tbsp each: salt, lemon juice, honey
½ tsp saffron, black pepper, crushed red pepper
16 oz clam juice
16 oz vegetable broth

Serve with Fresh Bread

In a large kettle, cook onion, carrot, and garlic until tender over medium heat. Add lobster, tomatoes, bay leaves and broth and bring to a boil. Cover and simmer for 15 minutes on low. Add shrimp, scallops, clam juice and everything else and simmer for anything 15-20 minutes longer and serve hot.

**Kitchens and Gardens are sacred spaces
And must be tended with care
Be most prudent with your behavior
And only plant good thoughts there!**

Mini Money Magick Spells

Keep a green glass mason jar in your cupboard and fill it with your spare change.

Always fold your money towards you to keep it coming back to you.

On the new moon hang green grapes in cheesecloth at every door and window.

Carry acorns or nutmegs in your purse, your pocket or set them on your windowsills.

Add spare change to your window sills on the new moon.

Hang a horseshoe above your doorway pointed up so the luck doesn't run out.

Leave a house through the same door you came in so you take your luck with you instead of leaving it behind.

If a black cat comes to you it brings fortune, accept it with open arms (better yet own one!) however if it turns and goes away it takes your fortune with it!

To be Momentarily Invisible

Some of the simplest spells work the best. For this one simply say "Turn their eyes away from me, make it so they can not see" while moving your power hand in a circular clockwise motion and the person or persons you want to avoid will be momentarily diverted.

Poultry

Stone Soup

1 lb of chicken, boned and skinned
1 Tbsp to 1/3 C olive oil
28 oz of chicken broth
28 oz of vegetable broth
1 C chopped carrots
1 C chopped celery
1 medium onion peeled and diced
½ tsp each: cumin seed, crushed red pepper, fresh grated ginger root, black pepper
3-5 cloves fresh garlic peeled and crushed
1 Tbsp dark raw honey
Variations: 5 large red potatoes peeled and diced or 8 oz egg noodles or ½ cup long grain white rice and ½ cup long grain wild rice or 1 cup barley

In a large 3-5 quart pot add in broth, vegetables and herbs and cook at a medium heat until boiling. If chicken isn't precooked, then pour 1/3 cup olive oil in a skillet and cook thoroughly about 10-15 minutes on each side and cube into bite size pieces otherwise cube chicken and add 1 Tablespoon of olive oil to the pot. At boiling point of pot add variations and boil 10-15 minutes, stir and then turn heat to low and simmer for another 10-15 minutes and add honey: Serves 4-6 people well.

Silverware and the Visitor

If a knife falls a gentleman calls
If a fork calls a lady calls
If a spoon falls a baby calls.

Red Hen Tortilla Soup

¼ C canola or grape seed oil
4-8 soft corn tortillas cut in half and then in strips
1 lb boneless skinless chicken breast
28 oz each chicken broth, vegetable broth
1 package taco seasoning
1 tsp each: cumin seed, black pepper
1 large can chopped green chilies
8 oz of sweet corn niblets
2-3 fresh avocados
1 Tbsp lime juice
1 bunch of green onions cleaned, roots off and chopped through to ½ greenery
1 large heirloom tomato cored and cubed
½ bunch of fresh cilantro chopped
1 oz package sour cream

In a large cast iron skillet pour oil and brown and stir tortilla strips until hardened and browned and set aside on paper towel. If chicken breast isn't precooked, brown in a cast iron skillet on both sides about 10-12 minutes and cube into bite size pieces. In a large 3-5 quart pot on medium heat bring broths, chicken cubes, herbs and seasonings, green chilies, and corn to boil and cook 5-10 minutes. Mean while peel, seed and cube the avocado and spritz with the lime juice and set aside in a bowl. In another bowl place the tomato, green onions, and cilantro, mix and set aside. When all is ready to serve put in individual bowls as follows: place a small handful of tortilla strips and a ¼ cup of avocados, and 1 ½ teaspoon of sour cream at the bottom of the bowl, then 1 ½ ladles of soup over the top and finish with the tomato and herb mixture on top and serve: Serves 5-8 well.

Hand Fasting Soup

1 lb ground turkey, kosher is best
4 0z grated romano and parmesan cheeses
1 tsp each: salt, black pepper
1 egg
28 oz vegetable broth
28 oz chicken broth
1 10 oz bag star pasta
4 – 6 oz frozen spinach
1 yellow onion peeled and diced
10-15 baby peeled carrots diced

In a large 3-5 quart mixing bowl put together the ground turkey, cheeses, herbs and egg and stir well. In a large cast iron skillet on medium heat brown the turkey mixture for about 10-15 minutes and cut into bite size pieces. In a large 3-5 quart pot add broths, spinach, onion and carrots and bring to a boil. Add star pasta and continue boiling for 8 minutes then turn heat to low and simmer. Add the turkey mixture and cook 10 minutes more. Serves 5-7 well.

The Elements, Directions and Arch Angels

Earth: Yellow Square, North, Uriel
Air: Blue Circle, East, Raphael
Water: Silver Crescent, West, Gabriel
Fire: Red Triangle, South, Michael
Spirit (Ether): Black Egg, Universe, Holy Spirit

Savory Soy Ginger Soup

¼ C 1st cold pressed extra virgin olive oil
1 lb boneless skinless chicken breasts
28 oz vegetable broth
28oz Trader Joe's Soy ginger broth
1 Tbsp dark raw honey
1 tsp each: sea salt, black pepper, crushed red pepper
2 C chopped each: baby peeled carrots, celery (cut at angle), whole sugar snap peas (ends off), crimini mushrooms & scallions (sliced)
8 oz linguine or other long pasta

In a cast iron skillet on medium heat, pour the olive oil and cook the chicken breasts for 10-15 minutes on each side or until done and cut into bite size pieces and set aside. In a large 3-5 quart pot add broths, honey, herbs, and vegetables and cook on medium heat until boiling then add pasta broken in half and continue cooking for 8-12 minutes until pasta is al dente: Serves 4-8 well.

The Elements, Seasons, Trees and Invocations

Earth: Summer, Oak, Adonai Ha Aretz
Air: Spring, Aspen, Shaddai El Chai
Water: Winter, Apple/Willow, Elohim Tzabaoth
Fire: Autumn, Almond, Jehovah Tzabaoth
Spirit (Esther): Cycles, Hazel, Eheieh Yeheshuah

Pho Pot Stew

1 lb Chicken/Beef on bone, skin removed
4 oz Rice noodle
1/4 tsp each: Ginger, Anise, Cinnamon, Cloves, Cardamom
1 small Onion peeled and diced
32-64 oz water or vegetable broth
2 oz Bean sprouts
½ tsp Coriander leaves, Basil
3 tsp fresh squeezed Lime juice
4-8 Green onions cleaned and chopped

In large stock pot or crock pot on low, cook chicken of beef for several hours in water or vegetable stock until the meat falls from the bone then check broth level and add accordingly. Remove all the bones and add the ginger, anise, cinnamon, cloves, cardamom and diced onion and bring to a boil. When it hits a boil add the rice noodles and cook for 8-10 minutes or until the noodles are soft. Add remaining ingredients and serve immediately.

Morning Angels

Dreams in the morning
Heed the Angels warning!
This is a very important thing to do
For this is when the Angels speak to you!
If they tell you stop don't go
Heed their words for they know!
If they tell you quiet be still
Heed their whispers until…
They tell you go on now grow
For the angels Always know!

Beef

Friendship Chili

1 Tbsp teriyaki sauce
1 Tbsp Kansas city barbeque sauce
1 lb ground round or kosher ground beef
1/3 C of 1st cold pressed extra virgin olive oil
1 medium yellow onion peeled and diced
1 15-16 oz can of refried black beans
2 cloves of garlic peeled and crushed
8-12 oz of jarred salsa – your choice
1 tsp each: cocoa powder, cumin seed, dried cilantro
½ tsp each: cayenne pepper, red pepper, chili powder
1/8 tsp each: cinnamon, ground cloves
1 can each: chili beans, kidney beans, drained
8 oz shredded cheddar cheese
1 medium red onion peeled and diced
1 bag of tortilla chips

In a large cast iron skillet brown ground beef with the sauces on medium heat about 10-15 minutes until done. In a Big Pot about 3-5 quarts on medium heat pour olive oil and cook yellow onion about 5 minutes, then add refried beans and stir. Add garlic, salsa, herbs and stir. Continue by adding beans and stir. Heat until boiling then turn to low and simmer for 20 minutes Top with cheddar cheese and onions and serve with tortilla chips. Serve 6 well or works as a dip for gatherings.

Fire Signs: Aries, Leo, Sagittarius
Earth Signs: Taurus, Virgo, Capricorn
Air Signs: Gemini, Libra, Aquarius
Water Signs: Cancer, Scorpio, Pisces

Sky Fire Chili

1 lb bacon
2 lbs dry pinto beans
1 large onion sliced
4 cloves garlic sliced
2 Ancho peppers
1 Tbsp chili powder
3 qrt water
2 ½ tsp salt
1 lb can tomatoes
12 Serrano peppers – either fresh or canned

Remove the fat (rind) from the bacon and cut into ½ inch squares and set aside. Put rind, beans, onions, garlic and Ancho peppers into a pot. Add water and bring to a boil, then lower flame, cover and let the beans cook gently for 1 ½ hours. Add salt and cook uncovered for 15 minutes. Dice remaining bacon, and fry in a separate pan until slightly crisp, add tomatoes and remaining ingredients to bacon. Cook mixture over a medium flame for 10 -15 minutes. Skim fat and add the mixtures to the beans for 45 – 60 minutes or until beans are tender. Great served with corn bread.

Mandrake:

Mandrake oh mandrake, how lovely and fair!
Prevents sterility, and causes the barren to bear;.
Compels true love, and promises visions rare,
Brings prosperity, and darkens the hair,
And all of this with so little care!

Farmhouse Soup

1/3 C 1st cold pressed olive oil
1 lb ground round, cooked
1 13-16 oz can green beans
1 13-16 oz can yellow beans
11-13 baby peeled carrots, diced
2 small or 1 large yellow onion, peeled and diced
½ stalk of celery, cleaned and chopped
3-7 red or white potatoes, peeled and chopped
1 C 15-24 oz crushed or diced tomatoes OR marinara sauce
26-32 oz vegetable broth
1 Tbsp each: raw honey, worchestershire sauce
1/2 tsp each: red pepper, basil, black pepper, salt

In a cast iron skillet brown hamburger over medium heat until fully cooked – about 10 minutes on each side and drain if necessary then set aside. Meanwhile, In a large 3 ½ - 5 quart cast iron pot place the olive oil on medium heat and sauté the onions, carrots and celery. Add the remaining ingredients and bring to a boil over a medium heat. Then lower heat and simmer for at least 20 minutes and serve.

Apple Harmony Spell

In a round bowl put an odd number of red apples and place in the center of your dining table or house. Write the name of the persons having issues with on a piece of parchment in red ink and place it under the apples for nine days. Soon harmony will once again restored between the two – whether it be between two friends or a relative and you!

Mountain Barley Soup

1 ½ lbs beef round steak, cut into strips
1/3 C olive or grape seed oil
4 C water or vegetable broth
2 C cleaned, chopped celery
2 C cleaned, sliced mushrooms
1 C cleaned, sliced carrots
1 medium peeled and diced white onion
16 oz crushed tomatoes
1/2 C quick barley
1 tsp each: salt, pepper
1 bay leaf (remove after cooking)

In a large stock pot cook steak in oil on medium heat until done, about 10-15 minutes. Add all ingredients except barley and bring to a boil. Once boiling add barley and boil 10 minutes then turn to low and simmer and additional 20 minutes. Remove bay leaf and serve.

The Orders of the Kabbalah

Metatron: Crown, Head, Violet, Rhodonite
Ratziel: Wisdom, Third Eye, Indigo, Sodalite
Tzaphqiel: Understanding, Throat, Blue,
      Turquoise
Tzadqiel: Mercy, Heart, Green, Adventurine
Khamael: Strength, Solar Plexus, Yellow, Jade
Mikhael: Beauty, Sacral, Orange, Carnelian
Haniel: Victory, Base, Red, Jasper
Shekhinah: Kingdom, Spirit, White, Crystal

Prairie Beef Stew

1 ¼ lb beef, cut into bite size cubes
3 lb red potatoes, peeled and chopped
1 large yellow onion, peeled and chopped
2 large carrots, peeled and sliced
¼ C olive or grape seed oil
¼ stick butter
6 cloves garlic, peeled and crushed
6 C beef broth
1 C dark beer
1 C red wine
2 Tbsp tomato paste
1 Tbsp each: sugar, thyme, worchestershire sauce
2 bay leaves
1/2 tsp each: salt, pepper, parsley

In a large cast iron skillet, fry the meat in the oil until done (10 minutes each side on medium). In a large stock pot sauté the onion and carrots in the butter for 5 minutes on medium then add the potatoes and simmer 5 minutes more. Add the meat to the mixture and also add the bay leaves, broth, beer and wine and simmer uncovered for 20 minutes. Remove the bay leaves and add the garlic, tomato paste, sugar, thyme, worchestershire sauce, salt, pepper and parsley then bring to a boil, lower heat and simmer for an additional 20 minutes and serve.

To Sell your House

Place anything that moves in front of it to draw attention to it – wind chimes, wind sock, pinwheels and soon you will the universe and many buyers will come running to your door!

Elf Banishing Stew

30 oz canned lentil beans
1 lb beef salami, chopped in bite size cubes
1/3 C Olive oil
1 large onion, peeled and diced
16 oz can crushed tomatoes
16 oz vegetable broth
1 C each: carrots, celery, spinach - chopped

In a stock pot put the olive oil, onion, carrots, and celery over medium heat for 5-8 minutes, add the spinach for 3 minutes, add the kosher salami and heat an additional 5 minutes then add the broth, crushed tomatoes, lentil beans, and seasonings and bring to a boil then simmer on low 10-20 minutes and serve hot.

Image Magick

Image magick is probably the easiest and oldest form of magick there is! Simply sit in a quiet and protected place with a potato in one hand and a pen and a small knife or other carving tool. Think about what you desire – be it love or money or friendship.

Next simply write and carve your desires into your potato, carefully and with great purpose.
Concentrate fully on what you want and be as exact as possible and then plant your potato, water it and watch it grow!

Mountain Bean Soup

2 cans cannellini beans
3 cans Italian style tomatoes
4 oz very small pasta
1 onion, cleaned and chopped
1 large garlic bulb, peeled and crushed
½ celery bunch, cleaned and chopped
1 C carrots, cleaned and chopped
¼ C cleaned and chopped fresh basil
¼ C shaved Romano cheese
1 tsp each: salt, black pepper, crushed red pepper

In a large pot add all ingredients except pasta and bring to a boil on medium heat. Once the soup is at a boil add the pasta and cook 10-15 minutes and serve.

Moon Blessed Water

You will need a scrying bowl and some natural water, be sea, lake, rain, dew or spring water and your special charging stone.
If you do not have a scrying bowl a mirror underneath a crystal or glass bowl will do. Place in the open on the full moon and chant or sing:
Lady of Light so beautiful and bright, charge and bless this water tonight! Repeating until you feel the charge you send up come back to you.
Keep your water in a green glass jar for your own personal use.

Gypsy Sea Spell:

To be done on the solstice or full moon by the sea as the tide is coming in. Write these words in the sand, light a candle, incense, bury 3 eggs and watch as your poverty melts away and your prosperity increases with every wave – feel the change coming on and filling you up – try to put the last line far enough away so it doesn't get taken as well.

```
       POVERTY
       POVERT
       POVER
       POVE
       POV
       PO
       P
       PR
       PRO
       PROS
       PROSP
       PROSPE
       PROSPER
       PROSPERI
       PROSPERIT
       PROSPERITY
```

Pork

Fire House Stew

8 bacon strips, diced
2 ½ lb stew meat, cubed
42oz can stewed tomatoes
16 oz can tomato sauce
2 C sliced carrots
1 C each :chopped Serrano or hot chili peppers, chopped celery
1 medium onion, chopped
½ C chopped green pepper
¼ C minced fresh parsley
1 Tbsp chili powder
1 tsp salt
½ tsp ground cumin
¼ tsp each: red pepper, black pepper

Cook bacon in skillet on medium heat until crisp, drain and set aside. Brown beef in bacon drippings in the skillet on medium heat until done - about 15 minutes. Combine all ingredients in a large pot and simmer until ready to serve – about 40 minutes.

Apple Love Spell

Take a red apple and your knife and peel it slowly and deliberately into one long slice. Now throw it over your left shoulder, and if it stays in one long slice it should reveal the initial of your very own true love.

Torremolinos Soup

4 celery ribs, cleaned and sliced
1 onion, peeled and diced
2 Tbsp olive or canola oil
16 oz canned tomatoes
1 C each: tomato puree, chopped parsley
1 lb chopped hot and spicy sausage
32 oz vegetable or chicken broth
3 bay leaves
1/8 tsp thyme
½ tsp basil
3 Tbsp sugar
Large pinch of saffron
2 C mashed potatoes
½ C Madeira wine
6 hard boiled eggs

In a large pot on low heat in oil, celery and onion until tender. Add the tomatoes, tomato puree, sausage and simmer for 10 minutes. Add the broth, bay leaves, thyme, basil, parsley, sugar and saffron and simmer for 30 minutes and remove bay leaf. In a mixing bowl blend the potatoes with 1 cup of the hot soup and the wine and mix back into the soup, stirring until smooth. Serve garnished with hard boiled egg slices.

Salty soup is a sign the cook is in love!

Ponaturi Soup

2 large carrots, peeled and diced
2 ribs celery, cleaned and diced
1 Each cleaned and diced: parsnip, onion, leek, ripe tomato
1 ham hock
1 ¼ dried split peas washed with stones removed
2 Tbsp olive oil
1 bay leaf
1 tsp dried thyme
4 C chicken broth
4 C water
2 tsp parsley
Salt and pepper to taste

Cut all vegetables and sauté in olive oil in a large stock pot for 10 minutes. Add remaining ingredients and simmer for 30-40 minutes or until peas are soft and malleable to eat. Serves 6-8 well – as a prelude to dinner or dinner itself!

Angelic Alphabet

B C G D F A E
M I H L P Q N
X O R Z U S T

Yes to you there are letters missing – however to the Angels they are unnecessary. Therefore, when you write your intentions asking for angelic helpers they would most like you to write clearly in their language as so to be best understood! Try it – you will be surprised!

To break a Curse:

There are three ways to break a curse, we all know those people whether they know it or not send the evil eye our way out of pure spite. It is best to do these spells periodically just to cleanse yourself, your magick and your surroundings.

Get some silver embroidery thread and tie a knot representing you and one end and 9 knots at the other end representing all the curses set against you (9 being the number of victory) Chant the spell and cut the string between you and the curses. Throw it into the middle of a crossroads, don't look or go back and set yourself free.

Get a silver or silver plated spoon and walk around your house absorbing all the negative energy that has happened to you in your life, chanting the spell as you do. Take it to a crossroads and either toss or bury it. Remember don't look or go back.

Take a brown egg and write the name of the person who cursed you or put the spell on the egg shell. Take it to crossroads or a river flowing away from you and break the egg in the midst of it while chanting the spell, again don't look or go back.

The Spell to break a curse: (chant 9 times)

I break all curses, Set against me
I bind all hexes, Three times three
No longer shall they, come against me
From this moment, I am set free
This is my will, And so shall it be! (or mote it be!)

Salads & Dressings
Flowering Herb Dressing

1 C light olive oil
½ C each: red wine vinegar, grated parmesan cheese
¼ C diced chives with flowers
2 crushed garlic cloves
2 sprigs each: of pineapple sage with pink flowers and rosemary with blue flowers; diced

Mix together in a bottle or Mason jar and let set at least 1 hour before using – also makes a great marinade.

Grow Strong Dressing

1 C light olive oil
½ C red wine vinegar
2 tsp each: dried burdock root, dried yellow dock root, dried lemongrass, cut rose hips

Mix together in a bottle or Mason jar and let set at least 1 hour before using - use daily when you are feeling puny and need strengthening.

Charm for a Fever
Good morning, dear Thursday! Take away from (name) the 77-fold fevers. Oh! thou dear Lord Jesus Christ, take them away from him! + + + .This must be spoken three times on first a Thursday, second a Friday, and third a and each time thrice. The Apostle's Creed has also to be said each time, and not a word dare be spoken to anyone until the sun has risen. Neither dare the sick person speak to anyone till after sunrise; nor eat pork, nor drink milk, nor cross a running water, for nine days.

Samhain Salad

½ head of cabbage finely chopped (red or green)
2 Tbsp each: salad dressing or mayonnaise
2 Tbsp each: sour cream, sugar
1 Tbsp apple cider vinegar
2 red apples, peeled, cored and diced
1 tsp lemon juice

Mix the apple pieces and the lemon juice together in a medium bowl and drain to help prevent discoloring. Mix the rest of the ingredients together, chill and serve.

What itches and twitches foretell:

If your nose itches, your mouth is in danger
You will kiss a fool and meet a stranger

If your right eye twitches, a birth will be
If your left eye twitches, a death in the family

If your right ear itches, someone speaks of you well
If your left ear itches, your secrets they'll tell

If your right palm itches, you will receive money
If your left palm itches, you will pay it out honey

If your rub your itches into wood,
All the ill will turn to good!

Summi Salad

1 small head of cabbage, finely chopped
¼ head of red cabbage, grated
2 packages top Ramon noodles
4 oz pkg of slivered almonds toasted
1C of toasted sesame seeds

In a large bowl crush the Ramon noodles (only - reserve seasoning for dressing) and add all the rest of the ingredients. Top with following dressing and stir. Refrigerate until ready to serve.

Summi Salad Dressing

½ C rice vinegar
½ C vegetable oil
4 Tbsp sugar
Seasoning from top Ramon

Mix all the ingredients in a small Mason jar and store until ready to serve salad then toss in. with the salad.

Lucky Vines

Ivy is luck to a woman as holly is to a man,
Grow them in your garden, or wherever you can
For it turns away the evil eye and injures the evil hand!

Lucky Clover

One in your shoe, brings good luck to you
Protects from the spells of magicians
And the wiles of fairies too!

Salad of the Earth Mother

1 lb curled pasta
3 peppers or various colors, top cut out, cleaned and diced
12 oz mini tomatoes, sliced in half
1 small red onion, peeled and diced
3 Persian cucumbers, peeled and diced
1 small can of sliced black olives 15 oz
8 oz mini mozzarella balls, drained
Options: one 14 - 16oz can garbanzo beans, or red kidney beans, or 1 C dry roasted peanuts, or sunflower seeds, or 4 oz capers, or 16 oz artichoke hearts or 8 oz dry salami cut into cubes.

Fill a large pot with salt water and set on medium heat until it boils and then add pasta for 8-12 minutes or until tender yet firm. Cool in a colander by draining and rinsing with cold water then set aside. In a large serving bowl prepare and mix all other ingredients. Add pasta and thoroughly mix. Keep refrigerated until serving until serving time. Just before serving ass 4 oz of Italian dressing.

Charm to end wound pain

Cut three small twigs from a tree--each to be cut off in one cut--rub one end of each twig in the wound, and wrap them separately in a piece of white paper, and put them in a warm and dry place.

Sicilian Antipasto:

1 lb cauliflower florets, roasted or pickled
4 sweet peppers, any color, roasted or pickled
4 oz miniature onions, roasted or pickled
1/3 C extra virgin olive oil - if roasting
8 oz of sliced mushrooms, canned, pickled or stuffed
½ lb sliced or cubed each: pepperoni, salami
1 lb cooked medium shrimp, cleaned, deveined and cooked
1 lb each: mozzarella, provolone, sliced or cubed

If roasting – fry in a large cast iron skillet with the oil until soft. Mix all ingredients together, add dressing (follows) and serve on a platter with toothpicks or on individual plates as an appetizer before meals.

Sicilian Dressing

1 C light olive oil
2/3 C lemon juice
1/3 C balsamic vinegar
2 tsp chopped fresh basil
¼ tsp cayenne pepper
2 cloves garlic, peeled and crushed
1 tsp honey

Best if made first and set aside in a bottle or Mason jar overnight before using.

To protect yourself from evil always wear a blue bead. From sickness wear an amber one.

Mermaid Salad

1 lb shell style macaroni
½ stalk celery, cleaned and cut small
1 small yellow onion, peeled and diced
12 oz albacore tuna or 12 oz small deveined, cleaned and cooked shrimp
¾ C salad dressing or mayonnaise
1 ½ tsp mustard
1 Tbsp dill pickle relish
1 tsp celery salt
½ tsp black pepper

In a large pot, fill with water, add salt, wait to boil and toss in macaroni for 8-12 minutes, or until firm yet tender to the bite. Strain and drain, run cool water over it and toss, strain and drain again and then set aside to cool. In a large serving bowl, mix remaining ingredients and when cool mix in macaroni and serve or keep in the refrigerator until needed.

Blessing of the Salt

May wisdom abide in this salt, may it preserve our minds and bodies from all corruption. By Hochmael and in the virtue of Rauch Hochmael, May the phantoms of Hyle depart from here, That it may become a heavenly salt, Salt of the earth and earth of the salt, That it may feed the threshing ox and strengthen our hope with the horns of the fighting bull – Amen!

Simply Devine Crab and Avocado Salad

1 16oz can crabmeat, drained with cartilage removed
½ C chopped celery
3 hard boiled eggs chopped
2 Tbsp pimiento
1 Tbsp chopped onion
½ tsp salt
½ C mayonnaise or salad dressing
4 small ripe avocados
1 Tbsp lemon juice
½ tsp salt
3 Tbsp dry bread crumbs
1 tsp melted butter
2 Tbsp slivered almonds

Heat oven to 400 degrees. Mix crab, celery, eggs, pimiento, onion, salt and the mayonnaise. Cut unpeeled avocados in half and remove the pits. Brush halves with lemon juice and sprinkle with salt. Fill avocado halves with crabmeat mixture. Toss bread crumbs in butter in a bowl and spoon over the crabmeat. Place on a ungreased shallow baking dish and bake for 10 minutes. Sprinkle almonds over the crumb topping and bake 5 minutes longer and serve.

Key of Secrets

```
      T
    O + A
      R
```

To Use:
Repeat on a piece of parchment and make circles with your finger while asking a question.

Shrimp & Spinach Salad

1 lb medium cooked shrimp with tails off
½ lb cooked apple cured turkey bacon, crumbled
1 lb fresh spinach leaves
3 shallots, peeled and diced
15 cherry tomatoes
3 Tbsp Balsamic Vinegar
1/3 C 1st cold pressed extra virgin olive oil
1 tsp each salt, white pepper

In a large serving bowl toss all ingredients together and serve immediately.

Angelic Blessing

Make a circle of Holy salt around you and your table then shout/chant/sing this mantra:

Angels of Protection, Angels who clear
Remove all the spirits, that don't belong here!
Take away all entities and all fear!
Trap them in the water here!

While you sing burn sage and a white candle and put a glass of water between them to collect the negativity. When the sage and candle are done burning, flush the glass of water down the toilet or if you have a septic system dispose of in a far away place.

Summer Spaghetti Salad

2 16 oz cans solid white tuna in water, drained
4 large shallots, peeled and diced
1 large clove garlic, peeled and minced
2 C broccoli florets
2 C sliced washed fresh mushrooms
½ tsp oregano
¼ C light olive oil
2 Tbsp butter
2 medium zucchini washed and diced
1 roma tomato, chopped
½ C sour cream
½ cooked left over spaghetti noodles
¼ C grated parmesan cheese
Black pepper to taste (1/4-1 tsp)

In a large skillet, sauté' onion, garlic, broccoli, mushrooms and oregano in the oil and butter until tender. Add tomato and zucchini to skillet and continue to cook. Break tuna into chucks and add to vegetables and heat through. Stir in sour cream and keep warm. Add leftover spaghetti and toss together with the vegetables along with the parmesan cheese, sprinkle with black pepper and serve.

Magickal Medal of Azoth

A B C D E
F G H I K
L M N O P
Q R S T V
 X V Z N

Copy on parchment and carry or divine your own uses.

Southern Shrimp Salad

1 lb medium shrimp, cleaned and deveined, tails off
1/3 C grape seed oil
2 ½ Tbsp ginger
3 shallots, peeled and minced
2 cloves garlic, peeled and crushed
1 Tbsp raw honey
8 oz black beans, drained
8 oz sweet corn, drained
1 lb mixed salad greens cleaned
Garnish: 1 cup scallions (ends cut off and chopped into white), ¼ C fresh cilantro leaves (chopped) and 2 heirloom tomatoes (cored and diced)

In a cast iron skillet on medium heat, cook shrimp, garlic, ginger and shallots in oil for about 3-5 minutes. Add the black beans, corn and honey and cook an additional 3-5 minutes until shrimp is pink and set aside. In a large serving bowl arrange lettuce, add mixture and top with garnish and serve.

Bibliomancy

Take the Holy Scriptures in your lap, concentrate on your question while holding the book to your heart, open at random and read

Auguries

Sit alone in a natural setting. Concentrate on your question, with your eyes closed. When you are ready, open your eyes and find symbols and pictures in the nature around you (clouds)

Greek Shrimp Salad

1 lb medium cooked cleaned
1 lb fresh mixed baby lettuce
3 Persian cucumbers, peeled and sliced
15 cherry tomatoes
6 oz crumbled Mediterranean feta cheese
1 C mixed pitted olives
1 small lemon sliced in four

In a large serving bowl toss all ingredients together except lime. Squeeze lemon over the salad and serve with following dressing.

Greek Salad Dressing

½ C olive oil
2 Tbsp red wine vinegar
½ C buttermilk
1 tsp each: sugar, oregano, basil, rosemary
1 Tbsp dill
½ tsp each: salt, pepper

Beat together with a whisk in a medium bowl or mason jar and use over the previous salad or store in a bottle until needed.

What Candle Flames Represent

Strong: Power, Energy, Winning, Strength
Weak: Heavy Opposition, Redo the Spell
Jumping: Fighting, Raw emotions, Arguments
Rainbow: Each color has a different meaning - look up on the color meanings on page 90

Thai Shrimp Salad

1 lb cooked large cooked shrimp, tails off
1 cantaloupe, cleaned and cubed, rinds removed
3-4 small red, yellow or orange peppers, cleaned and sliced
3 Persian cucumbers, peeled and cubed
1 lb fresh spinach leaves, cleaned and dried
¾ C pine nuts roasted at 325 for 10-15 minutes

Tossed together and drizzled with dressing just before serving.

Thai Shrimp Dressing

3 Tbsp each fresh squeezed lime juice, brown sugar, peanut oil
½ tsp each red pepper, chili sauce
2 Tbsp fresh ginger, grated
1 Tbsp fresh cilantro, chopped
2 green onions, end cut off and chopped whites only

Benefits of Mistletoe

Safe welcome for you and me
For no enemy can near it be
Untold good luck and fertility
Protects from thunder, lightning and disease
Antidote to poison, plant of peace

My Favorite Chicken Salad: hot or cold

1 ½ lbs leftover chicken or turkey, deboned, cubed
2 C vegetable broth
6 green onions, ends removed
1 C orange flavoured dried cranberries
½ stalk of celery, cleaned and diced
1 C chopped pecan pieces
1 ½ cup shredded medium cheddar cheese
1 C (or more to taste) organic mayonnaise or salad dressing
1 Tbsp turbinado sugar
1 ½ tsp mustard
1/2 tsp each salt, black pepper (or more to taste)
8 oz endive, cleaned and peeled into leaf cups (optional)

In a cast iron skillet, on medium heat combine the leftover poultry and fry in the vegetable broth until it is soft and fully pliable. Drain and remove from pan. Cool for cold salad, leave hot for not. Add remainder of ingredients and serve on endive leaf cups as a salad or without them for a main dish. Remember the cheese will melt if you serve hot and will become part of the sauce.

How a Rainbow predict tomorrow's weather

A rainbow in the eastern sky, the morrow will be fine and dry; A rainbow in the west that gleams, rain tomorrow – falls in streams

Golden Dragon Salad

1 ½ lb boneless skinless chicken breast
2 C vegetable broth
1 can 5-6 oz sliced black olives
1 can 16 oz mandarin oranges, cut in two pieces each
1 medium red onion, peeled and diced
8 oz grape tomatoes, sliced in two
1 lb herb salad greens (baby lettuces with mint, cilantro etc)
8 oz shredded mixed cheese
6 oz sesame dressing (feast from the east)

In a cast iron skillet on medium heat fry the chicken on both sides for 10-15 minutes each or until done and no longer pink. Drain and set aside to cool. In a large 5 quart bowl, add all other ingredients except dressing and chicken and mix thoroughly. Set in refrigerator until ready to serve and then mix in dressing at the last minute.

Candle Smoke goes …

North: Perseverance, you will need to work for what you want, Success will be difficult

South: Success and Recovery comes swiftly

East: Patience, Success only comes with careful thought and strategy

West: Clarity of issue is needed, meditate and see what you may be missing

Baja Salad

1 head romaine lettuce-remove core and
1 lb ground (turkey, beef, pork) cooked, drained
1 pkg taco seasoning mix
8 oz shredded light Mexican cheese blend
3 Heirloom tomatoes, cored and chopped
8 green onions-ends cut, sliced into green
16 oz black beans, drained
15 oz black olives-drained, sliced
8 oz sour cream
8 oz salsa
4 avocados-pitted, peeled and sliced
1 fresh lime
1 bag of organic tortilla chips or homemade

In a cast iron skillet on medium heat brown meat on all sides until done (about 10-15 minutes) and mix in the seasoning package with 2 Tbsp of water and set aside. In one large or four to six individual bowls place torn romaine lettuce, top with meat, cheese, tomatoes, green onion slices, black beans, and black olives. Top with salsa, sour cream and avocado slices and squeeze lime juice on it. Serve with Organic tortilla chips.

Candle Flame Pointing...

North: Physical manifestation, long duration
South: Spiritual manifestation, hot, aggressive
East: Mental manifestation, new ideas and intuition
West: Emotional manifestation, success

Angus Salad

8 oz cooked steak thinly sliced into 2-3 inch pieces
2 heirloom tomatoes thinly sliced
8 oz crumbled feta cheese
1 small red onion, peeled and thinly sliced
1 lb mixed lettuce with herbs
4 oz ranch dressing

Add lettuce to plate and place all slices neatly on top in a circle. Top with feta and serve with your favorite ranch dressing.

Broom (Besom) Legends

Fond of your special friend? Don't get too attached or don't move away too soon as a good broom sweeps up all evil in its path, so never lean it against a bed or a chair where you sleep or it will deposit the unhappy spirit there to torment your dreams.

Having nightmares or restless sleep – buy a new whisk broom and sweep your bed then toss it away. In fact buy several for when you move into a new place and as you go cleaning from room to room – scoop up the left behind bad luck and toss it out!

Never bring your old broom with you to a new home or the bad luck you sought to leave behind will follow you. Now of course there is always that pesky person in our lives who could probably use an old broom! Hmmmmmm….

Brownie Cobb Salad

1/2 head of lettuce, cleaned and torn to pieces
1 bunch each: watercress, chicory - cleaned, rib removed and torn
½ head romaine lettuce, cleaned and torn
2 heirloom tomatoes, cored and diced
6 strips apple smoked turkey bacon, cooked and crumbled
2 boiled chicken breasts, shredded or chopped
3 hard boiled eggs, peeled and sliced
1 avocado, peeled, seeded and sliced
½ C Roquefort cheese
2 Tbsp chives

Toss lettuce, watercress, chicory and romaine together in a large serving bowl. Top with the remaining ingredients arranged nicely then follow with the dressing before serving.

Brownie Dressing

¼ C each: red wine, extra light olive oil, opt. water
1 tsp lemon juice
2 tsp salt
¾ tsp each: white pepper, worchestershire sauce
¼ tsp each: dry English mustard, sugar
¾ C salad oil (like walnut, peanut, etc.)

Combine ingredients in a bottle and shake well. Serve over Brown Derby Cobb Salad.

Potpourri Potato Salad

5 lbs potatoes, baked, peeled and cubed
1 lb medium cheddar, cubed
1 lb Canadian bacon, cubed
1 medium yellow onion, peeled and diced
½ stalk celery, cleaned and diced
1 green pepper, cut of top, clean and dice
1 small can sliced black olives
3-6 medium eggs, hard boiled, peeled and diced
½ C salad dressing or mayonnaise
1 Tbsp each: mustard, kosher dill relish, turbinado sugar
1/2 tsp each: celery salt, seasoned salt, black pepper

Combine all ingredients in a large serving bowl and keep refrigerated until serving.

To Avert Danger and Drive Away Evil

Make the sign of the cross 3X in the air I the direction of the danger and spit 3X. For evil is stitched by a cross, can not enter a circle, is driven away by a cock's crow, the ringing of a church bell and the spit of a righteous person!

Mother Earth Potato Salad

5 lbs potatoes, baked, peeled and cubed
5 hard boiled eggs, peeled and diced
1 C green peas, cooked
1 red onion, peeled and diced
½ bunch celery, cleaned and diced
1 15 oz can of sliced black olives
½ C mayonnaise or salad dressing
1 Tbsp Dijon mustard
To Taste: salt, pepper, garlic powder, chopped dill

Combine all ingredients and refrigerate for at least 1 hour or overnight before serving.

Independence Day Potato Salad

2 lbs each red and white potatoes, scrubbed, baked, and cubed with skins on
8 oz crumbled bleu cheese
8 oz cooked and crumbled bacon
Petals from 3 passion flowers for decoration
½ C salad dressing or mayonnaise
2 tsp each: mustard, kosher dill relish
1 tsp each: kosher salt, mixed pepper

Combine all ingredients in a large serving bowl and keep refrigerated until serving.

Trying to get Pregnant?

Then never sweep under your bed – many religions believe that the child's spirit hovers near watching and waiting for the right moment to enter – sweeping under your bed may sweep them away!

Dutch Potato Salad

9 large potatoes, peeled an chopped
1 tsp salt
8 slices of bacon, cooked and crumbled
½ bunch of celery, cleaned and diced small
1 medium onion, peeled and diced fine
¼ C each: apple cider or balsamic vinegar, sugar
1/3 C water

In a 3-5 qrt pot, add water and potatoes and cook until tender – about 40 minutes. Drain and cool, meanwhile place bacon in a skillet and cook over a medium heat until crisp, turning once – about 15 minutes. Set aside bacon strips on a paper towel and then crumble and set aside. Reserve the bacon fat in the skillet and add the flour, sugar, water and vinegar to the skillet and cook in reserved bacon fat over medium heat until dressing is thick – 8-12 minutes. Add bacon, potatoes and green onions to skillet and stir until coated. Cook until heated and season with salt and pepper. Serve warm.

To Attract the Perfect Mate

3 parts Red sandalwood
2 parts Patchouli
1 part each: Orris root, Dragon's blood, Lemongrass

Crush together with a mortar and pestle. Cut into 3 parts – 1 part burn as incense, 1 part throw out to the four winds, 1 part carry with you in a little bag

Perfect mate, find me, come; Two hearts joining, spell begun; Do not stop until we are one; Two hearts bound and spell is done!

Sweet Summer Salad

2 small pkg of strawberry Jell-O
1 C boiling water
16 oz fresh strawberries (or frozen)
20oz can crushed pineapple, drained
1 C chopped pecans
3 medium ripe bananas, sliced thin
8 oz sour cream
¼ C mayonnaise or salad dressing or whipped cream
1 ½ tsp grated orange rind

Mix the Jell-O and water together in a medium size serving bowl and stir until dissolved. Refrigerate for 1 hour or until set. Cut into bite size pieces and add remaining ingredients – serve immediately or keep refrigerated.

Food of the Gods

15 oz can fruit cocktail drained
1 banana thinly sliced
15 oz can mandarin oranges, drained
15 oz can pineapple chunks, drained
16 oz extra creamy whip cream
8 oz mini marshmallows

Combine all ingredients in a large serving bowl and keep refrigerated until ready to serve.

To grow your hair long only trim on the new moon – to stunt your hair's growth only pluck or cut on the full moon.

True Love and Other things

To find your true love on New Year's Eve, lay a sprig of Ivy next to your breast, and the next one to speak to you their true love will last!

On New Year's Day a woman who looks out a window and sees a man passing by will marry before the year is out!

Kiss a passion fruit on February 1st and put it under your pillow and one of your most erotic fantasies will come true!

If on St. Valentine's Day you see a robin, then you will marry a man who will not have time to spend with you, if you see a sparrow you will marry a poor man but will be very happy, but if you see a goldfinch dear one, you will marry a millionaire!

On St. Valentine's Day put a silver coin under your pillow and your true love will propose by year's end!

To be kissed by the end of the day, tie a blue satin ribbon around your ankle in May!

If you see a falling star on St Lawrence day (8/10) you will dream of your future spouse!

Comfort Foods

Fried Green Tomatoes

3 green tomatoes, cored, cut in ¼ inch slices
1 C buttermilk
2 egg beaten
¼ C cornmeal or breadcrumbs
¾ C flour
1 tsp each: salt, black pepper opt cayenne
1/3-1 C oil

Core and cut the tomatoes and put aside. In a mixing bowl beat together the eggs and the butter milk and put aside. In another mixing bowl blend the cornmeal, flour and seasonings. Ready your cast iron skillet on medium heat with 1/3 cup oil and begin by dipping each tomatoes slice in the buttermilk, then coating it in the corn meal mixture than frying it on both sides until browned (2-3 minutes), and serve. You may need to lower the temperature of the pan after the first batch or two.

The Four Stages of Magickal Works

Discovery, Manifestation, Multiplication and Projection

The Four Stages of Magickal Creation

Numbers (how many of what), Writing (spell, desire, wish), Speech (the musical tones) and Action (to dance)

Then Release…

Herbed Rice Mix

1lb long grain rice
1/3 C dried minced onion
1.3 C dried parsley leaves
1 Tbsp each: dried chives, dried tarragon, celery seed
½ tsp salt
1 tsp pepper

Mix the ingredients together and store in small canning jars.

To use: put 1 1/3C of water into a pot and bring to a boil, add ½ C of rice mix and simmer on low for about 20 minutes stirring occasionally. Fluff with a fork and eat – Makes 4 - ½ C servings.

Sautéed Cucumbers:

3 Cucumbers, peeled and sliced ¼ inch thick
6 Tbsp flour
1 ½ tsp salt
1 tsp dill
½ tsp pepper
1/3-1/2 C butter
¼ tsp fenugreek

Mix together the flour, salt, pepper, and dill and coat the cucumber slices with it. Fry in a cast iron skillet with butter on medium until browned on both sides. Sprinkle with fenugreek and serve immediately.

All Incantations and Invocations require three substances; visualization, prayer and action.

Mountain Eggplant Casserole

2 medium eggplant, peeled and sliced ½ inch thick
6 Tbsp olive oil
2 large onion, peeled and diced
1 medium can tomatoes crushed
2 bay leaves
3 Tbsp tomato paste
2 cloves garlic, peeled and crushed
1 Tbsp sugar
½ tsp each: basil, tarragon, oregano, chervil, thyme, parsley
1/8 tsp cinnamon
½ C each: burgundy wine, cottage cheese
1 tsp each: salt, pepper
2 large eggs
½ C sour cream

Brush the eggplant slices with olive oil and broil to a golden brown on each side, and cut into cubes. Sauté in a large skillet, the onion in the remaining olive oil until transparent. Add the tomatoes, bay leaves, tomato paste, garlic, sugar, herbs and seasonings, and burgundy wine, then simmer gently for 30 minutes and discard bay leaves. Lightly oil a casserole dish and alternate layers of eggplant and sauce, ending with sauce. Blend together the cottage cheese, eggs, and sour cream and pour over the mixture. Bake at 350 until topping is bubbly about 45 minutes and serve from casserole.

To dance in the open air, in the forest, around the trees, ensures good health, true love, luck and prosperity!

Baked Beans

1 lb pkg dried white beans
6 C water
¼ C olive oil
1 medium sweet onion, peeled and diced
2 cloves garlic, peeled and crushed
32 oz tomato sauce
¼ C each: brown sugar, molasses
2 Tbsp cider vinegar
1 tsp each: salt, dry mustard, worchestershire sauce
¼ tsp each: black pepper, nutmeg, cinnamon

In a large pot soak the beans overnight in the water and drain the next morning. Again add clean water to the beans and now bring to a slow boil for 1 hour over medium heat and drain again. Remove to a casserole dish and combine with all other ingredients. Bake at 350 for 1 ½ to 3 1/2 hours (stirring every 30 minutes and add water if necessary) or until beans are soft and edible.

To Gain a Desire

Write your desire on anything you enjoy eating, like an apple, a carrot, a cupcake etc. Then place it in your scrying bowl under the full moon to charge so that your desire penetrates the food. Visualize Our Lady doing this as her vision penetrates the skies. Then speak the spell and eat with great relish.

It comes to me - Now mote it be! Aumn

Magic Quiche

3 scallions, chopped fine
5 slices bacon, cooked and crumbled
1 C grated sharp cheddar cheese
7 large eggs
1 to 1 ¼ C milk/cream (use whole milk or half whipping cream)
1/3 C crushed tea biscuits
1 tsp each: jasmine and pansy petals

Grease a square glass pan (9X9). In the bottom, sprinkle the onions, bacon, and cheese. In a mixing bowl, beat the eggs with the milk or cream and the tea biscuits briskly for 2-3 minutes and then pour into the baking pan. Top with flower petals and bake at 350 for about 35 minutes or until thoroughly set.

Dutch Hex Symbol meanings

Rosette – Protection and good Luck
Tulips - Triune Divinity, Faith, Hope and Charity
Hearts - Love, Friendship and Brotherhood
Scalloped borders - Smooth sailing in life
Crescent Moons – Four seasons
Pineapple – Welcome, hospitality
Star - Protection, energy, fertility, harmony
Triple Star – Success, wealth, happiness
8 pointed Star - Abundance
Sun wheel – Warmth, fertility, life force
Wheat – Abundance and good will
Oak Leaf – Long life, strength, endurance
Rain drops – Abundance, fertility, rain
Circle – Eternity , infinity, continuity
Tree of Life – Happy life and joyful memories

Leprechaun Pie

6 large green tomatoes
¼ C water
1 C sugar
3 Tbsp flour
½ tsp each: fenugreek, goldenseal
½ C diced onion
1 ½ tsp lemon zest
½ tsp salt
2 Tbsp butter
Pastry for a 2 crust pie
Additional sugar for topping

Blanche tomatoes in boiling water for 20-30 seconds each and remove. Core, peel, cut into pieces and place into a skillet on medium heat with water and bring to a boil for 5 minutes. Remove the tomato pieces from the liquid and set aside. Meanwhile add to liquid the flour, sugar, salt, spices and lemon zest until dissolved and then add the tomato pieces back in and cool for about 10-15 minutes then spoon into a prepared pie crust and top with the other pie crust crimping and sealing the edges. Cut venting slits in tops and sprinkle lightly with sugar. Bake at 40 minutes at 400 f. or until crust is golden brown.

Dutch Animal Meanings

Unicorn – Purity, Virtue, Piety
Eagle - Strength, courage, good health
Dove – Peace and contentment
Distlefinks/gold finch – Good luck and happiness
Horse head w/star – Protection for all animals

Brown Hen Casserole

6 slices white bread – 1 side buttered
3 C each: shredded cheddar & jack cheeses
8 eggs
3 C milk
8 oz can of diced green chilies
1 lb cooked sausage, drained
½ tsp pepper
¼ tsp each: garlic powder, dry mustard
1 tsp salt
2 tsp paprika

In a 13x9 pan, lay the buttered side of the bread down. Cover the bread with cheese, sausage and chilies and set aside. In a medium mixing bowl, beat together the eggs, milk and seasonings. Pour into the pan, cover and chill overnight in the refrigerator. Bake uncovered at 325 for 45 – 60 minutes. Let stand for 10 minutes and serve.

Dutch Color meanings

Red – love, emotion, life, passion
Green – growth, rebirth, luck, happiness
Yellow - divinity, life, sun, gentility, health
Blue - heaven, truth, beauty, protection
Brown – harvest, humility, pleasure, mother earth
White – purity, joy, everlasting life, moon
Violet – dignity, power, intuition, sacredness
Black – protection, binding elements together
Orange – career and success

Try writing your wishes or spells in colored ink!

Fairy Queen Quiche

1 – 9 inch pie crust
1 ½ C grated cheeses (cheddar, gruyere, Swiss)
½ C feta, ricotta or goat cheese
5 eggs
1 C light cream (half and half)
1tsp each dried: dill, parsley, Lovage (1 Tbsp fresh)
1 tsp each: chervil, chamomile flower petals

Preheat oven to 400 degrees. Line the pie pan (or quiche pan) with the pie crust. Place the grated cheeses in the pie shell. In a medium mixing bowl, beat together the eggs, soft cheeses and herbs for 2-3 minutes until well blended. Pour into the pie crust and top with the flower petals. Bake for 45 minutes or until a knife inserted in the center comes out clean. Cool for 5 minutes before serving.

Dutch Hex Signs

Now make your own – draw a circle on parchment or use a plain plate. Choose the colors, animals or symbols of your intentions (or those of a beloved friend) and complete your drawings on the new moon so the intentions will grow. Hang them throughout your house for protections and blessings and when you get good at it - give them as Samhain or New Year gifts to your friends!

Brownie Quiche

2 medium potatoes, peeled and sliced
1 C each, onion, red bell pepper, chopped
¾ tsp dried thyme
8 strips bacon, cooked crisp and crumbled
8-10 eggs
1/3 C cream
2 Tbsp olive oil
¼ tsp each: salt, pepper
4 oz grated smoked cheddar cheese
1/3 bread crumbs

Preheat oven to 350 degrees. Blanch potatoes into salted boiling water for 1 to 1 ½ minutes each and drain. When cool, slice and place in a single layer overlapping around and bottom of a pie dish – making a crust. In a skillet, place the olive oil, pepper, and thyme and sauté on medium heat for about 5 minutes. Spoon the mixture on top of the potatoes, crumble the bacon on top of the onions and spread the cheese on top of the bacon. In a medium mixing bowl, whip together the eggs, water, salt and pepper for 2 minutes and then pour into the pie dish. Top with bread crumbs. Bake for 35 to 45 minutes or until a fork comes out clean. Cool before serving.

To Perform a Invocation or Incantation

Thoroughly cleanse yourself, space, your spirit
Cast a circle with holy salt
Set up your space
Meditate and visualize your purpose
Create your action and let go

Lover's Quiche

1 – 9 inch pie crust
1 C each grated: Swiss, Monterey jack, mild cheddar cheeses
¼ C diced leek
1 C each: chopped scarlet runner beans, hyacinth bulb, crab apple (peeled and cored)
¼ tsp each: chervil, thyme, dill
1 ½ tsp mixed petals: daisy, hibiscus, jasmine
5 – 7 eggs
1 cup whipping cream

Preheat oven to 375 degrees. Put the pie crust into a tin and bake for 10 minutes on a cookie sheet then remove from the oven. Add the leek, beans, hyacinth, and apple. In a medium mixing bowl whip together the eggs and the whipping cream then add the herbs and mix. Pour into the pie tin and arrange the flower petals on top. Bake for about 40 minutes or until a fork comes out clean when inserted. Serve with Rye toast and eat together to insure your mate's lasting desire.

Talisman
A talisman is worn or carried to bring good fortune

Amber – brings love, purity, wisdom, health
Acorn – brings love, good fortune and monies
Four leaf clover – brings fame, wealth, love, health
Horn of plenty – prosperity
Jade – wealth, prosperity
Nefar – youth and happiness
Pennies – prosperity and luck

Imbolc Potatoes

8 medium potatoes, peeled and cubed
½ C each: sour cream, soft butter
4 oz cream cheese
1 C grated cheddar cheese
1 tsp each: salt, black pepper

Boil potatoes in salted water on medium heat until soft about 25 minutes, drain and then mash in a large mixing bowl. Add the sour cream, butter, cream cheese and seasonings then mash together until smooth. Place the mashed potatoes into a medium casserole dish and cover with the grated cheese and bake at 350 until the cheese is bubbly and melted – about 12-15 minutes then serve.

Beltane Potatoes

1 ½ lbs very small new potatoes
1 tsp first cold pressed olive oil
1 medium onion, peeled and diced
1 small garlic clove, peeled and crushed
1 C each: chicken broth, parsley
½ tsp pepper

Peel a strip of skin from each potato then clean and set aside in cold water. In a deep skillet on medium heat place the oil, onions and garlic and sauté for 5-8 minutes. Place the potatoes in a single layer in a deep skillet and add broth and ¾ C parsley and bring to a boil. Reduce heat and simmer covered for 10 minutes or until potatoes are tender. Place in serving bowl, cover with remaining parsley and serve.

Dijon Potatoes

3 lbs baby red potatoes
1/3 C olive oil
4 Tbsp mustard
2 tsp paprika
1 tsp each: ground cumin, chili powder
1/8 tsp cayenne pepper

Preheat oven to 400 degrees then coat a roasting pan with the olive oil. In a large mixing bowl add all mustard and seasonings and whisk together. Poke each potato several times and add to mixture. Coat potatoes thoroughly and pour into roasting pan. Bake for 45=60 minutes or until potatoes are tender – serve hot.

Amulet
An amulet crosses all religions and is a charm worn or held to bring protection against evil forces.

Alligator teeth – protects from sorcery and danger
Bell – wards of f evil eye and dispels spirits
Blue bead – wards off evil eye, dispels sickness
Cross – cure illness, drive away demons
Eye of God – protection from evil eye (jealousy)
Hexagram – wards off evil, protection, shield
Knot - wards off illness, evil and adulterous intent
Mirror – sends back negativity or absorbs it
Pentagram – protection from 5 elements
Tassels or fringes – ward off demons and evil

Lughnasadh Casserole

2 medium eggplant, peeled and sliced
6 Tbsp olive oil
2 large onion, peeled and diced
16 oz can crushed tomatoes
2 bay leaves (remove later)
3 Tbsp tomato paste
2 cloves garlic, peeled and crushed
1 Tbsp brown sugar
½ tsp each: basil, tarragon, oregano, chervil, thyme, parsley
1/8 tsp cinnamon
½ C burgundy wine
1 tsp each: salt, pepper
1 C ricotta cheese
¼ tsp ground nutmeg
2 large eggs
½ C sour cream

Brush the eggplant slices with olive oil and brown in a skillet on medium heat for 5 minutes on each side or until brown and set aside. Add the remaining oil to the skillet and sauté the onion until transparent (about 8 minutes) on medium heat. Add the tomatoes, bay leaves, tomato paste, garlic, sugar, herbs, seasonings (except nutmeg) and wine together in the skillet and simmer gently on low for about 30 minutes and then remove bay leaves. In a medium mixing bowl beat together the pot cheese (ricotta), eggs, nutmeg and sour cream. Lightly oil a casserole dish and alternate layers of sauce, eggplant, pot cheese, sauce, eggplant, pot cheese, eggplant, sauce. Bake at 350 until the tops is heated through and the top is bubbly – about 45 minutes and serve from the casserole.

Maben Casserole

11 peeled and sliced potatoes
10-12 slices (6 oz) Colby cheese
¼ cup butter
½ package fresh broccoli florets, sliced
1 lb package turkey bacon, sliced

In a 3-5 quart casserole baking dish, places 4 pats of butter on the bottom and follow with slices of potato until the bottom is covered. Layer as follows with half of the slices of broccoli and bacon and top with 4-slices of cheese and 4 pats of butter. Add another layer of potatoes, broccoli, bacon, butter and cheese. Bake at 350 for 45-60 minutes or until potatoes are tender: Serves 4-5 well.

Money Blessing

Every time you get paid and before you spend it bless your monies.

I bless thee times three (make 3 crosses)
Come back to me times ten (make circles)
Thy divine will to me
Mote it be
Amen!

Now always fold it towards you so it always returns back to you before you give it out!

Cati Mac

1 lb campanili pasta
1 15-16 oz jar Cheese Salsa

In a large 3-5 quart pot of salted water bring to boil and add pasta, cooking until al dente about 8-14 minutes. Drain, and put into a large serving bowl and pour the cheese salsa on top and mix well. Serves 4-6 well.

Variations:
1 lb cooked and cubed chicken meat
1 small can of sliced black olives 3-5 oz
1 small peeled and diced red onion
½ bunch fresh cilantro diced

Add chicken and olives and stir. Top with onion and cilantro and serve. Great for gatherings when fancy is good.

Magickal Macaroni and Cheese

1 lb large elbow pasta
3 Tbsp each: butter, flour
2 ½ C whole milk
10 oz extra sharp cheddar cheese, grated
4 oz grated gruyere cheese

Boil noodles on medium heat in a pot until al dente – about 10-12 minutes then drain. In a sauce pan, melt butter on low, add flour, blend, then add milk and whisk until it starts to thicken. Add cheeses slowly whisking until melted and smooth, pour over the macaroni and bake in a casserole at 350 for 35 minutes.

Bayou Voodoo (Gumbo)

1 ½ lbs large to medium shrimp, deveined, shell and tails cleaned off
1 lb crab meat
1 lb crawfish, peeled and cleaned
3 fat garlic cloves, peeled and crushed
1 Stalk celery, cleaned and sliced
2 large yellow onion or 8 ramps, peeled, cleaned and diced
1 red bell pepper, cored, seeded, cleaned and diced
2 Tbsp 1st cold pressed extra virgin olive oil
2 C chicken broths
24-28 oz crushed tomatoes
1 bay leaf (remove after using)
1 tsp each cumin, old bay seasoning, red pepper
2 C long grain rice cooked according to directions

In a large enameled pot simmer garlic, onion, celery and peppers in oil on a low heat for 10-12 minutes. Add broth, tomatoes, bay, cumin and seasonings and simmer for 30 minutes. Remove bay leaf and add shrimp and cook on high 5-8 minutes and serve over cooked long grain rice.

A Witch's Bottle – destroys evil and negativity

A large green or amber jar or bottle with a lid
Rosemary, red wine, pins and needles
Red and/or Black candles

Sing the spell (next page) as you add the rosemary, needles and pins to the jar. Pour in the wine, close the lid and seal it with the wax. Set it in a hidden place where it won't be disturbed or bury.

Swamp Witch Stew (Jambalaya)

1 lb shrimp, deveined, cleaned, skin and tails off
1 lb sausage (chicken, beef or pork) without skin
3 large heirloom tomatoes, cored and chopped
1 Vidalia onion, peeled and diced
1 celery stalk, cleaned and diced
2 C long grain rice cooked according to directions
1 Tbsp Old bay seasoning
1 ½ tsp red pepper

Prepare rice. In a large enameled pot cook sausage, onion, celery and tomatoes for 15 minutes on medium heat, stirring to get the sausage completely cooked on all sides and in the middle. Chop the sausage into bite size pieces and add shrimp and seasonings and cook an additional 7-10 minutes or until the shrimp is pink and serve immediately over cooked rice.

A Witch's Bottle Spell

Pins and needles, rosemary and wine,
In this witches bottle of mine
Needles and pins, wine and rosemary
Guard against harm and do not tarry
Wine and rosemary, needles and pins
Guard against evil and their Jinn's
Rosemary and wine, pins and needles
Guard against jealousy and all other evils
Witches bottle red and black,
Send all evil against me back
Witches bottle black and red
Destroy all evil, kill it dead
Witches bottle that I see
Destroy all evil, Mote it be!

Steamed Mussels

2 Tbsp butter
1 Tbsp olive oil
1 Tbsp each: onion, celery, carrots – diced
2 medium shallots, peeled and sliced
1 clove garlic, peeled and crushed
1 ½ tsp each: fresh tarragon, parsley, finely chopped
½ tsp each: salt, pepper
1/3 C vermouth
1 C dry white wine
2 lbs cleaned mussels

In a large skillet, over medium heat, melt the butter and olive oil and sauté' the onions, carrots, celery, shallots and garlic until they are tender – about 5 minutes. Add the tarragon, parsley, salt, and pepper to the vegetables and cook for 1 more minute. Add the vermouth and white wine and gently simmer for 4 minutes. Add the mussels to the wine sauce, turn up heat to medium, cover and steam the mussels for 4-9 minutes or until opened. Serve the mussels hot in the wine sauce.

The Eyes have it!

Grey: Prudence, practicality, moral strength
Hazel: Intelligence, sincerity, friendliness
Green: Impetuousness, passion, pride
Blue: Loyalty, modesty, gentleness, forgiveness
Brown: Consistency, nobility, truthfulness
Black: Self assurance, devotion, extravagance
Closely set: Intelligence
Large: Sincerity, loyalty, affection, industry
Small: Honesty, temper, recklessness

Grogochrs Lasagna

1 lb each: crab meat, shrimp, orange roughy
½ lb each: salmon, mahi tuna
1 box of fast cook lasagna noodles
1 lb each: ricotta, mozzarella – shredded
½ C grated cheese (parmesan, romano) for topping
2 tsp nutmeg
2 eggs
Grogochrs sauce – see recipe below

Combine and shred all seafood in a large bowl and set aside. Mix together in a separate bowl ricotta and mozzarella, nutmeg, eggs, nutmeg and set aside. In a 9 X 13 pan, layer as follows: ¼ sauce, 1/3 noodles, ½ seafood, ½ cheese, ¼ sauce, 1/3 noodles, remaining seafood, remaining cheese, 1/4 sauce, remaining noodles, remaining sauce, grated cheese. Bake at 350-425 for 45-60 minutes then cool 10 minutes and serve hot. Feed 6-8 well.

Grogochrs Sauce

8 oz each: shredded parmesan, cream cheese, mozzarella, muenster
16 oz sour cream
8 oz milk plus more for thinning
½ tsp garlic powder

In a sauté pan over medium light heat, melt together milk and cheeses and season, stirring constantly. Thin if necessary with additional milk by the teaspoonful.

Grogochrs Pasta

1 lb fettuccini pasta
Grogochrs Sauce: see previous recipe
1 lb chicken breast
½ C broccoli, chopped
¼ C carrots, peeled and diced
¼ C celery, cleaned and diced
1/3 C olive oil

In a large cast iron skillet pour in the oil and warm on medium heat. Cut the chicken breasts into cubes and place in pan and cook 15 minutes. Add vegetables and cook an additional 10 minutes. Add sauce and simmer on low for 10 more minutes. Meanwhile, bring a pot of salted water to boil and add the pasta and cook 8-12 minutes until al dente and drain. Serve sauce mixture on top of pasta: Serves 4-5 well.

Candle Colors and their meanings

Pink: Romance, friendship, affection
Red: Health, passion, love, courage, draws
Violet: Spiritual, power, success, psyche
Blue: Wisdom, harmony, healing, truth
Green: Prosperity, fertility, success, money
Yellow: Sun, creativity, persuasion
Orange: Creativity, career, law, ambition
Brown: Earth, study, telepathy, balance
White: Divinity, balance, substitutes for all
Black: Banishes evil, uncrosses curses
Gold: Understanding, attraction, fast luck
Silver: Removes negativity, develops psyche

Gypsy Pasta

1 lb (16 oz) fettuccini or other pasta
1 to 1 ½ lbs large precooked shrimp
1 Tbsp garlic & herb Old Bay Seasoning
1 tsp crushed red pepper
1 Tbsp 1st cold pressed virgin olive oil
1 C each: yellow and orange peppers cubed, grape tomatoes halved, red onions peeled and diced
1 small can sliced black olives 3-4oz
3 tsp infused truffle oil
1 package Mediterranean style feta cheese 5-7 oz

In a large 3 quart pot boil water and cook pasta until al dente (according to package directions) and drain. In a cast iron skillet, par cook shrimp 3 minutes in olive oil, then add peppers and onion and cook 3 minutes more, then add tomatoes and cook 3 minutes more. In a large serving bowl 5 quarts, add pasta, shrimp and vegetables, Old Bay Seasoning, crushed red pepper, olives, truffle oil, feta cheese and stir: Serves 5 well.

Candle Lighting

If a candle lighted as part of a ceremony blows out
Be assured that there are evil spirits about
Turn around three times, spit and shout
To the cross you unwelcome spirits – get out!

Black Forest Shire Chicken

4 boneless chicken breasts
1 ½ C forest (button) mushrooms, sliced
1 C shredded cheddar cheese, melted butter
8 oz heavy cream
1 tsp each: chervil, fenugreek, summer savory
½ tsp each: sage, rosemary, salt, pepper
2 C dried bread crumbs
1 ¾ C chicken broth
1 leek, diced
¼ Olive oil
3 Tbsp butter + 1 Tbsp

In a skillet, sauté' mushrooms and leeks in olive oil on low until all the water is out of them, then drain. Add 3 Tbsp butter, the cream, chervil, fenugreek, and savory and blend well, set aside. In a sauce pan mix the sage, rosemary, salt and pepper in the chicken broth and bring to a boil. Take off heat and add the bread crumbs and 1 Tbsp butter. Grease a 9X9 baking dish and layer ½ sauce, stuffing, chicken , ½ sauce and cheese then cover in foil and bake at 375 for 30 minutes, remove cover and bake another 20 minutes then serve.

Candle Dressing

Once you touched a candle you imprint your purpose upon it – to strengthen your purpose you may bless it, use essential oils, draw images on the candle, hold it and meditate your purpose to it etc – then be careful not to use it for anything else.

Hospitality Chicken

4 skinless boneless chicken breasts, cut into strips
16 oz pineapple chunks
3 Tbsp each: corn oil, corn starch
2 Tbsp soy sauce
2 tsp lemon juice
1 tsp salt
¼ tsp white pepper

Mix together the salt, pepper and corn starch and toss the chicken in it to coat. In a medium skillet, over medium heat, place the oil and when hot sauté each chicken strip for 10-12 minutes or until done. Drain the pineapple, but reserve the juice. Add the pineapples to the chicken, cover and simmer on low for 5 minutes. Mix the remaining ingredients and add to the chicken and mix. Bring to a boil and cook for 3-5 minutes and serve.

Simple Candle Magick

You will need: Beeswax candle, salt, essential oil, incense, paper, quill and ink

Cast a circle of salt around you. Dress your candle, draw images on it and place it on a safe surface to burn. Burn incense or play music if you like to put you in a soft mood. Write your wish or spell or intentions on a piece of unused paper with ink and quill. Meditate on your purpose and desire. Sing or chant your spell and then slowly fold the paper and burn it with the candle starting at the edge and placing in a fire safe bowl.

Southern Fried Chicken

1 cut up whole chicken
3/4 C each: flour, plain cracker crumbs
¼ tsp each: black pepper, parsley, sage, rosemary, thyme, poultry seasoning, seasoned salt, garlic salt, marjoram, cumin, dry mustard
½ C grape seed oil

In a medium large mixing bowl add the flour and cracker crumbs then add all the seasonings and mix thoroughly. Wash the chicken pieces and take damp (not dripping) pieces and roll into the mixture. Remove to a deep skillet with grape seed oil in it and cook on medium heat, turning occasionally for about 45-60 minutes or until thoroughly done.

French Baked Turkey Breast

1-2 large turkey breasts
1/3 C olive oil
2 Tbsp French herb blend
2/3 C water

In a large casserole dish, add the water. Place the turkey breasts sides up, brush with the oil and sprinkle with the herb blend (the one with lavender flowers works best. Bake at 425 for 45-60 minutes or until well browned and completely done.

Tossing someone an apple proposes marriage, catching one accepts the proposal – however – if you are given a green knotted ribbon as an answer then your proposal has been rejected!

Chicken and Dumplings

1 ½ lb chicken tenderloins
32 oz chicken broth
1 tsp each: salt, parsley, black pepper
2 C flour
½ tsp each: salt, baking soda
3 Tbsp butter - softened
¾ C buttermilk

In a large pot cook the chicken tenderloins, broth, salt, parsley and pepper on medium heat for 20 minutes and then bring to a boil. In a medium mixing bowl, add the flour, salt, baking soda, butter and buttermilk – mix thoroughly and set aside. When the chicken is ready, knead the dough and drop by tablespoonfuls into the boiling pot. Then turn heat to low and simmer for 8-20 minutes covered or until dumplings are firm and serve.

Full Moon Prosperity Rice

You will need: glass bowl, long grain rice, green food coloring, silver spoon and lace bag

Sit out on the first day of the full moon and concentrate on your desires, hold the bowl with the rice in it and drop food coloring in it and stir. Sing: Lady of mercy, Lady of grace, take my desires, and wrap them in lace – Bring me prosperity, abundance and luck, placed in my bag, at my will shall be plucked - As I spread it, out to be used – let me remember, to never abuse! Give now your will to me – My precious Lady – Now mote it be! Leave out the bowl and in 3 days place in your bag and use it at will wherever you need it!

Escalloped Chicken

4 chicken breasts, cubed
1/3 C olive oil
½ C each: celery, carrots, onions, peas
2 Tbsp parsley
1 tsp each: poultry seasoning, sage
4 Tbsp butter
2 C egg noodles, cooked
2 C Forest mushroom soup pg 28
1 C bread or cracker crumbs

In a large skillet brown the chicken breast in the oil and cube – about 15 minutes on medium heat. Add the celery, carrots, onions, peas and seasonings and cook an additional 5-8 minutes or until soft. Meanwhile, grease a large casserole dish with the butter. Add the soup and egg noodles to the meat and mix thoroughly. Remove to the casserole and top with the crumbs. Bake at 350 for 25-35 minutes and serve hot.

To break a spell or curse set against you

Take a length of red or black cord and your special knife. Tie a knot at one end representing you and knots at the other end representing those who are set against you – visualize and speak:

Between you and me this hex I break
For this hex was not right for you to make
So it's path I abruptly end
And back to you this hex I send!

Now cut the cord between you and them and throw in a crossroads and don't look back!

Roma Shack Steak

2-3 Cube steaks
3 eggs
1 ½ C flour
1 tsp each: salt, pepper
2 Tbsp soy sauce
½ stick butter

Melt butter on low in large cast iron skillet. Meanwhile beat the eggs together in a bowl. On a plate mix the flour and the salt and pepper. Now take the cube steak and dip in the egg and cover with the flour and put in the pan to fry. Continue until all cube steaks are in the pan, then add the soy sauce and put the rest of eggs on top of the cube steaks. Cover and fry 10 minutes or when browned. Remove cover and turn over and fry 10 minutes more or when browned. Continue frying until completely browned on both sides and serve.

Candle Magick to remove a Hex or Curse

You will need: an old cooking pot (that you can toss), a black candle, natural water

Cast a circle of salt around you, dress your candle, then place it in the center of the pot and fill the pot with the water leaving about 1-2 inches of candle left out to burn. Light the candle and sing: If truly hexed or cursed I came, then let it break with quench of flame! Stare at the flame until it is extinguished in the water and then say – Thy divine Will to me – Mote it be! Dig a hole and bury it all.

Shepherd's Pie

1 lb ground round
16 oz beef gravy
14 oz yellow or white corn
2-3 C leftover mashed potatoes

In a large cast iron skillet, brown the hamburger on medium heat until done. Make sure the hamburger is in bite size pieces. Add the gravy and stir. In a large pie dish put the meat mixture. Top with a layer of corn and then top that with a layer of mashed potatoes and bake at 350 for 25 minutes and serve: Serves 4 well.

Candle Magick for True Love

You will need: 3 candles – red, pink and white, essential oil of roses, apple and vanilla, string

Cast your circle of salt. Dress each candle separately with the essential oil. As you dress the red one envision what you would want in a mate – but don't look for physical characteristics. As you dress the pink on envision what you can give a mate. As you dress the white one, envision how the two of you will be able to work together as mates. Now tie the three together and light. Meditate on your own pure intentions and sing: Candles red, pink and white, search for my heart's delight! Candles pink, white and red, together will we both be lead! Candles white, red and pink, unite our destinies make them link! Forever will our Love be true – yours to me, mine to you!

Ghoul Mash

1 lb lean ground beef or sausage
1 small onion, peeled and chopped
1 green pepper, seeded and chopped
16 oz stewed tomatoes
8 oz elbow macaroni
½ tsp each: salt, red pepper, black pepper
1 tsp each: soy sauce, honey, balsamic vinegar
1 clove garlic, peeled and crushed
¼ C grape seed oil

In a large deep dish skillet, add the oil, soy sauce, and meat and cook over a medium heat for 10-12 minutes. Add the onion, garlic and green pepper to the skillet and cook for 8 minutes. Meanwhile in a large pot boil 6 qrts of water and cook the macaroni for 5-10 minutes or until soft but firm and drain. To the skillet add the tomatoes, seasonings, vinegar and honey and simmer on low of 12 minutes – add the macaroni and stir thoroughly and serve.

Summer Solstice Spell

You will need: a cloth bag, Lavender, Vervain, and all your worries and cares

What you do: Place the herbs in the cloth bag and either with pencil and paper or through meditation submit all your worries and cares into the bag.

The Spell: Mother of mine, Mother Devine, take all my worries, banish and bind, from now on, let them be Thine! - Now bury your worries with the bag.

Maben Meatballs

½ lb each: lean hamburger, chicken sausage
¾ C plain bread crumbs
½ tsp each: salt, black pepper
1 garlic bulb, peeled and crushed
¼ C Romano cheese, grated
1 large egg
1/3 C grape seed oil

Mix all ingredients (except oil) in a large mixing bowl until thoroughly mixed and smooth. Round into Tablespoon (or golf ball) size balls and either place in a deep dish skillet with the oil or a deep baking pan with the oil. If using the skillet then brown covered for 5 minutes and turn with a large spoon to keep it's shape. Continue process turning every 5 minutes for 20-25 minutes or until thoroughly cooked. If using a baking pan, turn oven to 425 and bake for 12 minutes, turn with a spoon to keep their shape and bake and additional 8 minutes.

Be my Valentine Love Spell I

You will need: 3 – 23 inch red strings, and one heart bead at the end to represent your true love then braid the strings while chanting the spell:

One for Love, One for Lust, One for harmony
As I braid these three strings, bring true love to me
Make him (soft, sweet, cute)
Make him (kind, generous, loving)
Make him love me true
Make him all the things, I need a man to do
Bring him swift, bring him fast,
But most of all, make love last!

Homemade Pasta

2 large eggs
1 ¼ C Semolina flour
Pinch of salt

On a clean surface, mix the flour and salt and make a well in the center. Place the eggs in the well and slowly knead the flour into the eggs until a soft dough forms. Roll out thin and cut. Dry on wooden dowels or clean towels and cook in boiling salted water until it floats or is done.

Pasta Sauce

32 oz crushed tomatoes
6 oz tomato paste
1 Tbsp balsamic vinegar
1 Tbsp brown sugar
1 Tbsp honey
1 Tbsp olive oil
1 tsp each: red pepper, black pepper, salt
1/3 C fresh basil leaves
3 cloves garlic, peeled and crushed
1 medium onion, peeled and diced
8 oz button mushrooms, sliced
1 green pepper, seeded and diced

Combine all ingredients in a large pot and cook on low for 3-8 hours or until all flavors are thoroughly mixed. Serve over your favorite pasta.

Jackstraw or a bonfire is lit on New Year's Eve to put an end to all of last year's evils.

Sky Fire Chili Burgers

2 lbs of lean ground beef
2 tsp onion salt
1 ½ C Sky fire Chili pg 45
6 oz shredded mild cheddar cheese

Mix lean ground with salt and divide into 12 balls. Flatten each ball into a 4 inch round. Spoon ¼ C chili on the center of each patty. Top with 1 oz of the cheese and top that with another beef round patty then press the sides together. Pan fry over medium heat or grill until done about 14-18 minutes, turning at least once. Serve on toasted buns with all the fixings! Makes 6 nice burgers.

The Seven that Stand before The Almighty One

Gnostics: Michael, Gabriel, Raphael, Uriel, Brachiel, Sealtiel, Jehudiel
Ethiopic Enoch: Uriel, Raphael, Raguel, Michael, Zerachiel, Gabriel, Remiel
Hebrew Enoch: Mikael, Gabriel, Shatquiel, Baradiel, Shachaquiel, Baraquiel, Sidriel
Solomon: Mikael, Gabriel, Uriel, Sabrael, Arael, Iaoth, Adonael
Talisman: Zaphkiel, Zabkiel, Camael, Raphael, Haniel, Michael, Gabriel
Tobit: Uriel, Raphael, Raguel, Michael, Sariel, Gabriel, Remiel
Hierarchy: Raphael, Gabriel, Chamuel, Adabiel, Haniel, Zaphiel
Persian: Truth, Right Order, Obedience, Prosperity, Wisdom, Health, Immortality

Merlin's Meatloaf

2 lbs lean ground beef
1 C either bread crumbs or oatmeal
1 tsp each: soy sauce, worchestershire sauce
1 tsp each: salt, black pepper, red pepper
1 tsp each: basil, chervil, Italian seasoning
2 eggs
2 cloves garlic, peeled and crushed
1 Tbsp balsamic vinegar
1 tsp honey
16 oz crushed tomatoes
4 Tbsp Olive oil

In a large mixing bowl, thoroughly mix the beef, bread crumbs (or oatmeal) sauces, seasonings, herbs and eggs and form into a loaf. In a Casserole dish add the oil to the bottom and then put the loaf on top. Now mix together the crushed tomatoes, vinegar, honey and garlic then pour the mixture on top of everything and bake at 375 for 35-45 minutes or until done, checking every 20 minutes and spooning the topping over the loaf again. Serve hot.

To Neutralize the Jealous Eye

You will need: 1 egg and 1 black pen
Write the name of the person who has vexed you or cursed you on the egg with the pen and speak:
Jealous person that I seek, I break thy hex, I make thee weak, I crush thy spell, I crush thy ways, I send thee into an endless haze!

Energize the egg to neutralize the power of the person involved with all your might – then smash the egg and put their evil to flight!

Pan Dinner

1 lb lean ground beef
1 small onion, peeled and diced
1 small green pepper, seeded and diced
2 C Forest mushroom soup pg 22
1 ½ C long grain rice, cooked
1 tsp soy sauce
½ tsp each: salt, black pepper, red pepper
1 C water or milk

In a deep dish skillet, brown meat with soy sauce and seasonings on medium high for 10 minutes and add the onion and green pepper and cook an additional 8 minutes. Add the soup and water (or milk) and stir thoroughly and heat an additional 5 minutes. Add the rice (already cooked according to package directions), mix thoroughly and serve.

Be my Valentine Love Spell II

You will need: 3 – 23 inch red strings and one heart bead at the end to represent your true love. Braid them together and sing the spell then wear on your wrist or ankle until it falls off.
Weave the magick, weave the spell
Make him love me, oh so well
Weave the joy, weave the tears
Weave a love, that lasts for years
Weave the days, weave the nights
Fill them with, sensual delights
Weave the days, weave the weeks
Make him the one, my heart seeks!

Fox Fairy Steak

¾ lb lean ground beef
¼ lb chicken sausage
2/3 C plain bread crumbs
1 egg
½ tsp each: salt, black pepper, chervil
1 Tbsp soy sauce
1/4 C olive oil
2 C brown gravy

In a large mixing bowl, combine the beef, sausage, bread crumbs, egg and seasonings until thoroughly mixed. Shape into four large patties. In a large skillet place the oil, soy sauce and then the patties and cook over a medium heat on each side for 10 minutes. Add the gravy, lower heat and simmer for and additional 10 minutes and serve.

Christmas Portends

Of all the days that Christmas falls,
Monday and Tuesday are not good at all
Wednesday foretells hard winter gales
Warm summer winds and bad ship sails
Thursday and Friday my child portend
A good summer harvest and a hard winter wind
Saturday says the winter I fear
Will be long, biting and severe
And the summer will faire no better
For endless wet will be the weather
However frost and snow at Christmastide
Shows signs of spring calm and mild
And while a new moon on Christmas Eve
Is lucky, be on your guard
For a green Christmas fills the church yard!

Enchanted Stroganoff

1/3 C 1st cold pressed extra virgin olive oil
1 lb beef round top steak, cut in 1-2 inch slices
3-4 oz shitake mushrooms sliced
1 small Vidalia onion, peeled and diced
1 Tbsp Worcestershire sauce
1 tsp each: sea salt, ground nutmeg
½ tsp each: black pepper, crushed red pepper
1 lb Barilla fettuccini pasta
8 oz of cream cheese

In a large 3 – 5 quart pot of salted water, bring to boil on medium heat and add pasta continuing boiling for 8-12 minutes until al dente. Mean while, in a large cast iron skillet on medium heat pour the oil and cook the steak 10-15 minutes or until mostly done. Add the mushrooms, onion, and sauce and cook until soft and turn to low heat. Stir in the herbs and cream cheese slowly. Turn off heat and drain pasta. Place pasta on each dinner plate and top with stroganoff mixture: Serves 4 well.

Candle Magick for Prosperity

You will need: 3 candles – green, orange and black, whole cloves for dressing, string

Cast your circle, dress your candles with designs in cloves, tie together with string and sing: Candles green, orange, black – send all poverty in me back; Candles black, orange and green – bring me endless money and means! This is my will, true it be, bless me with prosperity! And with the law of three, this is my will – Mote it be!

Tramp and Thief Beef

1 ¼ lb boneless steak, sliced
1 lb linguine
2 Tbsp olive oil
3 large garlic cloves, peeled and crushed
8 oz Portobello mushroom caps, sliced
1 medium red pepper, cut into strips
2 Tbsp thinly sliced fresh basil leaves
1/3 C grated Romano cheese

Cook pasta according to directions and drain, keep warm by placing it back in the pot with the lid closed. Meanwhile, cut steak into strips and heat with 1 Tbsp olive oil and garlic over medium heat in a large skillet for 2-5 minutes or until done to your satisfaction. Season with salt and pepper, and set aside. In the same skillet, heat 1 Tbsp olive oil, and stir fry mushrooms and red pepper for 3-4 minutes or until tender. Return the beef to the pan, add the sliced basil and toss. Place the pasta on a platter, spoon beef mixture on top, sprinkle with cheese and serve immediately.

Reverse Curse Spell

Red and Black send evil back
For it's been knocking at my door
Curse the one who so cursed me
To dwell in their wickedness as before
Let them see themselves clear as day
So they will mend their evil ways
Remove this curse when they are done
Learning the lessons of compassion!
This is my will, for them to see
By the law of three, Mote it be!

Wood Wife Steak

1 ½ C Wood Wife Soup pg 24
1 ½ lbs lean ground beef
½ C dry bread crumbs
1 egg
¼ tsp salt
1/8 tsp pepper
1 Tbsp flour
¼ C tomato paste
¼ C water
1 Tbsp worchestershire sauce
½ tsp dry mustard

In a large bowl mix together 1/3 C of the Wood Wife soup with the ground beef, bread crumbs, eggs, salt and pepper. Shape into 6 oval patties. In a large skillet over medium high heat, brown both sides of the patties, pour off excess fat and lower heat. In a small bowl blend flour and remaining soup until smooth. Add in water, tomato paste, worchestershire sauce and mustard powder and whip until well blended. Pour over the meat in the skillet, cover and simmer for 20 minutes, stirring occasionally then serve.

Onion and Garlic Protection Charm

3 whole onions with leaves attached
3 whole garlic bulbs with leaves attached

Weave together, hang in your kitchen and replace annually singing:
Layered bulbs of power and might, chase away all harm and spite!

Pixie Balls

2 lbs ground beef
2 eggs
1 ½ tsp garlic powder
1 tsp garlic powder
1 tsp seasoning salt
½ tsp pepper
¼ C plain bread crumbs

Preheat oven to 350. In a large bowl combine the seasonings, bread crumbs, and eggs until thoroughly mixed. With a teaspoon, scoop and shape into small meatballs. Cook in the oven for 30-35 minutes or until done. While meatballs are baking prepare the sauce. When meat balls are done, remove from the oven and cover with the sauce, return to oven for 10 minutes and serve.

Pixie Sauce

1 C Chili sauce – see page 10
1 C red currant or grape jelly

Mix together thoroughly in a medium bowl until thoroughly beaten and add to pixie balls.

Looking for a way to pass that impossible test?

Simply use the same pencil you studied with to take the test with and surely it will remember the answers!

Charmed Steak

2 lbs round steak
¼ C all purpose flour
1 tsp salt
¼ tsp ground black pepper
3 Tbsp olive oil
½ C diced onion
1 C diced tomatoes
1/3 C chopped bell pepper

Cut steak into bite size strips. On a cutting board combine, flour, salt and pepper and pound the steak into it with a mallet on all sides. In a large skillet, on medium heat, add the olive oil and brown the steak on all sides about 8-12 minutes. Add onion, tomatoes, cover and simmer on low heat for about 25 minutes or until tender. Add the bell pepper and continue simmering for 15 more minutes. Skim off any excess fat, taste and adjust seasonings then serve.

Midsummer Roast

1 well trimmed rib eye beef roast
2 Tbsp olive oil
2 tsp each: garlic and onion powder, black pepper
1 tsp each: kosher salt, sweet basil
½ tsp ground thyme

Preheat oven to 350. In a large mixing bowl combine all seasonings and olive oil then roll the roast in it - pressing the herbs into it. Bake in a shallow baking dish for 45-60 minutes or until done. in one inch of fresh water then serve.

Beltane Rack of Lamb

1 frenched rack of Lamb
1 Tbsp olive oil
1 tsp each: salt, pepper, crushed garlic
1 Tbsp each: thyme, marjoram, rosemary, chervil
¼ C fresh parsley leaves
6 Tbsp unsalted butter, softened
2 Tbsp Dijon mustard

Preheat oven to 425. Mix together olive oil, salt, pepper and garlic in a small bowl and rub the lamb thoroughly with it. Place in a roasting pan and bake for 15 minutes then remove. Meanwhile, mix together herbs (except parsley) with mustard and butter. When rack is cool (about 10 minutes) then cover with herb mixture and change oven setting to broil. Broil the lam rack until the crust is crisp and lightly charred about 6-12 minutes (depending on rare to well). Remove to a cutting board and slice rack apart then serve on a platter with fresh parsley leaves.

To prevent an unwanted guest from returning

Sweep out their room, where they stood, their chair
Sweeping them out the door and down the stair
Past the garden gate and on into nowhere
Stamp your foot and say: There!
Now as you start your way back
Sprinkle the holy salt in your sack
To ensure their spirit leaves
And their evil loses its tracks!

Maben Pork with Herbs

2 lbs pork tenderloins
12 springs each: fresh rosemary and thyme
2 tsp finely ground white pepper
½ C olive oil
½ C balsamic vinegar

Cut tenderloins crosswise into five or six thick pieces. Crush the rosemary and thyme leaves with a mortar and pestle then combine in a bowl with the pepper, oil and vinegar then use as a marinade for the pork. Marinade for anywhere from 1 hour to 1 day in a shallow baking pan, turning over periodically. From here you may either grill or broil the pork about 5-10 minutes on each side then serve hot.

Is it a boy or a girl?

Take off the mothers ring and place it on a string over the mother's stomach – if it swings in circle - it's a girl – a straight line – it's a boy! (Indicating the sex organs)

For a girl – carry wide, crave sweet and sour, have acne and intense early morning sickness.

For a boy – carry out front, your hair grows faster, clear complexion, your feet are cold, you crave meats and cheeses, your sickness is late in the day and Dad is carrying extra weight too.

Parsley, Sage, Rosemary and Thyme

2 lb pork roast
1 clove garlic, crushed
2 Tbsp rosemary leaves, finely chopped
3-4 sage leaves, finely chopped
1 Tbsp each: parsley and thyme leaves
2 cloves, ground
2 tsp each: salt, pepper
5 Tbsp extra virgin olive oil
½ C - 1 C vegetable broth
½ C dry white wine
½ Tbsp cornstarch

In a small bowl mix and crush together all garlic, herbs and seasonings. With a sharp knife make incisions in the roast and fill with the ½ herbs. With the other ½ herb mixture and rub into the outside of the roast. In a large skillet, heat the oil on medium heat for 5 minutes then brown and seal the roast on all sides (about 3-4 minutes per side). Add the wine and ½ C broth and bring to a boil. Lower heat and simmer for 1 hour or until done. Turn occasionally and add additional broth if necessary. Remove the meat to a platter , meanwhile in a small bowl stir together the cornstarch and 2-3 Tbsp of broth until smooth and add to the broth on the stove and heat on medium, whisking together to make a gravy sauce until thick. Serve warm sauce over the meat.

If a black cat comes to you, it brings you good fortune – however - if it walks away from you it takes your fortune with it!

Charm to make sickness melt away:

It was first recorded in a Latin medical poem De Medicina Praecepta by a Roman Physician Quintus Serenus. Its origins in Hebrew: ab (Father) ben (Son) ruach acadosch (Holy Spirit); or from the word avar k'davar "it will be according to what is spoken", abrakha adabra "I shall bless, I shall speak". The origins could be Chaldean: abbada Ke dabra "perish like the word, or it could be Aramaic: avra kehdabra "I will create as I speak" abhadda kedhabhra "disappear like this word . Or it could have originated from the Gnostic word for God "Abraxas". Regardless, this magickal charm has been used for thousands of years to cure sickness and make disease disappear. To use just write it on a piece of parchment and lay it on the sick person or under their pillow and as the letters descend it is said to draw away the sickness. Try singing as well.

```
A B R A C A D A B R A
 A B R A C A D A B R
  A B R A C A D A B
   A B R A C A D A
    A B R A C A D
     A B R A C A
      A B R A C
       A B R A
        A B R
         A B
          A
```

Crockpottery

2nd harvest zucchini

1 large zucchini, sliced
1 medium yellow onion, peeled and sliced
32 oz stewed tomatoes
½ tsp salt
1 Tbsp fresh basil leaves
8 oz shredded mozzarella

Layer half tomatoes, salt and basil on the bottom, alternate slices of zucchini with rings of onion, put remainder of tomatoes, basil and salt on top. Finish with the cheese on top of that and cook on low for 6-8 hours. Serve hot as a main dish or side dish.

Pixie Potato Puff

12 medium potatoes, boiled and mashed
1 C milk
6 Tbsp butter
¾ tsp salt
2 ½ C soft processed tube cheese, cubed
3 eggs beaten

Mix all ingredients together inside a crock pot and mash. Cover and cook on high for 2 ½ hours or on low for 3-4 hours. Stir and mix thoroughly after the first 40 minutes to produce proper puffing. Serve as a main dish or side dish.

**No matter what never leave a chair rocking,
For sorrow will follow and evil come knocking!**

Elfin Scalloped Potatoes Au gratin

2 C milk
1 ½ C flour
1/2 tsp each: salt, black pepper
¼ C butter
11-13 peeled and sliced potatoes
8 oz grated cheddar cheese
Optional: 1 lb Canadian bacon or lean ham or kosher salami cut into bite size cubes.

In a medium mixing bowl stir together milk, flour and herbs and place 1/3 of mixture on the bottom of a large 3-5 quart crock pot. Put down a layer of potato slices, followed by 3-4 butter pats and 1/3 of the shredded cheese (and ½ of the meat), top with 1/3 of the flour mixture, a layer of potato slices, followed by 3-4 more pats of butter. Add 1/3 of shredded cheddar cheese (other half of the meat), top with the rest of the potatoes, flour mixture, butter and remaining cheese. Put crock pot on low for 6-8 hours or high for 4-5 hours: Serves 4-6 well.

Saffron Rice

2 C uncooked long grain white rice
2 C each: water, chicken broth
¼ C melted butter
¼ tsp saffron threads
2 tsp salt
1 tsp garlic powder

Combine all ingredients in the crock pot and cover. Cook on low for 4-6 hours. Serve hot.

Moonshine Rice

1 ½ C uncooked long grain rice
½ C uncooked wild rice
1 envelope dry onion soup mix
1 Tbsp diced parley leaves
5 C water
1 bunch of green onion, cleaned and chopped
8 oz fresh button mushrooms, sliced
¼ C melted butter

Combine all ingredients together into a lightly greased crock pot. Cover and cook on high 2 ½-3 hours, stirring occasionally. Rice will become mushy if overcooked so watch carefully. Serve hot.

1st Harvest Eggplant Parmesan

2 eggplants, sliced
3-4 eggs
1 ½ C bread crumbs
1/3 C olive oil
16 oz pasta sauce
8 oz parmesan or parmesan Romano cheese
1 lb of your favorite cooked pasta

Put ½ the sauce on bottom of the crock pot. Mix eggs and reserve in a bowl. Spread bread crumbs on a plate. Take sliced eggplant, dip in egg, cover with bread crumbs and fry lightly in olive oil for 3-4 minutes on each side. Then remove eggplant to crock pot. Top with remaining sauce and cheese and cook on low 3-4 hours and serve with your favorite pasta: Serves 4-5 well.

Selkie's Herb Stuffing ***

1 C butter, melted
1 ½ C onion, peeled and diced
2 C celery, cleaned, diced
¼ C chopped fresh parsley leaves
8 oz mushrooms, sliced
8 C stale bread crumbs ***
1 tsp each: salt, dried thyme
1 ½ tsp dried sage
½ tsp ground marjoram
¼ tsp ground black pepper
4 C chicken broth***

Combine all ingredients, mixing thoroughly in a crock pot and set on high for 45 minutes – stir thoroughly and change to low to keep for up to 3-6 hours longer. Great alternative for Thanksgiving.

Your own Candle

The easiest way to make your own candle is simply to buy sheets of beeswax and roll a wick into it. As long as you are at it – roll different herbs, flowers, and oils into your candle related to its specific purpose – see the Herbal reference in back.

Any Purpose Candle

Into your sheet of beeswax press the following: frankincense, myrrh, rosemary, hyssop, cassia, cinnamon and spikenard. Place the wick at one end and roll tightly. Trim wick and burn on a fireproof surface.

Divination Pasta

1 lb ricotta cheese
8 oz shredded mozzarella
8 oz frozen spinach
2 eggs
1 tsp each: nutmeg
½ tsp each: salt, pepper
1 lb large shell pasta
1 jar pasta sauce

In a large pot of salted water, cook pasta according to package directions. In a large bowl combine cheeses, spinach, nutmeg, eggs and seasonings. Line the crock pot with ½ jar of pasta sauce, fill the pasta with the mixture and stack on top of each other. Cover with the rest of the sauce and heat on low for 4-6 hours and serve: Serves 4-5 well.

On the Job!

Never place your shoes under your desk or a table as it will bring you bad luck for a day, bring trouble with your mate and cause you to lose your job!

If you are having trouble with jealous or vindictive coworkers, hang a mirror that reflects on anyone who passes by or enters your space. This will reflect their evil eye and designs back at them and they will soon be seen for the trouble that they bring!

Wicked White Lasagna

1 lb box of quick lasagna noodles
1 C zucchini, cleaned and chopped
1 C carrots, peeled and chopped
1 C mushrooms, sliced
1lb ricotta cheese
8 oz mozzarella cheese, shredded
Alfredo sauce: see chicken fettuccini Alfredo recipe
2 eggs
1 tsp: nutmeg
½ tsp each: salt, crushed red pepper

Mix together cheeses, eggs, and seasonings in a bowl and set aside. Mix together zucchini, carrots and mushrooms and set aside. Layer crock pot as follows: ¼ sauce, noodles, ½ vegetable mixture, ½ cheese mixture, ¼ sauce, noodles, ½ vegetable mixture, ½ cheese mixture, 1/4 sauce, noodles, remaining sauce. Cook on low 4-8 hours and serve: Serves 6 well.

Other great combinations: Spinach, mushrooms & carrots; Sweet peppers, yellow onions and sausage; Poultry, mushrooms, carrots or make your own.

New Moon to Full Moon

This is a time for hidden knowledge and new beginnings. This is also a time when you want to attract something or want something to grow, good for love, money, career and all endeavors.

Italian boats on a Mediterranean Sea

16oz large shell pasta
1 lb ground turkey
1/3 C 1st cold pressed extra virgin olive oil
1 medium red onion peeled and diced
8oz diced crimini mushrooms
1 C fresh basil cleaned, stems removed and sliced
1/2 tsp each: kosher salt, ground pepper, nutmeg
2 C shredded mozzarella cheese
16 oz pasta sauce
6 oz Mediterranean feta cheese
5 oz sliced black olives

In a large 3-5 quart pot on medium heat in salted water cook pasta al dente according to package directions, drain and cool. In a cast iron skillet on medium heat pour olive oil and brown ground turkey for 10-15 minutes or until done and remove to large 3 quart mixing bowl. To bowl add onions, basil, mushrooms, herbs and mozzarella and mix thoroughly. In a large crock pot (3-5 quarts) put 1/3 of Barilla sauce then fill each pasta shell with meat mixture and layer on the bottom of the crock pot. Top with 1/3 of the jar of sauce, ½ of the feta cheese and ½ of the sliced black olives, then add another layer of stuffed pasta. Top again with 1/3 of the jar of sauce, ½ of the feta cheese and ½ of the black sliced olives and cook on low for 2-4 hours: Serves 4-6 well.

A bird in the house portends death
While a bee meanwhile brings a guest
Do not kill it or they will be a pest

Country Hen Provolone

4 boneless skinless chicken breasts
16 oz pasta sauce
4 slices of provolone cheese
Your favorite pasta, cooked according to directions

In a crock pot layer ½ the sauce, chicken breasts, ½ the sauce and the cheese and set on low 3-4 hours. When ready cook your favorite pasta according to directions and serve on top: Serves 4 well.

Crock Pot Enchiladas

1 lb boneless skinless chicken breast
1/3 C olive oil
5 oz sliced black olives, drained
1 small onion, peeled and diced
1 C long grain rice cooked according to directions
12 oz red enchilada sauce
8 oz shredded Mexican blend cheese
8-12 small corn tortillas

In a large skillet, place the oil and cook the chicken breast and onion over medium heat until done, about 15 minutes. Mix in the rice, olives, and ½ the sauce with the meat, turning off heat and set aside. Put ¼ of the sauce on the bottom of the crock pot. Take a tortilla, put in cheese, then mixture then roll and put in the crock pot. Repeat until all the meat mixture is finished. Top with enchilada sauce, cover and cook on low 2-3 hours and serve: Serves 6 well.

Mountain Forest Chicken

6 boneless skinless chicken breasts
6 slices of Swiss cheese
6 tbsp Gruyere cheese
6 slices of black forest ham
2 Tbsp butter
2 C Forest Mushroom Soup pg 28
3 Tbsp milk
¼ tsp mixed pepper
String

Slice each chicken breast in half and beat with a mallet until thin. Cover each half with 1 slice Swiss, 1 Tbsp gruyere, 1 slice ham and top with the other half of the chicken breast and tie together with string. Brown each side in butter on medium heat in a skillet (about 5 minutes each side). Mix together the remaining ingredients in a small bowl and put half into the crock pot. Add Chicken and top with remainder of the sauce. Cook on low for 3-5 hours and serve hot.

Full Moon to New Moon

This is a time for banishing things, letting go, leaving behind, breaking curses and worn out attachments, getting rid of things, getting rid of negativity, breaking bad habits, etc.

This is also a time when your wishes on the new moon should begin being spilled out in your life so expect to see what happens next!

Charmed Chowder

1 lb bacon, diced
½ lb ham, fat trimmed and cubed
2 C each: celery, onions, peeled and chopped
½ tsp each: salt, pepper
2 C potatoes, peeled and cubed
2 C chicken meat, diced
4 C chicken broth
2 bottles clam juice
4 C milk
¾ C flour
16 oz can creamed corn
4 C shredded Colby jack cheese
2 Tbsp fresh parsley leaves, chopped

Sauté bacon, ham, onions and celery in a skillet on medium heat until bacon is crisp and onion and celery are limp. Reserve milk, flour, cheese and parsley and add all other ingredients to crock pot. Cover and cook on low for 6-8 hours. When almost ready, whisk together the milk, flour, cheese and parsley together and stir into soup. Cook one more hour on high and serve hot with bread.

Aura Color Meanings

White: Purity, protection
Violet: Spiritual, psychic ability
Blue: Devotion, spiritual, noble, religious
Green: Empathy, jealousy, deceit
Yellow: Intellect, logical thinking
Orange: Pride, noble living, irritability
Red: Passion, sensuality, love and anger
Brown: Materialism, selfishness
Black: Malice, depression, fear

Crazy Crock pot Lasagna

40 oz pasta sauce
9-12 quick lasagna noodles
16 oz ricotta cheese
16 oz shredded mozzarella cheese
2 eggs
1 ½ teaspoon each: ground nutmeg and ground peppercorns
1 lb ground round or kosher ground beef
1 lb kosher salami, cubed
2 oz grated Romano cheese

In a large cast iron skillet brown ground beef and salami for about 10-15 minutes or until done. Add one jar of Barilla sauce to the mixture, stir and set aside.. In a large mixing bowl add the cheeses, eggs and herbs and mix thoroughly and set aside. Now add 1/3 jar of Barilla sauce to the bottom of a large 3-5 quart crock pot and then place 3-4 lasagna noodles to the bottom, top with ½ of the meat mixture and ½ of the cheese mixture, then follow with 1/3 jar of the sauce, 3-4 lasagna noodles, ½ of the meat mixture and ½ of the cheese mixture and follow with 3-4 lasagna noodles and last 1/3 of the sauce and top with grated Romano cheese. Cook on high for 2-3 hours or low 5-7 hours: Serves 5-8 well.

To Cure a Sty

Go to a crossroads and say: Sty, sty, leave my eye: take the next one walking by!

Winter Green Peppers

1 C basmati rice
28 oz marinara sauce
1 lb ground round or kosher
1 large heirloom tomato, cored and chopped
1 medium yellow onion, peeled and diced
3 cloves garlic, peeled and crushed
1 tsp each: salt, black pepper, crushed red pepper
3 C of water (2 for rice, 1 for sauce)
5 green bell peppers, tops cut off, seeds cut off/out

In a cast iron skillet on medium heat cook onion, tomato, hamburger, garlic and peppers for 10-15 minutes or until done. Put the rice in a sauce pan and rinse several times pouring out the colored water with each time until the water runs clear. Add only 2 cups of water to the pan of rice and cook on medium low heat for 10-20 minutes depending on brand. Add the rice to the meat mixture and add 1/3 of the marinara sauce and stir. Place the rest of the marinara sauce in the crock pot with 1 cup of water. Place meat mixture by tablespoonfuls into each bell pepper and put the top back on placing it on top of the marinara sauce in the crock pot. Repeat until all are filled and topped off. Place the lid on the crock pot and cook on high 2 hours or low 3-5 hours: Serves 5 well.

Fidelity Feather

A swan's feather sewn into your mate's pillow will ensure fidelity as swans only mate with one partner their entire life!

Mayan Shredded Beef

3 lbs very lean round roast
1 Tbsp olive oil
16-24 oz mild or medium salsa
1 large onion, peeled and diced
3 cloves garlic, peeled and crushed
Opt: 1-3 Serrano peppers, seeded and diced (HOT)

Cut the roast into sections and put all ingredients in the crock pot on high for 6-8 hours. If possible check and pull apart after 3-4 hours. Can be used for tacos, burritos, enchiladas, Taquitos or any other dish. Great served with tortillas, guacamole and shredded cheese.

Mayan Guacamole

4 avocados, peeled, seeded and mashed
1 tsp sea salt or more to taste
3 tsp lime juice
1 C sour cream
1 C salsa

Mix together in a bowl, cover and chill until ready (ok for up to 4-6 hours) and serve.

Mayan Salsa

1C each: tomatoes (red) or tomatillos (green)
1/3 C each: onions (green or white), green chilies peppers (mild) or jalapeno peppers (medium) or Serrano (hot), fresh cilantro leaves
1 crushed garlic bulb - optional

Mix together and eat with chips or as condiment.

Dutch Boiled Dinner

2-3 lbs corned beef
1 C carrot, chopped
1 C onion, peeled and sliced
2 C cabbage, chopped
16 oz stewed tomatoes
4 corn cobbets
3-4 garlic cloves, peeled and crushed
1 tsp each: crushed red pepper, celery salt
1 Tbsp each: balsamic vinegar, sugar

Combine all ingredients in a crock pot and cook on high for 2 hours then cook on low for 4-6 hours more: Serves 4-6 well.

Winter Solstice Stew

1lb beef round - cubed
1 small onion, peeled and diced
¼ C barley
3 large potatoes, peeled and cubed
4 ribs of celery, cleaned and cubed
15 oz red kidney beans, drained
1 tsp salt
½ tsp worchestershire sauce
¼ tsp each: pepper, chili powder
1 C tomato sauce
½ C water

Remove all ingredients to crock pot and cover. Cook on low for 6-8 hours and serve.

Yuletide Stew with Venison

1 lb venison cubed, and set in salt water overnight in refrigerator then drained
2 C red potatoes, scrubbed and quartered
1 C carrots, peeled and sliced
1 medium yellow onion, peeled and sliced
1 bunch lettuce, cleaned and chopped with leaves
16 oz stewed tomatoes
¼ C fresh basil or ½ tsp dried basil
½ tsp red pepper
3 cloves garlic, peeled and crushed
½ tsp each: salt, black pepper, rosemary
2 C water

Put everything in the crock pot on high for 2 hours then on low for 6 hours and serve hot in bowls, Serves 5 well.

Sealing the Six Directions

Stand in your circle of salt, with your three fingers of your power hand make the form of the cross and say:

Above me I seal the Heavens + **IHV**
Below me I seal the Earth + **IVH**
Before me I seal the East + **HIV**
Behind me I seal the West + **VHI**
On my right I seal the South + **VIH**
On my left I seal the North + **HVI**
AUMN

Upon release extend your desires to the 6 directions.

Hoppin' John

1 lb ham or chicken hot sausage
1 C onion, peeled and chopped
30 oz black eyed peas, canned and drained
1 ½ C uncooked long grain rice
    (for wild rice add 1 C more broth)
2 C cabbage, shredded
1 C vegetable broth
2 C crushed tomatoes
½ C parmesan cheese, grated
1 Tbsp each: worchestershire sauce or say sauce
1 Tbsp each: raw honey, olive oil
2-3 cloves garlic, peeled and crushed
¼ tsp each: crushed red pepper, oregano, celery salt
    (more or less to taste)

Combine all ingredients in a crock pot and put on high for 2-3 hours, then on low for an additional 1-4 hours and eat on any new moon, New years day or Samhain for prosperity.

First Footer's Basket

A dark haired boy should be the first to enter your house on the New year with a basket filled with a lump of coal to keep your hearth warm, a silver coin to bring prosperity, a bit of bread so you will always be fed, a sprig of evergreen to ensure your life, a bit of salt to rid all evil and a token of a wish from each person to give them! For instance – a heart for love, a house ornament for a new residence, a harmonica for song and joy!

Faerie Folk Pork Roast with Cranberries

3-4 lb pork roast
1 tsp each: salt, pepper
1 C fresh cranberries, ground
¼ C each: Port wine, raw honey
1 tsp grated orange peel (zest)
1/8 tsp each: ground, cloves, nutmeg

Rub salt and pepper into roast and place in the crock pot. Combine all other ingredients in a small bowl and mix thoroughly then pour over roast. Cover and cook on low for 8-10 hours.

Winter Pork with fennel and sage

3 lb pork loin roast, trimmed and sliced
¼ tsp each: salt, pepper
1 C water
4 Tbsp fresh chopped sage
2 fennel bulbs sliced
2 Tbsp cornstarch
½ C white wine or herbed liquor

In a small bowl combine the salt, pepper and sage and use for a rub on the pork before placing it in a crock pot. Add water, and sliced fennel bulbs, cover and cook on low for 7-8 hours. Remove the fennel and pork onto a platter. Place the drippings in a sauce pan on medium heat. Dissolve the cornstarch in the wine and slowly stir in until thickened. Spoon sauce over the fennel and pork slices and serve.

When worn thyme attracts good health!

To Bless a Scrying bowl

You will need:

A silver or silver plated dish, bowl or glass that reflects the moons light.

When to do it:

On the new moon and the full moon after, fill or dowse with holy water.

The Charm:

Michael, Gabriel, Raphael and Uriel, I call on thee
To bless this scrying glass, for me to see
May all its visions be pure and true
May they show avenues of what to do
May these Thy Angels lead me best
And with Thy power this bowl be blest
Thy Almighty will to me
The spell is done, So mote it be!

To Use:

Fill with holy water, sea water, rain water, spring water or any natural water and sing or chant:

The Charm:

Michael, Gabriel, Raphael, and Uriel, I call on thee – this (bowl/glass/plate) is blest so make it see!

Now look into the water and see.

Old Fashioned Breads

Bread that is fresh and warm out of the oven perks up any meal or occasion. Grandma would always suggest that the darker the bread – the better it was for you and she wasn't far off. I've included some warm dark breads that I've found to magickally compensate for lost love, make just about situation more clear, and are generally improve your health better than the store bought variety. Now say it with me – real butter is not my enemy – fast food, manufactured food, preservatives, artificial ingredients, hydrogenated oils, dyes etc. are! The health of your household and all those you hold dear depends on you, use your strength!

Dumplings

1 C all purpose subtract 2 Tbsp flour
2 tsp baking powder
¼ tsp salt
1 egg
¼ C milk
2 Tbsp parsley or chervil, finely chopped
Optional: 2 Tbsp soft butter

Beat together the egg and milk, beat in the salt and baking powder and then beat in the parsley and then the flour until well mixed. Whatever you are dropping it on should be simmering but not boiling. Drop by spoonfuls and try not to touch each other. Cover and simmer 5-7 minutes on each side and serve hot with the meal: Serves 4-8 dumplings.

Southern Biscuits

2 C all purpose flour
2 tsp sugar
4 tsp baking powder
½ tsp salt
½ C butter or vegetable shortening, softened
2/3 C milk

Combine all dry ingredients into a large bowl and mix thoroughly. Pound in the butter and slowly mix in the milk and stir until the sides of the bowl are clean. Knead lightly on a floured surface, pat or roll out to about ½ inch thick and place on ungreased baking sheet. Bake at 450 for 10-12 minutes. Serve warm with dinner or honey butter: Makes about 16 biscuits.

Popovers

1 C bread flour
¾ tsp salt
1 C milk
3 eggs
opt: 4 Tbsp parmesan

Preheat oven to 450. Grease a 6 cup muffin tin. In a medium mixing bowl mix the flour and salt together. With a wire whisk beat in the milk. Continue beating the mixture until smooth and then slowly beat in one egg at a time. Pour into prepared pan and bake for 20 minutes then reduce heat to 350 (375 if you are not using a black pan) and bake 15-20 minutes more. Remove from pan and serve immediately: makes 6 popovers.

Southern Pecan Muffins

1 ¾ all purpose flour
2 tsp baking powder
¼ tsp cinnamon
1/8 tsp nutmeg
2 eggs
1/3 C sugar
¼ C melted butter, cooled
¾ C milk
¾ fresh Georgia pecans

In a bowl beat the eggs together, then beat in the sugar. Next beat in the butter and the milk. Now beat in all the dry ingredients and finish by folding in the pecans. Put in a prepared cupcake pan and sprinkle with sugar. Bake in a preheated 375 oven for 20-25 minutes: makes 12 muffins.

Corn Muffins

2 eggs
1 C milk
1/4 C melted butter
1 C all purpose flour
1 C yellow cornmeal
¼ honey
4 tsp baking powder
½ tsp salt

Mix all ingredients one by one in order in a bowl. Grease a cupcake pan. Preheat oven to 425 and cook muffins for 20-25 minutes: makes 12 muffins.

Hot Cross Buns

1 C all purpose flour
¼ C each: graham flour, brown sugar
1 tsp each: salt, cinnamon, water, sugar
½ tsp nutmeg
¼ tsp ginger
1 C warm milk
1 pkt active dry yeast
1 egg
1 egg yolk
¼ C softened butter
1 ¾ - 2 C more flour
¾ C dried cranberries, confectioner sugar
1 egg white
1 Tbsp each: lemon juice, melted butter

In a small mixing bowl stir together 1 C flour, graham flour, brown sugar, salt, cinnamon, nutmeg and ginger and set aside. In a Large mixing bowl combine the milk and yeast, stir and leave alone for 10 minutes. Then add the flour mixture, egg, egg yolk and softened butter and cream together. Slowly add the remaining flour and scrape the dough down and around the bowl. Cover and let rise about 45-60 minutes in a warm place or until doubled in size. Knead in the currants (or cranberries) and turn onto a floured surface and toss until no longer sticky. Roll out into ½ inch thickness and cut rounds placing them on a baking sheet. Preheat oven to 350. Brush the tops with egg white, water and sugar. Bake in for 15 to 18 minutes and cool on wire racks. While still slightly warm, combine the confectioner's sugar, lemon juice and melted butter and make a cross in each bun: Makes 12 buns.

Tortillas

Corn: ordinary cornmeal can not be used – you must use and instant corn mesa mix like Quaker masa harina instant mesa mix or MaSeCa instant corn mesa mix or if you are incredibly lucky freshly prepared mesa.

2 C instant corn mesa mix or fresh
½ tsp salt
1 1/8 – 1 ¼ C lukewarm water

In a large mixing bowl combine the corn mesa and salt and slowly add the water mixing well until the right consistency is reached. All the four should be moistened and the dough should be soft not sticky.

Divide the dough into 12 equal halves. On a piece of waxed paper, flatten one of the balls and top with another piece of waxed paper. Now roll out with your rolling pin (or a wine bottle) roll into a 6 inch round. Remove wax paper and cook inside a heated greased cast iron skillet on medium to low heat. Cook on the first side until the edges begin to curl and then toss over and cook on the second side just a bit longer than the first – until lightly browned. Remove to a plate and cover with a kitchen towel and repeat the process or have the children do the rolling while you do the cooking!

Lower the heat if necessary. Stack on top of one another to retain heat and flexibility, best used with tacos and enchiladas: Serves 4-6 well.

Tortillas

Flour: No special ingredients needed and great warm with butter!

2 C all purpose flour
1 tsp salt
1 tsp baking powder
¼ C butter softened
½ C very warm water (approximate)

In a mixing bowl stir together the flour, salt and baking powder. Fold in the butter until well mixed. Add just enough water to make a soft dough that is not sticky. Cover the bowl and let rise about 5 minutes. Divide into 12 parts and roll into balls. Toss each ball lightly with flour, cover and let set 15-30 minutes. Turn onto a board and roll out into a 6 inch circle (for burritos combine 2 balls together and roll into 12 inch circles). Cook on a dry, medium hot cast iron skillet until blistered. Flip over and cook until browned. Lower the heat if necessary and continue until all are done. Tortillas may be stored in a plastic bag until needed in the refrigerator or freezer. Great for burritos or Taquitos.

Ancient Knowledge Grows Here!

Always make the sign of the cross over bread before baking so the evil spirits won't keep it from rising. Always rub an apple before eating it to let the evil spirits out as it is thought to be the food of the dead.

Homemade Pizza

Tomato Pizza Sauce

1 can tomato paste 6 oz
2 cans water 12 oz
4 Tbsp brown sugar
1 large clove garlic, peeled and crushed
2 tsp basil
1/2 tsp each: oregano, crushed red pepper
1 Tbsp balsamic vinegar

In a sauce pan combine all ingredients and simmer slowly for about 10-20 minutes. And then spread on your pizza.

Pesto Pizza Sauce

5 oz parmesan cheese
3 crushed garlic cloves
4 C basil leaves, washed and dried
1 C olive oil

Finely chop and crush all basil leaves then remove to a medium mixing bowl and add the garlic cloves crushing them together. Add the cheese and the oil and whisk until smooth then spread on your pizza.

Never let your front door face your back door – or – money in – money out!

Homemade Pizza

Pizza Dough

1 ¼ C warm water
1 pkt active dry yeast
1 tsp sugar
1 tsp salt
2 ½ Tbsp olive oil
1 C bread flour
1 ¾ C all purpose flour

In a large bowl add the yeast to the warm water and sugar and let set 5-10 minutes. Then stir in the salt and 2 Tbsp olive oil. Mix in the bread flour. Slowly little by little add in the all purpose flour until you feel the dough is stiff enough – or it comes off the sides of the bowl. Remove dough to a floured surface and knead until smooth. Place back in the bowl and cover with ½ Tbsp (2 tsp) olive oil. Cover the bowl and let rise for 30-45 minutes.
Roll onto a large pizza pan and continue with your sauce and toppings. Bake at 450 for 15-22 minutes or until crust is browned and cheese is bubbly.

New Year's Lore

Anything you do on New Year's Day you'll do the whole year through! So no arguing, crying, spending money, taking out the trash or doing the laundry! Make sure there is money in your bank account, your purse, your penny jar and on your window sills! Make sure your cupboards are stocked and your debts are paid!

All purpose Buttermilk Baking Mix

2 C all purpose flour
1 Tbsp baking powder, baking soda, salt
6 C all purpose unbleached flour
1 ½ C shortening

In a large bowl mix together 2 C flour, baking powder, soda and salt. Mix in thoroughly the rest of the flour and cut into the shortening and you will have 10 C of mixture. Divide mixture evenly between 4 sandwitch Ziploc bags, label and refrigerate. When ready to bake bring the bag up to room temperature and use for the following biscuits, pancakes and waffles.

Buttermilk Biscuits

¾ C buttermilk
1 pkg buttermilk baking mix

Preheat oven to 450. Empty a package into a bowl and with a fork beat in the buttermilk until doughs cleans the bowl. Toss on a floured surface and knead lightly. Roll into ½ thickness and section into rounds and placed on a ungreased cookie sheet and bake for 12-15 minutes: makes 12-15 biscuits.

Be sure to open all the doors at midnight to let the old year out and the New Year in!

Buttermilk Pancakes and Waffles

2 eggs
1 Tbsp sugar
2Tbsp oil
2 C buttermilk
1 pkg buttermilk baking mix

Beat the eggs together in a bowl until frothy, add the oil, sugar and buttermilk and beat again. Mix in the baking mix and let batter stand 5 minutes before using. Use ¼ C batter per cake, bake on a lightly greased cast iron skillet on medium – low and turn only once: makes 12 pancakes. For Waffles make the same as pancakes only bake in a preheated waffle iron until steaming stops: Makes 3-4 waffles.

To Heal a Friend

You will need 3 strands of light blue cord at least 2 feet long and a healing bead of blue – now lift your voice and sing as you weave the string:

Weave these cords with healing power
Make it grow with every hour
Weave it well and weave it fine
Infuse the power of the Great Divine
Weave it nice and weave it fast
Make the healing power to last
Weave a cure for my good friend
Healing power to never end!

Now give it to them to carry or wear!

Pretzels: The original Lenten bread

1 C hot water
1 tsp barley malt extract
1 pkt active dry yeast
¾ tsp salt
1 Tbsp softened butter
½ C wheat gluten
1 C all purpose flour
½ - ¾ C all purpose flour

In a mixing bowl stir the hot water with the barley extract and cool until warm (or you will cook the yeast). Add the yeast, salt, butter, gluten and flour and mix thoroughly and quickly for 3 minutes. To stiffen dough add the rest of the flour slowly until it forms a soft dough that isn't sticky. Turn onto a floured board and knead until smooth. Put in a dry bowl and cover for 30 minutes to let rise. Turn out and press flat the let the air out. Divide into 8 pieces of equal size. Roll each piece into a long 20 inch tapered rope. Fold each rope into praying hands (originally this was done with the right arm over the left arm and crossed at the wrists). Press ends firmly to seal. Lightly grease baking sheets and place the pretzels on top. Leave uncovered for 30 minutes to rise once again. Meanwhile preheat oven to 425. As well place 1 quart of water and 4 Tbsp baking soda in a enameled pot and set to boil on medium heat. Then lower heat to simmer and simmer each pretzel (1-2 at a time) for 30 seconds on each side. Remove from pot and place on baking sheet (salt if desired) and bake at 425 for 15 minutes or until well browned. Serve with English mustard or melted cheese. For a change top with cheese before cooking.

Fritters

1 ½ C all purpose flour
1 tsp salt
1 tsp season salt, Creole seasonings or paprika
12 oz beer
½ C all purpose flour
Options: 1 C one of the following: drained canned corn, sliced zucchini, peeled and chopped onion, whole button mushrooms, boiled and mashed sweet potatoes, string beans, boiled and mashed eggplant, elderberry flowers or fish.
1/3-2/3 C oil

Mix together in a bowl, flour salt and seasoning. With a wire whisk, whip in the beer and set aside. In a separate bowl place the remaining flour. Take the food desired and coat it with the flour and dip it into the batter. Heat a frying skillet on medium heat and add oil. Place each fritter into the skillet and brown on both sides. Remove to a paper towel and serve warm: serves 6 well.

Into your Scrying Bowl

Fill your scrying bowl with natural water then add marigold or buttercup petals, sage or thyme flowers and stir in a clockwise motion and chant:

Into the threads of time I cast my thoughts
To cast a glimpse of what will be
O God/Goddess of All bring to me
The lovely gift of your prophesy!

Zucchini Bread: the Original Friendship Bread

2 C shredded zucchini
1 C shredded carrots
3 C flour
1 C packed brown sugar
¾ C dark molasses
¾ C butter or oil (olive, vegetable, canola or for a kick walnut)
3 eggs
3 tsp vanilla extract
1 tsp each: baking soda, baking powder, salt, crushed cloves, ground nutmeg, and ground cinnamon, opt Cardamom
Optional: 1 C nuts (walnut or pecan)

Turn oven onto 350-400 depending on your altitude. Grease and flour 2 bread pans or one 10 inch cast iron skillet (if using a 15 inch cast iron skillet then double mix). Bake for at least 45- 60 minutes, check if done by pulling out the rack and inserting a fork. If the fork comes out clean it's done – if it shakes or the fork does not come out clean it needs to bake longer. Share with friends.

On New Years do something small related to your occupation but make sure it is something you can finish quickly!

Gingerbread

1 C flour
1 tsp baking soda
¼ tsp salt
2 tsp ground ginger
1 egg
5 Tbsp dark brown sugar
½ C each: molasses, buttermilk
¼ C melted butter

In a large mixing bowl mix together dry ingredients (first four). Then add wet ingredients (remaining) and mix together thoroughly. Grease and flour a 9 inch square pan and remove mixture into pan. Bake at 350 for 30 minutes or until a fork inserted comes out clean. Cool and serve with powdered sugar and applesauce or whip cream.

Rosemary Tea Bread

2 C water
2 eggs
3 ½ C flour
1 tsp each: baking soda, baking powder, salt
½ C butter
1 C Romano cheese
1 Tbsp each: crushed garlic, fresh rosemary

Preheat oven to 325-350. sift together all dry ingredients and set aside. In a separate bowl beat together all wet ingredients and then by spoonfuls mix the two bowls together. Divide batter into two and grease two 8-9 inch loaf pans and bake for about 1 hour.

Pumpkin Bread

1 ¾ C all purpose flour
¾ C packed brown sugar
1 tsp each: baking powder, baking soda, salt
½ tsp each: cinnamon
¼ tsp each: cloves, nutmeg, ginger
1/3 C each: oil, molasses
2 eggs
1 C canned pumpkin

Preheat oven to 350. Grease and flour a 9x5 baking pan. In a large bowl mix together the flour, sugar, baking powder, soda, salt and spices until thoroughly mixed. Then mix in one by one the remaining ingredients, mixing thoroughly. Pour into prepared pan and bake for about 1 hour or until a fork comes out of the middle clean. Cool in pan for 5 minutes and on a wire rack or board until complete. Wrap in foil to store: makes 1 loaf.

Planetary Perfumes

Sun: black pepper, civet, wolfs bane, dragons
        Blood and magnolia
Moon: mandrake leaves, roots of bentain, valerian
Jupiter: sandalwood, agrimony's leaves, cloves, and
        Henbane powder
Mars: white poppy, chamomile, camphor
Mercury: seed of the ash tree, wood of aloe, leaves
        Of skull cap and mandrake root
Venus: musk, juniper berries, wood of aloes, dried
        Red roses, and dries leaves of elder
Saturn: aloes, saffron, aloe wood, elder wood, pine
        Wood and grain of musk

Apple Bread

2 ¼ C unbleached flour
½ tsp baking soda
1 ¾ tsp baking powder
¼ tsp salt
1 tsp cinnamon
½ C butter, softened
1 1/2C sugar
2 eggs
1 C buttermilk
2 C apples, peeled, cored, chopped
½ pecans, chopped (or walnuts)

Preheat oven to 350, sift together flour, baking soda, powder, salt and cinnamon. In a separate bowl cream butter and sugar until fluffy. Beat eggs until foamy and ad to the butter mixture until mixed thoroughly. Ass dry ingredients and buttermilk alternately, starting and ending with dry ingredients. Beat until smooth. Fold in apples and nuts and pour into two greased and floured bread pans. Bake 50-60 minutes and let cool for 10 minutes in the pan before removing onto racks. Serve with Apple butter for a great taste sensation.

Friends

If a friend a knife doth give
Return a coin and both shall live!

If upon a bridge you part
Forever shall you have separate hearts!

Carrot Bread

½ C all purpose flour
1 tsp baking powder, grated lemon zest
½ tsp each: baking soda, salt, ginger
1/3 C oil
¾ C sugar
2 eggs
2 C raw grated carrots
opt: 1 C golden seedless raisins

Preheat oven to 350. Grease and flour a 9x5 baking pan. In a large bowl mix together the flour, baking powder, soda, salt, ginger, and lemon zest until well blended. Then mix in each of the next ingredients in order until all are well blended together. Pour in prepared pan and bake for about 1 hour or until a fork put in the center of the loaf comes out clean. Cool in pan for 5 minutes and then on a rack of board until complete. Wrap in foil to store: makes 1 loaf.

Sacred Space

These sacred things I see
Make them all a part of me
Wash me, cleanse me of every doubt
Banish negativity, inside, outside, all about
Help me raise the energy
This is my will, so mote it be!

German Sourbrot

Starter

2 C warm water
1 pkt active dry yeast
2/3 C each: stone ground rye flour, stone ground wheat flour, unbleached all purpose white four

Begin starter 3-4 days before baking and combine in a large bowl and set covered in a warm area like the kitchen. Walk by and stir several times a day. It may form a crust. Every morning mix in the crust plus 3 Tbsp of flour and 3 Tbsp of water to keep it going. To soften on baking day mix ½ c warm water and 1 packet of yeast together and let set for 10 minutes and then add to the starter.

Bread

½ C very warm water
1 pkt active dry yeast
1 Tbsp salt
1 Tbsp oil
2 Tbsp molasses
2/3 C each: stone ground rye four, stone ground wheat flour and unbleached white flour
2/3 C each again: stone ground rye flour, stone ground wheat flour, and unbleached white flour
1 egg
1 Tbsp water

Then mix in the salt, oil, molasses and first set of flours and beat until smooth. Gradually add the second set of flours and make a stiff dough. Turn out on a floured surface and knead until elastic. Place in a greased bowl, cover and let rise until doubled – about 1 hour. Knead dough down in the bowl and divide into half. Shape each half into a ball and place in a prepared round cake pan and cover and let rise for 45-60 minutes or until doubled again. Brush with egg and water, cut a cross in the top with a knife and bake in a preheated oven 375 for 40-45 minutes and cool on wire racks: makes 2 loaves.

Harvest Bread

2 C flour
½ tsp salt
1 C sugar
½ tsp each: baking powder, baking soda
1 orange – juice and grated peel only
2 Tbsp butter, melted
1 egg
1 C walnuts, chopped
1 C raw cranberries

Put orange juice in a ¾ Cup measure and add enough boiling water to fill. In a large mixing bowl add the juice, orange zest, butter and stir until softened then set aside. Beat sugar, and egg together, add orange mixture and beat until well blended then fold in cranberries and nuts. Sift together flour, salt, baking soda and powder and stir into orange mixture. Pour into greased loaf pan and bake at 325 for 45-60 minutes or until a toothpick comes out clean. Cool on rack and serve.

Russian Black Bread

3/4 C molasses
2 C flour
1 C rye flour
2 Tbsp cider vinegar
1 tsp salt
¾ C packed dark brown sugar
3 Tbsp cocoa
1 tsp instant coffee
¼ tsp fennel seed
2 packages either active dry yeast or 1 package bakery yeast
¼ very warm water

In the very warm water, put the yeast and set aside for 10 minutes undisturbed. In a large mixing bowl, mix the dry ingredients and blend in the wet ingredients then add the yeast water and mix together thoroughly. Set loaf onto a board and cover in a warm area (kitchen) and let rise (about 1 hour). Punch down, and place in a covered, greased and floured bread pan to rise again. When risen place in a warm oven on 400 and bake 25-30 minutes or until browned and done. May be served warm or cold.

Goddess Prayer

Goddess from the heaven's above
I pray thee fill me with thy love
With life fluid, with life force
Fill me with thy heavenly course
With thy heavenly blessing divine
To your will I forever bind!

Dark German Rye

3 cup flour
3 ½ C rye flour
¼ C cocoa
1 Tbsp each: caraway seed, salt, sugar
½ C molasses
2 Tbsp butter
2 pkg yeast
2 C warm water
2 Tbsp Oil

In a large mixing bowl combine the white flour, salt cocoa, yeast and caraway seed. In a saucepan heat together molasses, butter, sugar, water and oil until very warm but not boiling and add to dry mixture. Mix thoroughly then add the rye flour and continue stirring until soft. Flour a surface , kneed, cover and let rise in a warm place for about 20 minutes. Punch down, divide in half and brush with oil. Cover until doubled in size (about 45-60 minutes). Bake in greased and floured loaf pans at 400 for 25-30 minutes.

Snakes

Snakes fear ropes of the knotted kind
For they tie up evil and they bind
So 'tis well for sure
To put one by your garden door
Put one on your house as well
A snake's disguise you may not tell
It could come knocking at your door
Saddened friend or hobbled poor
That is why 'tis best to keep
A name the snake can not speak!

Pumpernickel

2 C soft water
1 oz dark chocolate
½ C cider vinegar
½ dark molasses
2 Tbsp caraway seeds
2 tsp instant coffee

2 pkg yeast
½ C warm water

1 Tbsp each: salt, sugar
4 C dark rye flour
1 C spelt
3 C white flour
1 egg
2 tsp salt

Mix yeast with the warm water and set aside. Meanwhile in a large mixing bowl mix the second set of ingredients and set aside. In a large pot on medium heat bring the first set of ingredients up to a boil. Add the first set of ingredients to the second set of ingredients and mix thoroughly. Blend in yeast water and mix well, cover and set aside to rise in a warm place for about 30 minutes. Punch down, divide into 3 oiled and floured bread pans and let rise again in a warm place for 45-60 minutes and bake at 400 for 25-30 minutes.

**While choosing a name remember to do
One for the world and one for you!**

Dusty Potato Bread

2 C warm potato water (water you cooked potatoes in)
1 packet active dry yeast
3 Tbsp sugar
1 Tbsp salt
3 C all purpose flour
2 Tbsp shortening or butter, melted and cooled
2 ½ - 3 C more flour

In a large mixing bowl combine the water and yeast and stand for 10 minutes. Then stir in the salt, sugar and 3 C of flour and mix well. Beat in the shortening or butter and gradually add the rest of the flour to make soft dough. Turn onto a floured surface and knead until smooth, place in a greased bowl and cover top and let rise. It should double in bulk in 1-1 ½ hours. Divide dough in half and shape into balls and place on well greased round cake pans. Cover and let rise again until almost doubled – about 45-60 minutes. Dust loafs with flour and bake at 400 for 35-40 minutes. Cool on wire racks: Makes 2 loaves.

Home Blessing

Who comes to me I shall keep
Who goes from me I set free
Yet against all I shall stand
Who are not freely given my hand!

Cherries and Chocolate Bread

2 C flour
1 tsp baking soda
½ tsp salt
½ C butter
1 C sugar
2 eggs
3 medium bananas mashed
½ C chocolate chips
½ C maraschino cherries, chopped
½ C walnuts, chopped

Preheat oven to 350 and grease and flour a loaf pan. Sift together in a medium mixing bowl all the dry ingredients and set aside. In a large bowl beat together the butter and the sugar until fluffy. Add one egg at a time and continue beating, until smooth. Fold in the mashed bananas, fold in the flour mixture, then fold in the chocolate chips, cherries and walnuts and pour into the loaf pan. Bake for 45-60 minutes or until a fork comes out clean and cool for 10 minutes before removing from pan and serving.

The direction of the wind on New Year portends

South: Fine weather and prosperity the year through
North: Bad weather and bad news
East: A year filled with famine and calamites
West: Lots of milk and fish there will be,
But the death of an important person you will see
No wind is the best news of all
For it portends joy and prosperity to all!

Honey Bear's Pear Bread

3-4 pears, peeled and chopped
2/3 C shortening
4 eggs
2/3 C each: honey, brown sugar packed
2 ½ C flour
1 tsp each: salt, baking soda, cinnamon
¼ tsp each: allspice, crushed cloves
1 ¼ C dates, chopped
1 tsp finely ground orange peel

Core, peel and chip enough pears to make 3 Cups. Cream together the shortening with the brown sugar until fluffy. Add eggs one at a time and then blend in the honey. In a separate bowl, sift together the flour, salt, salt, baking soda, cinnamon, all spice and cloves and add to creamed mix and blend until moist and well blended. Stir in dates, orange peel and pears. Turn into a greased and floured bundt pan and bake at 350 for 50 – 65 minutes or until the tsp springs back when touched lightly in the center. Cool in pan for 30 minutes, remove and drizzle with brandy glaze.

Brandy Glaze

1 C powdered sugar
2 tsp brandy
1-2 tsp orange juice

Mix together and pour over the cake before serving.

Bunny Bread

½ C all purpose flour
1 tsp each: baking powder, lemon zest
½ tsp each: baking soda, salt, ginger
1/3 C vegetable oil
¾ C sugar
2 eggs
2 C raw grated carrots
Opt: 1 C golden seedless raisins

Preheat oven to 350 and grease and flour a bread pan. In a large bowl mix together the flour, baking powder, soda, salt, ginger and lemon zest until well blended. Then mix in the oil until smooth, then the sugar until light, and the eggs and carrots last. Pour into the pan and bake for 45-60 minutes or until a fork pushed in the center comes out clean. Cool in the pan for 5 minutes then remove to a rack. Either wrap in foil and reserve or serve.

Earth Love Spell

Upon the earth this spell I doth cast
For true love to come and ever last
O course a name I write upon
The earth aflame dare ne're be gone
Circle it, cast it , out to thee
True love now return to me!

Onion Bread

2/3 C milk
1 tsp salt
1 ½ Tbsp butter
½ pkg baking yeast
2/3 C plus 1 Tbsp warm water
4 Tbsp onion, minced

Warm the milk in a sauce pan and add the salt and the butter. Sprinkle the yeast over the flour, stir in the water and then add the milk until you form a dough. Add the onion and mix until the dough is soft. Cover and let rise in a warm place. Thoroughly knead for 1-2 minutes and remove dough to a greased 8 inch pan and let rise again for 45 minutes. Bake at 350 for 55- 75 minutes or until done and serve with fresh butter.

Water Love Spell

Within this scrying glass, I swirl and cast
A love so true, forever to last
True intention, now I speak
Make him come to me this week
And if he dare speak my name
Set our hearts forever aflame!

Indian Fry Bread

2 C flour
1 C sugar
½ C butter
3 large eggs
2 tsp baking powder
½ tsp salt
2 tsp vanilla
¾ C milk

Preheat oven to 350°F. Grease and flour two 9-inch cake pans. In medium bowl, combine flour, baking powder, and salt then beat with a wire whisk. In a large bowl cream butter and sugar until light and fluffy. Beat in eggs, one at a time. Add vanilla and mix until completely combined. Slowly add flour alternately with milk, batter should be smooth. Divide between 2 pans and bake for 20 to 25 minutes. Cool 5 minutes in pan, then invert onto a rack and cool completely before frosting. For a 9 x 13 pan – Bake for 30 to 38 minutes.

Irresistible Spell

1 red candle	Scrying bowl
Natural water	7 peppercorns
3 drops vanilla	9 rose petals
5 mulberries	11 seeds of thyme

Pour the water and ingredients in your scrying bowl, light your candle and swirl it slowly around your scrying bowl 9 times: Irresistible fires to me flow, Irresistible were 'er I go, Irresistible waters surround me about, as I put this candle out – now douse the candle with the water and go.

Dark German Rye

3 C flour
3 ½ C rye flour
¼ C cocoa
1 Tbsp each: caraway seed, salt, sugar
½ C molasses
2 Tbsp butter
2 pkg yeast
2 C warm water
2 Tbsp vegetable oil

In a large bowl combine the white flour, salt, cocoa, yeast and caraway seed. In a sauce pan heat together the molasses, butter, sugar, water and oil until very warm but not boiling and add to dry mixture. Mix thoroughly then add the rye flour and continue stirring until soft. Flour a surface, kneed, cover ad let rise in a warm place for about 20 minutes. Punch down, divide in half and brush with oil. Set in greased and floured loaf pans and cover then let rise until doubled (about 45-60 minutes). Bake at 400 for 25-30 minutes or until done.

Air Love Spell

Love upon the air divine
Send this spell ore space and time
Send it through both wind and air
Cast it well my heart doth bare
Open up the channels met
Make it so true love will set!

Now whisper your desire to the wind!

Why some Magick doesn't work

Never pit one element against another (fire, air, water, earth, spirit). For instance, never blow (air) out a candle (fire) or dowse a fire with water or earth – it must be smothered instead.

Do all your magick in a circle of salt so evil and jealousy can not see you, hear your intentions or disrupt your spell. It not only protects you from the wandering spirit but makes sure evil can not fly against it.

Remember in all things there is balance especially the Divine – Male and Female; God and Goddess; Holy Trinity and the Holy TrinoSophia – equal and ONE.

Always know who or what you are asking to do your bidding and bind them well. Never invite unfamiliar spirits will nilly for they have their own agenda and you may not be able to control them or their deeds otherwise.

Take heed of the magickal principals and know the most important thing is RELEASE! You spend all your time and energy gathering the correct ingredients and amounts and then if you don't let go of it, then it will manifest to nothing! Rather like putting together a pot of stew and expecting it to cook on its own with out any means of doing so. RELEASE is the most important magickal lesson – release, walk away and believe!

Sandwitches

Toasted Cheese Sandwitch: the original Panini

8 pieces of your favorite bread
8 tsp butter
8 slices of cheese (white American, provolone, mild cheddar)

Variations: 8-12 heirloom tomato slices, 12-18 red onion slices, or 4 scallions halved. Also try various herbs and flowers for flavour.

Make Sandwitches by putting 2 pieces of cheese and any vegetables, herbs or flowers in between 2 slices of bread. Place a pat of butter in a cast iron skillet and fry the sandwitch on medium heat until brown watching carefully (depending on the heat in your pan 2-5 minutes). Lift sandwitch with a spatula, placing a second pat of butter in the skillet and flip sandwitch over on top of the butter. Continue frying on medium heat until brown (1-3 minutes) and remove to a plate. Finish by frying each sandwitch the same manner. Serves 4 well.

SHHHHH – Ancient Knowledge Grows Here!

Do you have rusted pots, pans, utensils? There is a very simple and easy way to clean them without much scrubbing at all. Simply rub salt into them – any iodized table salt will do and watch the rust magickally disappear before your very eyes!

Cucumber Sandwitch

3-4 Persian cucumbers, peeled
8 oz cream cheese, softened
4 tsp sweet butter, softened
8 pieces of white bread

Variations: 2-3 green onions, whites diced only or 1 teaspoon EACH chives and dill or ¼ C mint washed and sliced

Cream together cream cheese and butter then decide if you which variation you prefer and whether you desire your cucumber sliced or grated. If grated add to cream cheese mixture, if not slice thinly and set aside. Take four of the pieces of white bread and spread ¼ of mixture on each. If using slices, top the mixture with the slices. Put the other four bread pieces on top of the sandwitch and cut into four triangles or fingers and serve. Serves 3 - 4 well.

SHHHHH – Ancient Knowledge Grows Here!

Apple cider vinegar is not only good as a vegetable wash as it removes pesticides and debris it is also good as a household cleaner especially for mirrored surfaces. Don't like the smell – add orange zest or peel to a bottle and steep for a week before adding it to your spray bottle – the added orange oil makes the cleaning properties even stronger!

Guacamole Sandwitch – Open face

1 large avocado, mashed
1 medium tomato, seeded, chopped
3 green onions, sliced
1 Tbsp lime juice
½ tsp garlic salt
6 slices dark rye bread, buttered
3 C shredded lettuce
1 C tortilla chips, crushed
¾ C creamy bleu cheese salad dressing
6 slices turkey bacon, cooked crisp, halved

In a small mixing bowl combine the avocado, tomato, onion, lime juice and garlic salt, mash together and set aside. Toast each slice of bread and top with ½ C lettuce, avocado mixture, and the tortilla chips then top it all with about 2 Tbsp salad dressing on each sandwitch then finish with the bacon and serve.

Indian Summer Sandwitch

4 ½ oz deviled ham
1 tsp horseradish, prepared
6 thin slices oatmeal bread
4 Tbsp mayonnaise
12 cucumber slices

In a mixing bowl combine ham, horseradish, and mayonnaise. Divide onto 3 slices of bread. Top with cucumber and then the other 3 slices of bread.

TLC Sandwitch

3 slices Heirloom tomato
1 small handful Mixed lettuce
6 slices Persian cucumber
1 tsp Organic mayonnaise
Pinch each: salt, black pepper
2 sprigs each: fresh cilantro, mint
2 slices white variety bread

On one slice of bread layer the tomato, lettuce and cucumber. On the other slice spread the mayonnaise and sprinkle with salt and pepper to taste. Finish with the sprigs of cilantro and mint laid out on the first side, cover with the mayo side and enjoy!

Watercress Sandwitch

½ C watercress, without stems
¼ C parley, without stems
¼ C butter, softened
4 oz cream cheese, softened
2 Tbsp chopped chives
8 slices white bread
Variation: Omit chives and substitute pimento stuffed green olive

Chop watercress and parsley, mix together and set aside. In a small mixing bowl cream together butter and cream cheese and fold in either chopped chives or sliced green olives. On each of four bread slices spread ¼ of the cream cheese mixture and top with ¼ of the watercress mixture. Add the other four slices of bread on top and cut off crusts, slice. Enjoy!

Egg Salad Sandwitch

6 hard boiled eggs (cool in iced water for best effect)
1 Tbsp dill relish
2 tsp mustard either yellow or Dijon
¼ tsp celery salt
¼ tsp dill
¼ tsp paprika
¼ tsp black pepper
2 Tbsp mayonnaise or salad dressing

Peel and discard egg shells and dice eggs. If you have cooled them in ice water the insides should be a nice bright yellow – if not oxidation will make them greenish. In a bowl combine the eggs and the remainder on ingredients and mix well. Serve on toast or bread as desired. Enjoy!

Tuna Salad Sandwitch

1 can albacore tuna
¼ C minced celery
¼ C minced onion
¼ C minced sweet pepper
¼ tsp lemon pepper
¼ tsp sea salt
2 Tbsp mayonnaise or salad dressing
1 tsp mustard, yellow or Dijon

Drain tuna from juice in can and put in bowl. Add remaining ingredients and stir completely. If eating cold, place between bread slices and enjoy. If eating hot, place open face in oven and top with mild cheddar cheese on 350 for 10 minutes and enjoy!

Crab Elegant'

7 ½ oz crab meat, drained, flaked, cleaned
1 medium avocado, peeled, pitted, mashed
2 green onions, finely chopped
2 Tbsp lemon juice
2 Tbsp mayonnaise
1/8 tsp pepper
3 English muffins, split and toasted
3 leafs of lettuce
3 hard boiled eggs sliced
2 oz black caviar

In a bowl, combine, crab, avocado, onion, lemon juice, mayonnaise and pepper and chill. Top each muffin with lettuce, arrange egg slices over lettuce, spoon crab mixture over egg slices and top with a rounded tsp of black caviar. Finish with remaining muffin top and serve.

Party Sandwitch:

1 C American cheese, grated
3 eggs, hard boiled, chopped
3 Tbsp olives, chopped
3 Tbsp each: green pepper, onion, diced
2 Tbsp pickle relish
½ C mayonnaise
15 oz crab meat or shrimp
8 potato rolls

Combine all ingredients and put on potato rolls, bake at 350 until the cheese melts (about 10 minutes) and serve hot.

California Turkey Sandwitch

¼ lb sliced turkey
1 romaine lettuce leaf, rib removed
1- 2 large slices of heirloom tomato
3 slices fresh avocado
2-3 slices of red onion
2 slices wheat berry bread

On fresh or toasted bread arrange lettuce, turkey, tomato, onion and avocado and serve.

Chicken Salad Sandwitch

1 lb shredded cooked chicken breast
¼ C orange flavored dried cranberries
¼ C chopped celery
¼ C chopped red onion
4 mild cheddar cheese slices
8 Endive lettuce leaves
1/3 C mayonnaise or salad dressing
1 Tbsp sugar
1 tsp yellow mustard
½ tsp each: salt, pepper
8 pieces of wheat bread

Combine in bowl all ingredients except cheese and bread and mix thoroughly. Put between slices of bread topped with cheese and serve.
Serves 4 well.

Always rub an apple before eating it as it to shake off any lingering spirits as it is often called the food of the dead and you do not want to consume any spirits that may be attached to it!

Chicken, Tomato, Spinach and Asiago Panini

1 cooked chicken breast
1-2 heirloom tomatoes sliced
¼ C fresh chopped spinach with stems removed
½ C asiago cheese
¼ C peeled and chopped red onion
½ tsp each: salt, pepper
2 pieces of White bread

In a bowl combine spinach, cheese, onion and seasonings. Place chicken breast on the bread, spread with mixture, top with tomato and add the other piece of bread and toast at 350 for 10 minutes.

Curry Chicken Pinwheels

10 oz canned chicken spread
¼ C pimiento, finely diced
½ tsp mustard
¼ tsp curry powder
1 loaf of bread, unsliced
9 Tbsp butter, softened

In a small bowl combine the chicken spread, pimiento, mustard and curry powder. Remove crust from the loaf and cut lengthwise 9 times. Take each slice and butter then add 2 Tbsp of the filling, spread and roll. Wrap in foil and chill. When ready cut pinwheels and serve on a platter.

It is very lucky if perchance you meet
A happy go lucky chimney sweep
So make a wish on one if you do
For you know for sure it's bound to come true!

Lamb Salad Pita

1 lb cooked lamb
1 C sour cream
1 C Mediterranean feta cheese
¼ C mint leaves, chopped
½ C peeled shredded cucumber
½ tsp each; salt, pepper
4-5 pitas

Combine all ingredients in a mixing bowl and then fill each pita with the mixture. Should make about 4-5 pitas. Eat well!

Meatball Sub Sandwitch

4 sub sandwitch rolls
8 provolone slices
1 C spaghetti sauce
12-16 meatballs (beef, pork, turkey or meatless)

Cut and arrange rolls on a cookie sheet. Put spaghetti sauce and 3-4 meatballs on each roll. Top with 2 slices provolone per roll. Bake on 350 for 10 minutes or until cheese bubbles and browns. Serve and enjoy!

Charm against Warts

Roast chicken-feet and rub the warts with them; then bury them under the eaves.

Pastrami Panini

2 slices rye bread
3 slices pastrami
2 slices tomatoes
2-3 red onion slices
1-2 slices Swiss cheese

Arrange ingredients on the bread and toast until cheese melts about 2-4 minutes. Serves 1, live well!

Rueben

3 slices corned beef
1 Tbsp sauerkraut
2 slices Swiss cheese
2 slices rye bread
1 Tbsp deli mustard

On a baking sheet put both slices of bread, spread with the mustard and top with the cheese. On one put the meat, on the other the sauerkraut and toast at 425 for 10 minutes or until the cheese is bubbly. Put both sides together and serve hot.

To Keep Love Strong

Find a twin or double strawberry and eat one half of yourself and give the other half to your lover eat together then kiss.

Two halves as one, The spell begun
Two halves as two, The spell renews
Two halves as one, The spell is done

Philly Steak and Cheese

3 ultra thin cut steak slices
1/8 C green pepper slices
1/8 C yellow onion slices
1/8 C white mushroom slices
2 slices American white cheese
Season salt and pepper to taste
1 Tbsp oil
1 steak roll

In a cast iron skillet, pour the oil and cook the steak, pepper, onions and mushrooms until done. Season while cooking. The steak should be browned and the others should be limp. Gather the ingredients together in the pan and top with the cheese and let melt. Remove to a roll and serve. Enjoy!

And Her Holy Name: Holy TrinoSophia

Asherah – Mother Goddess; Eema, Mother Earth, Queen of Heaven, Bride of God, All Life, Union, Physically, Sacrality, Cyclical Renewal, Eternal Life, Divine Will, Sacredness, Divinity, Branch, Tree of Life

Shekhinah – Daughter Goddess, Bride of the Sabbath, Bride of the Son, Sophia, Wisdom, Truth, Sabbath Queen, Holy Spirit, Holy Ghost, Creation, Order, Intellect, Study, House of Divine Study, Illumination.

Pneuma - Goddess of the Holy Soul, Divine Soul, Bride of Humanity, Soul, Breath, Love, Psyche, Courage, Vigor, Movement, Light, Inspiration

Teas and Special-Teas
Tasseomancy - reading tea leaves see additional Grimoire in the back of the book page ***

InFLUenzTea

5-10 sage leaves
3 slices of fresh ginger root
2-3 sprigs fresh thyme
1 Tbsp clover honey
½ juice from a fresh lemon
Dash of cayenne pepper

Steep 5-10 minutes, strain and sip slowly for best effect.

Medicinal Charms Tea

Use a combination of any of the following:
Burdock root, chickweed, dandelion, Echinacea, ginger, juniper berries, ladies mantle, licorice root, mint, red clover, sage and thyme.

Comberry Tea

½ C each comfrey leaves chopped, elderberries
1 C clover or raw honey
1 C water

Simmer for 30 minutes, strain and take as needed to produce perspiration and reduce fever. Also eases discomforts, soothes mucus membranes. Actions: demulcent and expectorant.

Dandelions Tea

1 oz dandelion greens
1 pt water

Steep 10 minutes, strain and sweeten with honey. Good for bilious infections and dropsy.

For Liver: add 1 oz horseradish
For Gallstones: add 1oz each parsley root, balm, ginger and licorice root

Elder flower Tea: Influenza, Bronchitis, Asthma

3 Tbsp elder flowers
1 tsp cinnamon

Steep 5-10 minutes, strain, breathe in as you sip slowly.

Ginamon Elixir: at the first sign of a cold

1 C scalded milk
1 Tbsp honey
½ tsp crushed ginger root, cinnamon

Steep5-10 minutes, strains and drink hot.

Friendship Wish Bracelet

Collect assorted colorful beads to representing your friend. Wish on each bead for happiness, tie the beads together and give! See page ***

Hopermint Tea

½ tsp each hops, peppermint, rosemary and sage
2 C boiling water

Steep 10-15 minutes, strain and add ginger or sugar to taste and drink warm.

St. Hildegard's Chai: great drink for your heart

In a wide mouth green jar place:
1tsp each: galangal, star anise, cardamom, cinnamon, ginger, black pepper
5 Tbsp china black or earl grey tea
Mix thoroughly and add 1 tbsp to your tea ball for every two cups or try it in hot buttered rum.

Royal Tea: for severe colds

1 C each catnip, horehound, pennyroyal, sage, spearmint, and dried white yarrow, mix and set aside in a jar.

To use: pour 1 pint boiling water over 2 ½ tsp of mixture, cover, steep 10-15 minutes, strain, sweeten and reheat. Drink 1 C every 1-2 hours as needed. This tea was used extensively by royalty in Europe for many centuries.

For any Spell

With harm to none, this spell is done
Your will to me, now mote it be!

Tea Tonic

3 slices each fresh ginger root, burdock root
1 Tbsp red clover
1 tsp each chamomile, nettle, rose hips

Steep 5-15 minutes, remove and keep in a jar. Drink on cup daily.

Willow Bark Tea

Soak ½ tsp dried white willow bark in 2 C cold water overnight. Bring to a boil and simmer for at least 20 minutes. Strain, cool and contain. Sweeten if desired. Dosage is ¼ C every 4 hours.

Flowermint Curative Tea

1 Tbsp each peppermint, elder flower, feverfew, white yarrow
2 C boiling water

Cover and steep 15-20 minutes. Strain, sweeten and reheat. Drink hot, it will expel the sickness through your pores, dispel the mucus and help ease the aches and pains.

Gold and silver coins of mine
Appease the spirits I call on to bind
With me in my circle cast
I throw these coins to them at last
Presenting themselves to
To do my will so Mote it BE!

Love Divine Tea

1 Tbsp Orange Pekoe tea
1 tsp each raspberry leaves damiana
2 tsp each chamomile, mullein, rose hips

Steep 3-5 minutes, strain and add honey to taste.

Aumn Tea

1 Tbsp Yorkshire gold tea
1 tsp each: chamomile, elder flowers, rose hips
1/8 tsp nutmeg

Steep 5-10 minutes, breathing in the aroma, strain and drink.

Linden Tea

4-5 linden flowers
2 leaves scented geranium
1 tsp each chamomile, lemon balm, mint, skullcap

Steep 5-10 minutes, strain and sweeten with clover honey

Chamomint Tea

1/2 tsp each chamomile flowers, lemon rind, mint leaves

Steep 3-5 minutes, strain and drink 1 cup slowly before bedtime for a sweet night's sleep.

Divination Tea

1 Tbsp Red tea
2 tsp lemon balm
1 tsp each eyebright, mugwort, rose hips OR nutmeg and thyme

Steep 5-10 minutes, strain and relish the aroma before drinking.

Purification Tea

! Tbsp Green tea
1 tsp each valerian, chamomile
2 tsp each fennel, hyssop

Steep 5-10 minutes, strain and sweeten.

Psychic Healing Tea

1 Tbsp White tea
1 tsp each elder flower, nettle
2 tsp each burdock root, mullein, rose hip

Steep 5-10 minutes, strain, sip slowly and reflect.

Strawberry leaves carried in your pocket will bring you fast fortune, and good luck.

Unwind, Detach and Let pass

1 Tbsp English breakfast
2 tsp each rose hips, hops
1 tsp each chamomile, valerian

Steep 5-10 minutes, strain, sip slowly for best effect.

Cease, Relinquish and Let go

1 tsp each chamomile, lemon balm, linden flowers, valerian, skullcap

Steep 3-5 minutes, strain and sip slowly.

Asian Adventures Tea

4 rose blossoms
3 slices of fresh ginger
2 scented geranium leaves
1 tsp each clove, clover, hibiscus, lemon balm, orange peel

Steep 5-10 minutes, strain and sweeten with raw honey

Sweet Summer Slumber

Take nine fresh flowers with no thorns and wrap with mistletoe. Place under your pillow for a good nights sleep and to have your dreams come true by summer's end.

Love Potion Tea

2 tsp black tea   1 pinch rosemary
3 fresh mint leaves   3 C cold water
6 fresh rose petals   6 lemon leaves
3 pinches each: thyme, nutmeg
1 tsp each: fairy sugar, honey

Brew this tea on a Friday during the waxing moon in a copper kettle. Steep 7 minutes and blow these words across it "By the light of the moon waxing I brew this tea (drink some tea) Goddess of Love now hear my plea and let dear (name) desire me!" Now share a cup with your intended and it will light their desire for you!

Aphrodite (to increase the passions)

3 tsp fresh red rose petals
1 tsp each: clove, nutmeg, lavender, ginger

Brew in cool water and steep 3-7 minutes and serve to our lover or drink yourself to increase passions.

Love Sweet and Innocent (first love)

1 C water
3 fresh cherries-pitted, crushed
3 white rose petals
3 Tbsp each: peach juice, oregano
3 drops of clover honey

Brew water just to boil and steep ingredients for 7 minutes then drink yourself to have love find you or together to have love bind you.

Great Combinations

Green Tea with jasmine flowers
Chamomile with linden flower and rose hips
Chrysanthemum petals with blackberry leaves
English breakfast with dandelion root, elder flower,
      hops and rose hips
Orange Pekoe with lavender, pineapple mint and
      peppermint leaves
Mint with chamomile, hibiscus and lemon verbena
Scented geranium leaves with hibiscus, rose
      blossoms, citrus peel

Bring 2-4 Cups of water to boil and remove from heat then steep for 3-5 minutes and strain. Drink hot or chill for iced tea and sweeten if desired.

Fountain of Youth

3 C spring water
½ tsp each: sarsaparilla, licorice root, burdock,
½ tsp Pau D'Arco

Bring water to a gentle boil and remove from heat, steep herbs for 10 minutes and sip a cup slowly 3-4 times per day to improve the quality of your skin.

Chills be Gone

½ tsp each: Echinacea root
½ tsp leaves of each: peppermint, hyssop, yarrow
½ tsp flower petals of elder
½ tsp Schisandra berries

Bring your tea water to boil and steep for 20 minutes. Sip slowly throughout the day.

Honey Cough Syrup

1 Tbsp each root: licorice, marshmallow
1 Tbsp plantain (greater) leaves – bruised
1 pt water
4 Tbsp raw honey
1/8 tsp anise

Put the water into a glass pot and simmer the licorice, marshmallow, anise and plantain for 20 minutes. Strain and stir in honey until dissolved. Remove to a dark bottle and keep in a refrigerator (can be kept for several months). To use take 1 Tbsp every 2 hours.

Southern Sweet Tea

5-7 tea bags orange pekoe or black tea
1/8 tsp baking soda IF using black tea
2 C boiling water
¾ C to 1 ½ C sugar
6 C cold water

Bring 2 cups water to boil in a small sauce pan then turn off and add tea bags to steep for 10-15 minutes. Remove tea bags and add a pinch of baking soda (if using black tea to remove bitterness) and sugar to dissolve. Put syrup into a large pitcher and add remaining water, stir and chill until ready to serve. Makes two quarts - Serve with Ice.

Sweet Southern Peach Tea

5-7 bags orange pekoe or black tea
1/8 tsp baking soda IF using black tea
2 C boiling water
½ - ¾ C sugar
33.8 oz bottle of peach nectar
6 C cold water

Bring two cups of water to boil in a small sauce pan, turn off and steep tea bags in it for 10-15 minutes. Remove tea bags and add baking soda (if using black tea) and sugar to create syrup. In a galleon pitcher add syrup, nectar and remaining cold water. Stir and chill. Serve with Ice.

Raspberry Tea

5-7 bags orange pekoe tea
4 C boiling water
12 oz frozen raspberries, unsweetened
1-1 ½ C sugar
¼ C lemon juice OR mint leaves
8 C cold water

In a saucepan bring 4 cups of water to boil and remove from heat. Steep tea bags and berries in the boiling water for 5-10 minutes and strain. Dissolve sugar in the water creating syrup and add lemon or mint. Put syrup in a gallon container, add the remaining water and chill. Serve over ice.

The seventh son of the seventh son,
     Magic to others, Vampires to some!

Christmas Cranberry Punch

1C each: sugar, water
4 oz whole cloves
2 cinnamon sticks
3 qrt orange juice
1 qrt cranberry juice cocktail
3 oranges, whole

Stud the oranges with the cloves. In a crock pot on high for 1 hour or on low heat in a stockpot add the sugar, water, and juices and simmer for 20 minutes – add the oranges and cinnamon sticks and simmer 10 minutes more and serve hot in cups.

Wassail: a Yuletide Specialtea!

2 quarts apple cider
1 ½ cups orange juice
¾ cup pineapple juice
1 Tbsp brown sugar
½ tsp lemon juice
1 Tbsp raw honey
Cheese cloth bag
3 cinnamon sticks
3 slices fresh ginger
4-6 whole cloves
Opt: decorate with clove studded tangerines when finished

Combine first six ingredients plus a cheese cloth bag with the next three ingredients and bring to a boil on medium heat in an enameled, stainless or glass pot. Set to simmer on low for 20-30 minutes, then turn off, take out cheese cloth bag and add decorations. Serve and enjoy!

Stones and their Vibrations

Abalone: Cleansing, Offerings, Prayers
Agate: Strength, Courage, Balance, Insight
Amazonite: Success, Communications, Soothes
Amber: Uplifting, Luck. Love, Change, Healing
Amethyst: Master Heal, Spiritually, Dream recall
Apache Tear: Vision Quest, Dissolves Negativity
Aquamarine: Sea, Creativity, Self Awareness
Aventurine: Abundance, Luck, Joy, Money
Azurite: Divination, Truth, Cell growth, Wisdom
Barite: Spiritual, Dreams, Cleanses Toxins
Beryl: Depression, Elimination, Circulatory
Black Onyx: Protects
Bloodstone: Strength, Circulatory, Abundance
Boji: Balances energy, Reduces Pain
Calcite: Transition, Tranquility, Astral Projection
Carnelian: Focus, Motivation, Cleansing, Success
Charoite: Prosperity, Transformation, Detoxify
Chrysoberyl: Wisdom, Prosperity, Amplifier
Citrine: Clarity, Sexual Balance, Digestion, Wealth
Clear Quartz: Concentration, Dream stone
Copper: Strength, Energy, Amplifier, Inflammation
Coral: Sea, Diplomacy, Regeneration, Compassion
Corundum: Insight, Intuitive, Stimulates, Peace
Diamond: Absorbs and Amplifies Good and Bad
Emerald: Love, Fortune, Abundance, Growth
Fluorite: Dreams, Magick, Balances, Intuition
Fossil: Elemental
Garnet: Wisdom, Creativity, Passion, Fertility
Gold: Abundance, Amplifies, Conducts, Energizes
Granite: Water and Earth, Protection, Abundance
Hawk's Eye: Vision, Insight, Physic Awareness
Hematite: Soothing, Grounding, Survival, Repels

Stones and their Vibrations (continued)

Jade: Beauty, Longevity, Health, Wealth
Jacinth: Friendship
Jasper: Solutions, Cleansing, Visualization
Kunzite: Empowering, Radiation, Stress
Lapis Lazuli: Joy, Spirituality, Guidance, Intuition
Lepidolite: Mood Swings, Manic Depression
Malachite: Visions, Radiation, Aura Cleansing
Moldavite: Cosmic, Psychic Awareness, Telepathic
Moonstone: Divination, Spirituality, Stress, Travel
Mother of Pearl: Protection, Sea, Relaxes, Sooths
Obsidian: Fire and Water, Grounding, Conversion
Onyx: Reduces Sex Drive, Banishes Grief, Absorbs
Opal: Water, Amplifies, Clarifies, Mirrors
Pearl: Water, Absorbs, Cleanses, Balances
Peridot (Olivine): Health, Wealth, Protection
Petrified Wood: Longevity, Past Life Regression
Pyrite: Grounds, Conducts, Energizes, Increases
Rose Quartz: Love, Beauty, Peace, Forgiveness
Rhodocrosite: Giving and Receiving Love, Soul
Rhodonite: Love of Self, Heals Heartache
Rock Crystal: Centering
Ruby: Wealth, Joy, Love, Sex, Power
Sapphire: Insight, Intuition, Inspiration, Wealth
Sardonyx: Change, Transformation, Love
Selenite: Astral, Cancer, Mental, Emotional
Serpentine: Meditation, Vibration, Regeneration
Snowflake Obsidian: Calm, Clairvoyance, Aware
Sodalite: Night, Divination, Meditation, Wisdom
Sugilite: Spiritual Guides, Psychic Abilities
Tiger's Eye: Money, Psychic Protection, Luck
Topaz: Warmth, True Love, All Success
Tourmaline: Transmits Thought, Radiates Light
Turquoise: Heals, Conducts, Opens, Protects

Homemade Happiness: Snacks and Desserts

Baklava for the Gathering

12 breadsticks made from biscuit recipe pg 141
2 Tablespoons dark raw honey
4 Tablespoons butter plus 1 Tablespoon to brush
½ cup dark brown sugar
1 ½ cups of fine ground walnuts (reserve ¼ cup)
1 ½ cups chunky applesauce

In a small sauce pan on low heat, melt butter then turn off. Add honey, sugar and nuts. In a Bread pan layer 4 breadsticks, mixture, ¾ cup chunky applesauce, 4 bread sticks, mixture, ¾ cup chunky applesauce, 4 breadsticks, brush with butter and top with reserve nuts. Bake at 350 for 12 – 18 minutes or until light brown and done. If family and small gatherings serve in slices, if for larger gatherings each slice should naturally fall into 4 pieces, place each piece on a small dish and drizzle with caramel.

Gingered Almonds

1 C almonds
1 tsp salt
2 Tbsp butter
½ tsp ginger

Preheat oven at 350 degrees. Place the nuts and butter in a shallow baking dish. Bake for 20 minutes stirring occasionally. Drain on paper towels. Sprinkle salt and ginger over nuts and toss together in a medium sized bowl. Enjoy!

Gingerbread Candy

1 lb honey
1 lb toasted bread crumbs (or day old dried)
1 Tbsp each: ginger, cinnamon
½ tsp white pepper
Pinch saffron

In a medium saucepan on medium heat bring honey to a boil. Lower heat and skim anything on top off. Add the spices and slowly add the bread crumbs, stirring to evenly coat. Remove to a lightly greased (in butter) square pan and spread evenly. When cooled cut into small squares and serve.

Sugar Spiced Pecans

2 C pecans
1 Tbsp egg white
¼ C sugar
1 Tbsp cinnamon

Preheat oven to 300 degrees. In a large bowl mix the egg white and pecans, stirring until completely coated and sticky. In a separate bowl mix sugar and cinnamon together and sprinkle the mixture over the nuts. Stir until thoroughly coated. Spread on a ungreased baking sheet and bake for 30 minutes. Cool and serve.

Curse the cook while you eat,
        And you will die quickly in your sleep!

My little Monkey Bread

2 dozen buttermilk biscuits (141) cut and uncooked
¼ lb of butter melted in a bowl
1 ½ cups dark brown sugar
1 teaspoon cinnamon
Optional: ½ cup of nut pieces (walnut or pecan)

Preheat oven to 375. In a cereal bowl melt butter in the microwave on high about 1 minute more or less depending. In a Bundt pan, pour 1 teaspoon of the butter into the bottom with 1 teaspoon of the sugar and if using nuts 3 teaspoons of nuts. Mix remainder of the sugar and cinnamon together in a bowl and set aside. Open biscuits and peel apart – with a fork stab each biscuit, dip it in the butter, then dip it in the cinnamon sugar and coat on all sides. Place in the bundt pan and do not worry about perfect layers just continue around and around until done. If using nuts sprinkle the nut pieces half way through between the layers. Bake at 35-45 minutes or until crispy golden brown and done. Remove the bundt pan and place a dinner plate on top of it and flip it over, remove slowly . Serves 6-8 well.

Password Magick: Magick is everywhere and in everything and since constantly changing your passwords is a must in today's society – why not have them work for you? Try things like: Lovef1ndME, SoulmateC0m3, Moneyc0meNow1, and keeping your mind concentrating on your desires helps the universe manifest them more quickly!

Cheese Glazed Walnuts

1 ½ C walnut halves
1 Tbsp melted butter
¼ tsp each: salt and hickory smoked salt
¼ C shredded parmesan cheese

Preheat oven to 350 degrees. Spread nuts in a shallow baking pan and bake for 10 minutes. Mix butter, salts and toss with walnuts. Sprinkle cheese over the top and bake an additional 3=4 minutes. Cool and enjoy!

Candied Jack

1 small pie pumpkin
4 C apple juice
½ stick butter
1 tsp pumpkin pie spice
1 C packed dark brown sugar
½ Package mini marshmallows

Peel (or shred the skin off) cut, core, clean and cube pumpkin and place it in a large pot. Add the Apple juice, on medium heat and bring to boil. Boil for 15 minutes or until soft. Add remaining ingredients, reduce heat to low and simmer for 20 minutes longer or until thick.

Dogs howling in the dark of night,
    Howl for death before day's light!

Southern Florida Pan Cake

½ cup butter
3 eggs
1 cup packed dark brown sugar
¼ cup chopped pecans
1 20oz can pineapple slices drained
10 fresh cherries stemmed and pitted
1 box Lemon cake mix
1 ¼ cup Orange juice with pulp
1/3 cup butter, vegetable or grape seed oil
1 orange peel shredded

Preheat oven to 350. In a 10+ inch by 2 inch deep cast iron skillet melt the butter on low heat and turn off. Stir in the brown sugar and pecans until well mixed and flatten to bottom and up the sides of the pan. Drain pineapple slices and arrange into a flower pattern (1 center, 6 petals) on the bottom and 6 halves of pineapple along the sides so that when you flip it over they will form a scalloped edge design. Place 1 whole cherry (stemmed and pitted) in the middle of each of the pineapple slices on the bottom and 6 - ½ cherries into the scallops on the sides of the pan. In a mixing bowl pour cake mix and add the orange juice, oil and eggs. Mix well – on low speed 30 seconds, then on medium speed for 2 minutes, scraping the bowl occasionally. Pour into cast iron skillet on top of the toppings. Bake at 350 for 25-40 minutes or until a fork inserted in the center comes out clean. Remove from oven and wait 5 minutes. Take a cake platter or a large dinner plate and place on top of the cake and flip over in one fell swoop, remove pan slowly keeping top intact. Replace any fallen pieces, cool and serve.

Spiced Monkeys

8 Bananas, peeled (whole, halved or sliced)
3 C sugar
1 ½ C wine vinegar
½ C burgundy wine
1 Tbsp ground cloves
2 tsp cinnamon

In a pot on medium heat bring to boil the sugar, vinegar, wine, cloves and cinnamon. Once boiling, drop in the bananas one by one, turning once, for 2-3 minutes or until well glazed. Serve immediately while hot.

Ginger me Sweetly Cookies

1 stick butter, softened
½ C packed dark brown sugar
1 Tbsp fresh ginger, grated

½ tsp Vanilla
1 ¼ C flour
¼ tsp baking soda
Pinch salt

3-4 pieces crystallized ginger

Mix together the first three ingredients and blend in the next four ingredients and form into a dough log. Wrap and chill the log in the refrigerator for 1 hour (or next day). Preheat oven to 350 and slice ¼ inch rounds onto greased cookie sheets and top with crystallized ginger. Bake 8-10 minutes or until browned. Makes about 30 cookies.

Bunny Rabbit Bars

1 ½ C whole wheat flour
½ tsp each: baking powder, ground cinnamon
½ C each: chopped walnuts, light brown sugar
¾ C vegetable or walnut oil
2 large eggs
2 C carrots, shredded
Cream Cheese frosting
Optional: ½ C toasted coconut

Preheat oven to 350 and grease a 13 by 9 baking pan. In a small mixing bowl combine the flour, baking powder, cinnamon and walnuts. In a large mixing bowl beat together the sugars, oil and eggs until well blended then add the grated carrots to the mix. Gradually add the flour mixture to the sugar mixture beating together until smooth. Scrape into the prepared pan and bake for 35 minutes or until a fork comes out clean when inserted. Cool thoroughly then top with cream cheese frosting and coconut if desired before serving.

Cream Cheese Frosting

16 oz cream cheese, softened
½ C butter softened
2 C confectioners sugar
1 tsp vanilla extract
1 C heavy whipping Cream

Beat together the vanilla an whipping cream until fluffy then beat in the cream cheese and butter. Slowly add in the sugar ½ cup at a time until well blended and keep refrigerated before use.

Blueberry Morning Cake

2 C blueberries
2 ¼ C flour
2/3 C granulated sugar
2 ½ tsp baking powder
½ tsp salt
1/3 C plus 2 Tbsp butter
¾ milk
1 egg
¼ C chopped nuts
¼ C packed brown sugar
½ tsp ground allspice

Beat together the sugars, salt, butter, milk and eggs in a large mixing bowl. Add in the baking powder and allspice and mix well. Slowly add in the flour and mix until well blended. Fold in the blueberries and nuts and remove to a well greased baking pan and bake at 350 for 30-55 minutes or until a fork inserted come out clean and serve after cooling.

Treasure Trove

Put to soak a squaw root (black cohash), mandrake root, and 3 whole nutmegs or acorns in a muslin bag. Hang in a small jar of spring water on the new moon and cover. Leave for 7 days. Then remove from the water and place both the water and the bag in your cupboard for 7 days while you whisper to it everyday. On the full moon, wash the souls of your shoes with the water and carry the bag while going for a walk and repeat to yourself: find it, gain it, give it – Win it, retain it, live it! And it will lead you to money. Remember – one to share, one to spare and one for my livelihood to bear!

Desire Me Completely Cake

1 pkg Chocolate cake mix
1 C chocolate chips
¼ C pecans, chopped
8 oz pkg instant chocolate pudding
1 C sour cream
½ C pecan oil
¼ C heavy whipping cream
4 eggs
1 tsp vanilla

Preheat oven to 350. Grease and flour a bundt pan. In a small bowl place 2 Tbsp of the cake mix, chocolate chips, and pecans in a bowl, toss and set aside. In a large bowl place remaining cake mix, pudding mix, sour cream, whipping cream, oil, eggs and vanilla and beat together until well blended. Fold in the chocolate chip mixture until thoroughly mixed and remove to the bundt pan and bake for 50-55 minutes or until a fork inserted comes out smooth. Cool for 10 minutes and place on a cake platter and turn upside down to remove cake. Frost when completely cooled.

Desire Me Completely Frosting

1 C brown sugar, packed
1 stick butter, softened
¼ C heavy whipping cream
1 Tbsp cocoa
2 C powdered sugar

Cream together and whip until soft, fluffy and completely mixed. Serve on the cake and enjoy!

Daisy Cake

¾ C pecans, ground
3 C flour
½ tsp each baking soda, salt, vanilla
1 C each: milk, butter - softened
2 Tbsp each, Lemon zest, lemon juice
2 C sugar
1 pkg lemon gelatin
6 eggs

Preheat oven to 350 degrees. Place pecans in a 13 x 9 greased baking dish. In a medium mixing bowl sift together flour, baking soda, and salt. In another mixing bowl whip together milk, lemon juice, lemon zest and vanilla. In a large mixing bowl cream together the butter, sugar and gelatin until light and fluffy. Add one egg at a time while continually beating, ¼ of each the flour mixture and milk mixture until well blended. Pour batter into the pan and bake for 45 minutes to 1 ½ hours or until the top is lightly browned and a fork inserted comes out clear. Cool for 20 minutes on a wire rack, then flip over and turn out on a serving plate while still warm and poke holes in the top before pouring on the glaze allowing it to cover the top and drizzle down the sides the let cool completely.

Daisy Glaze

1 ½ C powdered sugar
2 ½ Tbsp lemon juice
2 Tbsp lemon zest

In a medium bowl whip together until well blended and syrupy then pour over the cake and serve.

Wandering Gypsy Bars

1 ½ C flour
1 C quick cook oats
½ C each: brown sugar, pecans or walnuts chopped
¾ C tsp cinnamon, ground
1 C butter, softened
1 egg yolk
8 oz dates, pitted and chopped
½ C each: water, orange juice
1 tsp orange peel, grated

Preheat oven to 350 and grease a 13 X 9 baking pan. In a medium saucepan, put water, juice, peel and dates over medium heat for about 15 minutes or until dates are tender and set aside. In a large mixing bowl mix together the flour, oats, sugar, walnuts, and cinnamon. Cream in butter in the mixture until crumbly then add the egg and toss until thoroughly mixed. Place ¾ of the mixture on the bottom of the pan, then spread the fig mixture on top ending with the remaining crumbly tossed lightly and evenly on top. Bake 35 to 45 minute or until lightly browned and cool in pan on rack – makes 24 bars.

Natural Air Purifiers

You should have a minimum of 1 plant (in a 8-10 inch pot with activated carbon in the soil) for every 100 square feet of your house. Place them in the Eastern (health and family: consider Bamboo, Lady or Parlor palms), Southeastern (prosperity and abundance: consider English ivy or Spider plant) or Northeastern (spiritual growth: consider Peace lily, Gerber daisy, or Moth orchid) part of each room.

Fertility Pudding

½ C each: dried cranberries, golden raisins
1 Tbsp cornstarch
2 C each: milk, cooked long grain rice
¼ C brown sugar
1 tsp vanilla
2 eggs
Pinch of salt

In a mixing bowl add the cornstarch, milk, sugar, vanilla and eggs and beat until well mixed. Stir in the rice until well blended and fold in the cranberries and raisins. Pour into a 8 x 8 greased baking dish and place that inside a 13 x 9 baking dish and add hot water up the sides between the two dishes (but not over). Bake at 350 for 50-60 minutes or until well set and serve..

Harvest Cake

3 C flour
½ C each: sugar, milk
1 tsp each: salt, baking powder, cinnamon - ground
1 C shortening
2 Tbsp butter
1 egg
5 apples, peeled cored and minced
1/3 C brown sugar

Blend sugar and shortening until smooth then beat in egg and follow with salt, baking powder. Add in the milk until it forms dough and place in a 13 X 9 greased baking pan. Top with the apples, brown sugar and cinnamon and bake at 375 for 45-60 minutes or until a fork inserted comes out clean.

Garden of Eden Cake

3 eggs
3 C each: flour, apples – peeled, cored, diced
2 C sugar
1 ½ C nut oil
1 C each: golden raisins, crushed pineapple
1 C coconut flakes
1 tsp each: baking soda, salt, vanilla

Preheat oven to 350. In a large bowl mix all the ingredients together until well blended and place in a 13 x 9 baking pan and bake for 45 – 60 minutes or until a fork inserted comes out clean and serve.

Mudslide Bars

1 C plus 1 Tbsp flour
½ tsp each: baking soda, salt
½ C each: butter - softened, pecans – chopped
¾ C brown sugar
1 tsp vanilla extract
1 egg
12 oz chocolate chips (6 oz plus 6 oz)

Mix 6 oz of chocolate chips with remaining ingredients and place in a greased 9 x 9 baking pan and bake at 350 for 20-30 minutes. Remove from oven and top with remaining chocolate chips and let them melt. Serve hot with ice cream.

Bring harmony to your household by clearing clutter, playing music, adding natural light, fresh air and beauty. Now take the lesson outside.

Blackberry Cobbler

3 C blackberries   1 ¾ C sugar
1 C flour   ½ C milk
1 tsp each: baking soda, baking powder
¼ lb butter- melted

In a large mixing bowl combine blackberries and 3/4 cup sugar, then mix in the flour, 1 cup sugar, baking powder, and milk. Pour melted butter into a 8 x 8 pan or cake round and spread evenly. Pour berry mixture on top then bake at 375 degrees for about 1 hour. Serve warm topped with milk or ice cream.

Feng (gentle wind) Shui (clear water) – Directions and Elements

North: water; blue, black, career, life path, mirror, Aquarium (red, orange, yellow fish), knot
Northeast: earth; beige, light yellow, spiritual Growth, self cultivation, bamboo, tigers eye
East: wood; brown, green, health, family, mirror, Aquarium, bamboo, knot, amethyst
Southeast: wood; brown, green, prosperity, mirror, Bamboo, abundance, pyrite, citrine, Aquarium, knot
South: fire; red, strong yellow, orange, purple, Fame, reputation, carnelian, obsidian
Southwest: earth; beige, pink, light yellow, tan, Sand, love, marriage, pink quartz, knot
West: metal; glass, gray, white, creativity, children, Tumbled hematite, knot, Adventurine
Northwest: metal; glass, white, gray, helpful People, blessings, clear quartz

Sunnyside Cheesecake

16 oz each: cream cheese, sour cream
1 pt heavy whipping cream
1 ½ C sugar
4 eggs
1 ½ Tbsp lemon juice
1 tsp vanilla
3 tsp cornstarch
¼ lb butter, melted
8 graham crackers, crushed fine
1 Tbsp sugar
2 Tbsp butter, melted

In a large mixing bowl combine the cream cheese, sour and whipping creams. Beat in the sugar, eggs, vanilla, cornstarch and lemon juice until smooth. In a pie tin mix together the graham crackers, sugar and butter and press onto bottom and sides. Put cheesecake inside and bake at 350 for 45-65 minutes then turn off oven and leave the cheesecake in for 2 hours DO NOT OPEN DOOR and serve.

Mystic Knot

The Mystic Knot represents eight times infinity (as it is an infinity symbol wound eight times with no beginning or end) and benefits one by providing a harmonious flow of energy through your life path without misfortune. This magickal knot is beneficial as an amulet for love, abundance, protection, career and luck. The knot can be carried or hung and made of any material.

Knave of Hearts Tarts

8 oz cream cheese, softened
1 C each: pecans – chopped, butter - softened
2 C each: flour, brown sugar
2 eggs
2 Tbsp vanilla

In a small bowl cream together cream cheese, butter and flour then chill for 1 hour in refrigerator. In a medium bowl blend brown sugar, eggs, vanilla and pecans. In a mini muffin tine add a small ball of dough and work it around the bottom and up the sides. Fill with pecan mixture and bake at 350 for 30-40 minutes then remove and cool before serving.

Buttermilk Socks

To cool down after a heated argument, to calm a child's fever, reduce swelling in feet and ankles, calm the lightheadedness of pregnancy, fatigue or just to cool off in the dog days of august simply soak an old pair of sock in cold buttermilk and wear for 20 minutes while resting. The socks will absorb all the heat and inflammation in your body and allow it to cool it down. This is a great remedy for just before bed on a hot night – try it – what have you got to lose? An old pair of socks and some buttermilk! Please – you may be surprised!

Cream Cheese Frosting

16 oz cream cheese
1 C powdered sugar
1 tsp vanilla extract

Cream together and spread on cake before serving.

Cottontail Cake

¾ C brown sugar
1 C each: sugar, walnuts, chopped
1 ½ C walnut oil
2 C each, flour, carrots – peeled and grated
3 eggs
1 tsp each: cinnamon, nutmeg, allspice
2 tsp baking soda

Cream together sugars, oil and eggs in a large mixing bowl. In a separate bowl combine the flour, baking soda, salt and spices. Slowly add the dry mixture to the wet one and then fold in the grated carrots and walnuts until mixed thoroughly. Bake at 350 for 45-65 minutes or until a fork inserted comes out clean. Cool completely on wire rack and frost. Serve at leisure.

Mirrors

A convex mirror has protective qualities, consider using a round convex mirror with a gold frame in the southeast corner of a room for abundance but do not have any mirror face your main door or bed never use it in the south corner of any room.

Grasshopper Brownies

1 C plus 1 Tbsp flour
½ C each: peanuts – chopped, butter – softened
¾ C brown sugar, packed
1 tsp vanilla extract
½ tsp each: baking soda, salt
1 egg
6 oz chocolate chips

Combine all ingredients in a medium mixing bowl and blend thoroughly. Place in a 9 by 9 greased baking pan and bake at 350 for 20-30 minutes.

Grasshopper Frosting

3 C powdered sugar
1/3 C butter, softened
2 Tbsp each: crème de menthe, crème de cacao
1 ½ squares unsweetened baker's chocolate, grated

In a medium bowl combine the sugar, butter and liquor and beat thoroughly. Cover the cooled brownies and tope with the grated chocolate.

Aquariums

Like bamboo embody all five elements of Feng Shui - water, plants (wood), metal structure placed inside, pebbles (earth) and fish (fire). Choose the stones to reflect the color of the placement –north (blue and black), northeast (yellow, beige), east (brown and green) etc. Since the fish represent the fire element they should always be red, yellow or gold. Never place in your bedroom or kitchen.

Catch me if you can Gingerbread man

2 ½ C flour
½ C each: brown sugar, butter – softened
¼ C molasses
1 egg
1 tsp each: cinnamon, ginger, cloves – ground
¼ tsp baking soda
Raisins, chocolate chips, cream cheese frosting 204

Cream butter and brown sugar together in a large mixing bowl then add molasses and egg and mix thoroughly and set aside. In a medium mixing bowl combine flour, baking soda, and spices and mix well. Slowly combine both mixtures into the large bowl until it forms a dough. Roll between sheets of wax paper and cut into shape. Place on a greased cookie sheet adding raisins for eyes, chocolate chips for buttons, and bake at 350 for 8-12 minutes or until lightly browned and firm. Cool and decorate.

Lucky Bamboo

Bamboo (wood) should be grown in a glass pot (water), with a red ribbon (fire) and coin (metal) tied around it, with stone pebbles (earth) surrounding it, and teaches the wisdom of being flexible and open on the inside so your spirit can flow freely and heal your being.

2 shoots: love and marriage, southwest
3 shoots: happiness, northeast
5 shoots: health, east
8 shoots: wealth and abundance, southeast
9 shoots: good fortune and happiness, northwest

Ginger cookies

1 ¼ C flour
1 stick butter, softened
½ C dark brown sugar, packed
1 Tbsp fresh ginger, grated
½ tsp vanilla extract
¼ tsp baking soda
pinch of salt
3-4 pieces crystallized ginger

Cream together the butter, sugar and grated ginger in a large bowl. Blend in the flour, vanilla, baking soda and salt and mix thoroughly. Roll into a log shape and wrap in waxed paper to chill for 1 hour to 1 day. When ready preheat oven to 350, and slice into ¼ inch rounds onto a greased cookie sheet. Top with crystallized ginger cut into miniature pieces and bake for 8-10 minutes or until browned.

The Singing bowl, the Magic bell and the Gourd

The singing bowl (placed on a cushion) and magic bell are both comprised of metal and used to purify your space by ringing it three times with a wooden mallet. The gourd is tied with a red ribbon and used to catch the blessings from above.

Gold: Sun and ultimate source of yang energy
Sliver: Moon and ultimate source of yin energy
Copper: Venus, female (yin), love
Iron: Mars, male (yang)
Tin: Jupiter
Lead: Saturn
Zinc: Mercury

Basic Cake Recipe

½ C butter   1 C sugar
1 tsp vanilla   2 eggs
2 ¼ C flour
1 tsp each: baking soda, baking powder

In a large mixing bowl cream together butter and sugar, then add vanilla and eggs blending well. Add flour and baking powder until thoroughly blended and bake in 350 for 25-45 minutes or until a fork comes out clean in 8x8 pan or round.
To change flavor add: 3 Tbsp cocoa or 1 tsp cinnamon with 2 C chopped apples or ½ C black walnuts or ¼ C butter, ½ C brown sugar and 1 C crushed pineapple mixed together in bottom of pan or ½ tsp pumpkin pie spice with ¼ C walnuts.

Basic Pound Cake

2 ½ C sugar   1 tsp vanilla extract
1 C butter-softened   5 eggs
3 C flour   ¼ tsp salt
1 C evaporated milk
1 tsp each: baking soda, baking powder

Cream together in a large mixing bowl the sugar, butter, vanilla and eggs. In separate bowl, mix flour, baking powder and salt. Slowly combine the flour mixture into sugar mixture alternately with milk mixing slowly until well blended. Spread into a greased and floured 13 x 9 cake pan and bake at 350 for 35-50 minutes or until a fork inserted comes out clean. Cool in pan for 5 minutes then invert onto a rack to completely cool. Serve as is or with whipped cream and fresh berries.

To Breathe Chocolate Air

2 square unsweetened chocolate, cut up
3 egg yolks
3 egg whites
¼ C each: sifted flour, butter
¾ C milk
½ C sugar
¼ tsp each: salt, cream of tartar

In a medium sauce pan on low heat melt the butter then add the flour and salt and remove from heat. Whisk in the chocolate and milk then return to heat and bring to a boil for 1 minute – then remove and cool. In a large bowl beat together the egg yolks and sugar then slowly add the cooled chocolate mixture to the egg mixture. Beat the egg whites and cream of tartar in a separate bowl until stiff and gently fold into the chocolate mixture. Pour into a greased 2 qrt baking dish and set that in a pan of hot water in the oven at 350 for 45-50 minutes. Serve in squares.

Sweet Leaves of Summer

1 C mint leaves
½ C semi sweet chocolate chips
1 Tbsp sweet butter

In a small sauce pan on low, melt butter and then add chocolate and stir until melted. Place leaves on waxed paper over a plate and gently brush with chocolate onto the backs of the leaves. Refrigerate until firm. You may use as is in coffee or hot chocolate or peel the mint leaf gently from the chocolate leaf and use as a decoration on cakes, etc.

Divinity Dip

1 C heavy whipping cream
14 oz bittersweet or dark chocolate bars, grated
1 tsp bourbon vanilla extract
¼ C hazelnuts, finely chopped

In a small saucepan on low to medium heat, bring ½ c of cream to a slow boil and remove from heat. Add chocolate and wait 5 minutes then whisk together with the cream. Stir in the vanilla and hazelnuts and transfer to a mixing bowl set above a small lit candle to keep warm. As the fondue thickens add the reserved cream 1 Tbsp at a time until desired consistency. Arrange marshmallows, strawberries, banana slices, apple pieces, pretzels and pound cake pieces on a platter with bamboo skewers and have fun – great for parties and kids love it too!

Fevered Fudge Bars

2 C flour
1 ½ C butter, softened
2/3 C brown sugar, packed
1 C chocolate frosting page 288
8 oz cream cheese
2 eggs
¾ C slivered almonds

In a small bowl combine flour, sugar and butter and stir into crumbs then line a 13 X 9 pan with them. In a small bowl blend cream cheese and frosting, then beat in eggs until smooth. Spread over crust and sprinkle with nuts and bake at 350 for 30 minutes.

Good Marrow Cake

2 C each: flour, sugar
2 eggs
20 oz crushed pineapple with juice
1 C pecans, chopped
1 ½ tsp baking soda
1 tsp vanilla

Sift flour with baking soda and set aside. In a large bowl cream sugar and eggs together. Add pineapple, juice and vanilla until thoroughly mixed. Slowly add the flour in and blend well. Fold in pecans and pour into a greased and floured 9 x 13 pan and bake at 350 for 30-45 minutes or until a fork inserted comes out clean, cool and frost.

Good Marrow Frosting

8 oz cream cheese, softened
1 stick of butter
1 tsp vanilla extract
1 ½ C powdered sugar
½ pecans, chopped

In a medium bowl cream together cream cheese, butter, vanilla and sugar until well blended and fluffy. Frost cake and top with pecans.

**To knit one of your own hairs into a garment
Knits the recipient to you!**

Dutch Apple Strudel

2 C flour
1 egg
2 Tbsp butter, melted
¼ - 1/3 C warm water
½ tsp salt
6 red delicious apples-cored, peeled, sliced
6 granny smith apples-cored, peeled, sliced
1 ½ C walnuts, ground
¾ C raisins
½ C each: sugar, brown sugar – packed
¼ tsp each: cinnamon, nutmeg
1 ½ sticks butter

Preheat oven to 350. In a medium mixing bowl beat egg and cream with melted butter. Add flour salt, and water and work into a dough. Knead on a floured board for 10-12 minutes, cover and keep warm for 30 minutes. In a large bowl combine the brown sugar, nuts, raisins and apple slices then roll dough as thin as possible. In a small shaker combine the sugar, cinnamon and nutmeg. Sprinkle on the dough, top with mixture, Sprinkle more sugar spice on mixture and roll into a loaf. Place on a greased cookie sheet and bake for 1 hour at 350 and baste with melted butter then top with sugared spice and serve – makes two loafs.

If your scissors drop away from you
    It's a sign your lover's been untrue!

Monkey Bars

2 C flour
1 ½ C sugar
1 C sour cream
½ C butter – softened
2 eggs
1 tsp each: vanilla, baking soda
¼ tsp salt
2 medium ripe bananas – peeled, mashed

In a large mixing bowl cream together the butter and sugar then beat in the eggs, sour cream and vanilla. In a separate bowl combine together the flour, baking soda and salt and slowly add to the large mixing bowl then whip in the bananas. Spread into a greased 13 x 9 baking pan and bake at 350 for 20-25 minutes. Cool and frost.

Monkey Frosting

8oz cream cheese, softened
½ C butter, softened
2 tsp vanilla
3 ¾ C powdered sugar

Cream together all ingredients in a medium bowl until fluffy and frost the cake when cool.

Who gives the third gift,
    And I don't mean maybe,
        At a bridal shower,
            Will have the next baby!

Summum Bonum Cookies

2 C each: sugar, brown sugar, butter – softened
4 eggs
4 C flour
5 C quick oatmeal
2 tsp each: vanilla extract, baking powder and soda
24 oz chocolate chips
8 oz dark chocolate bar, grated
3 C pecans, chopped

Preheat oven to 375. In a large bowl combine flour, oatmeal, salt, baking powder, baking soda and set aside. In a separate bowl, cream together; butter, sugar, brown sugar, eggs and vanilla. Add both bowls together and fold in chocolate chips, grated chocolate and nut pieces. Make into golf size balls and place 2 inches apart on a cookie sheet and bake for 5-8 minutes or until browned.

Seven Sages of the Druids

The Knower: Gautama, Marici Uesos
The Researcher: Bharadvaja, Angiras Uocomarcos
Wisdom: Visvamitra, Pulaha Eulacsas
Truth: Jamadagmi, Kratu Uirionos
The Overly: Vasistha, Pulastya Ueros
The Superior: Kasyapa, Bhrgu Andiatis
The Dazzling: Atri, Dksa Uindonos

Lemon Moon Cookies

4 C flour
1 C each: sour cream, butter – softened
2 egg yolks – whipped
2 Tbsp lemon juice
1 tsp each: salt, cinnamon
2 egg whites
½ C sugar
8 oz ground nuts (walnut, almond, pecan)
2 ½ tsp cinnamon
2 Tbsp grated lemon rind
2 tsp lemon juice
1/8 tsp salt

Sift together in a large mixing bowl flour, 1 tsp salt, 1 tsp cinnamon then cut in butter. Add sour cream, egg yolks and 2 Tbsp lemon juice and combine into a dough and chill overnight. The next day in a small mixing bowl beat the egg whites and gradually add sugar until meringue forms peaks. Fold in the nuts, lemon rind, remaining lemon juice, cinnamon and salt. Dust a table with confectioner's sugar and roll out the chilled dough and work until thin. Cut into 3 inch squares and spread 1 tsp of filling on each square. Roll up diagonally to form a crescent and bake at 325 on a cookie sheet for 28-30 minutes or until lightly browned and firmed.

Celtic Knots

Are typically 8 knots continuously strung together as a symbol of sacred geometry that shows the interconnectedness of all things and continuous cycling of existence as seen on the Book of Kells.

Celtic Astrology of the Woods

The Reed: October 28 – November 24 (the Owl, the White Hound)

Magickal Strengths: Fertility, love, protection, family, hunting, gathering, regeneration, keeper of secret treasure, divine power, the other world.

Favored Wands:
October 28-November 11: the Walnut
November 12-21: the Chestnut
November 22-24: the Ash

Spiritual Purpose: To produce order where others have caused chaos, use this skill and take charge, to keep any given target in sight and not be distracted, realizing your results are only as sure as the intentions of which they were begun, to expect surprise encounters and upsets as these tools you use to overcome them will become as valuable as the journey itself.

The Elder: November 25 - December 23 (the Black Horse, the Badger, the Raven)

Magickal Strengths: Exorcism, banishment, prosperity, healing, is in opposition to and yet part of the light, thievery, winter, rebirth, seasonal magick, weather magick, earth, sky, moon and sun magick, reiki and stone magick.

Favored Wands:
November 25-December 1: the Ash
December 2-11: the Hornbeam
December 12-21: the Fig
December 22: the Beech

Spiritual Purpose: To learn that with the passing of each aspect of life another begins anew, to learn that new creativity and inspiration can come from old thoughts and ideas, to learn that renewal comes as links are continually formed and as new phases of life and experience repeat themselves in different ways so lessons can be renewed with fresh perspectives and points of view.

The Birch: December 24 – January 20 (White Stag, Golden Eagle)

Magickal Strengths: protection of children, purification, creativity, grain harvest, light, fire, sun, metallurgy, weaving, medium, hidden treasure, leprechauns and fairies.

Favored Wands:
December 24-31: the Apple Tree
January 1 – 11: the Fir tree
January 12 – 20: the Elm tree

Spiritual Purpose:
Focus on new beginnings, concentrate on personal desires and get rid of negativity, unuseful influences and bad thoughts to accomplish your goals. Practice meditation and concentrate on your firmly on your desires and keeping the image of the wanted result in your mind's eye despite any distractions or obstructions and you will create new beginnings with your focus.

The Rowan: January 21 – February 17 (the Crane, the Green Dragon)

Magickal Strengths: healing, personal empowerment and divination, fertility, poetry, arts and crafts, healing, learning, love, hearth and home, agriculture, witchcraft, occult knowledge

Favored Wands:
January 21 – 24: the Elm
January 25 – February 3: the Cypress
February 4 – February 8: the Popular
February 9 – February 17: the Cedar

Spiritual Purpose:
Focus on keeping hold of your senses to distinguish good from bad, harm from help, refuse to be swayed tricked or beguiled, strive to possess strength of character to turn away from anything that threatens purpose or serenity – be unafraid.

The Ash Tree: February 18 – March 17 (the Adder, the Seagull, the Tern, the Seahorse)

Magickal Strengths: prosperity, protection, healing, singing enchantments, music magick, magician, storyteller, trickster, illusion, cultural arts, learning.

Favored Wands:
February 18: the Cedar
February 19-29: the Pine
March 1- 10: the Weeping Willow
March 11-17: the Lime or the Linden

Spiritual Purpose:
Focus on the realization that the world and you are interconnected – and every ripple in the pond of the cosmos you cause creates an effect of circumstance, therefore all your actions warrant careful consideration. Learn to ask questions of others to see your problems in a wider context and get opinions to see different sides of a controversy. Balance is your primary goal in all things.

The Alder: March 18 – April 14 (the Fox, the Bear, the Falcon, the Hawk)

Magickal Strengths: Spirituality, weather magick, teaching, duty, mental prowess, prophecy, art, war, writing, bard, minstrel, musicians, defense, protection, invasion.

Favored Wands:
March 18 – 20: the Lime or the Linden
March 21: the Oak
March 22 – 31: the Hazel
April 1 – 10: the Rowan
April 11-14: the Maple

Spiritual Purpose:
To open your minds eye to see the deeper qualities within you and of others, acknowledge the unusual, put to use that which is overlooked, enhance your oracular and intuitive nature to be able to offer spiritual aid and protection in disputes.

The Willow: April 15 – May 12 (the Adder, the Hare, the Serpent, the Sea Serpent)

Magickal Strengths: Romantic love, healing, protection, fertility, female magick, moon magick, nature, inspiration, astrology, herbs, science, poetry, spells, prophetic powers and divine knowledge.

Favored Wands:
April 15-20: the Maple
April 21-30: the Walnut
May 1–12: the Popular

Spiritual Purpose:
Change and values go hand in hand are paramount for your growth. You are encouraged to become comfortable in the material world. Repetition and a steady accumulation of facts is often the foundation of true understanding. You are called on to progress to periods of rest and reflection so as not to miss the lessons learned during continual activity.

The Hawthorne: May 13 – June 9 (the Bee, the Owl, the Chalice)

Magickal Strengths: Fertility, peace, prosperity, cleansing, protection, chastity, unfailing protection, immortality, perpetual health, brew crafting, jewelry, fire, metal work, blacksmithing, earth magick, gardening, fairies.

Favored Wands:
May 13-14: the Popular
May 15-24: the Chestnut
May 25-June 3: the Ash
June 4-9: the Hornbeam

Spiritual Purpose:
You are called to maintain a healthy diet, exercise, work on your physical condition and betterment of yourself, open and cleanse your mind from falsehoods and ignorance, learn that through the most dire of circumstances comes knowledge and strength, for it is upon these that your spirit will be renewed.

The Oak: June 10 – July 7 (the Wren, the Otter, the Hawk, the White Horse)

Magickal Strengths: All positive purposes, fidelity, masculine magick, cookery, defense, love, humanity, and the ability to see the merits of an individual, seasonal and cyclical magick.

Favored Wands:
June 10-13: the Hornbeam
June 14-23: the Fig
June 24: the Birch
June 25-July 4: the Apple
July 5-7: the Fir

Spiritual Purpose:
You are to learn by doing, use a hands on approach to nurture your skills, accumulate and share your acorns of wisdom to watch them grow mightily, become strong, wise, tough, resilient and yet able to bend to become resilient in your nature.

The Holly: July 8 – August 4 (Cat, Unicorn)

Magickal Strengths: Protection, prophecy, animal magick, sexual magick, universal wisdom, magick, seasonal magick, nature, tree magick, fertility, bounty, abundance, prosperity, plenty, harvest, purification and blessing of the earth.

Favored Wands:
July 8-14: the Fir
July 15-25: the Elm
July 25-August 4: the Cypress

Spiritual Purpose:
To learn if the cause is just and that all things may be overcome by unity and concerted effort, learn daily and train others, cultivate instinctive intuition and dynamic ability in fast moving situations, accept the reality of here and now.

The Hazel: August 5 – September 1 (the Stalking Crane, the Rainbow Salmon)

Magickal Strengths: Manifestation, spirit contact (medium), protection, fertility, communication, writing, literature, eloquence, poetry, direction, wisdom, optimism, chameleon, shape shifter, disguise, cookery, medicine, regeneration, healing, invisibility, separation.

Favored Wands:
August 5-13: the Popular
August 14-23: the Cedar
August 24-September1: the Pine

Spiritual Purpose:
To muse, to inspire others to go beyond their limits in poetry, divination, mediation, to be aware that example is the best teacher, practice the intuitions ability to bring forth ideas, to then follow the intuition to the Source and your reward will be boundless wisdom and your soul will sing out in poetry for joy!

The Vine: September 2 – September 29 (the Lizard, the Hound, the White Swan)

Magickal Strengths: Dependant on the type of vine; Blackberry (prosperity and protection), Blueberry (spirituality, dream magick), Grape (fertility, inspiration, prosperity, binding), Thistle (courage, protection, strength; All – beauty, love, sexuality, sea magick, light and goodness – but beware the jealous nature of others who will lie and blame you for their deliberate acts of malicious mischief.

Favored Wands:
September 2: the Pine
September 3-12: the Weeping Willow
September 13-22: the Lime or the Linden
September 23: the Olive
September 24-29: the Hazel

Spiritual Purpose: Learn to allow your intuition to guide you at any given moment in any situation where it is necessary to act in a certain way, to open your senses to allow inner development, place trust in your senses and act strongly – do not stop to reason, open your inner self so that all signs and omens may be harvested and gathered in your realm of understanding.

The Ivy: September 30 – October 27 (the Boar, the Goose, the Butterfly)

Magickal Strengths: Healing, protection, cooperation, exorcism, star, full moon, reincarnation, silver, time, karma, weaver, creation, magickal practices, helping others find their feminine powers, birds, horses, enchantments, song magick, charms, lull the living and wake the dead; beware those who would steal your children and watch over them carefully.

Favored Wands:
September 30-October 3: the Hazel
October 4-13: the Rowan
October 14-23: the Maple
October 24-27: the Walnut

Spiritual Purpose: To link with others and recognize that the group consciousness does have influence, to absorb, go inward and learn about yourself, to enter into the group mind with joy, to assist others in their spiritual journey so they can in turn assist others, to learn that all is intertwined.

Pied Piper's Pickles and Charms

Pied Piper's Pickles: cucumber or cauliflower, peppers, carrots, and onions

1 Tbsp Alum
2 bunches of fresh Dill
¼ cup Kosher salt
Several Garlic bulbs, peeled and crushed
1 tsp Dry mustard per jar
1 ½ C Apple cider vinegar per jar

In a large stockpot add several cucumbers or other vegetables, ¼ cup salt, 1 Tbsp alum and bring to boiling on medium heat. Continue boiling until the cucumbers or vegetables are the softness of your liking. Pack in a glass jars and add dill, 1-2 cloves crushed garlic, 1 tsp dry mustard and 1 1/2 cup vinegar to each jar, finishing with water to the top. Seal jars and leave undisturbed for 2-3 months and serve.

Pickled Easter Eggs: eggs, onions and beets

Hard boil eggs in hot salted water for 10-15 minutes and cool quickly in cold water with ice. Peel eggs and put in a gallon container, add peeled and sliced onions and canned beets with juice to container. Add 1 tbsp each: sugar, dry mustard, salt and dill. Fill with 2 cups apple cider vinegar and water and seal container. Let set in refrigerator undisturbed for from Palm Sunday until Easter Sunday and eat as desired.

Asian Pickles

½ C rice vinegar
3 Tbsp sugar
juice of two limes
1 tsp salt plus more to taste
1 small garlic clove, peeled and crushed
fresh hot peppers, seeded and julienned (amount of peppers determine spiciness)
6 pickling cucumbers, sliced
1 head of Napa cabbage
½ C shallots, peeled and thinly sliced
¼ C cilantro, chopped (optional)
1 large round flat rock

In a large bowl combine vinegar, sugar, salt, lime juice, and garlic in a large bowl. Slice shallots, cucumbers, cabbage and cilantro thinly and coat thoroughly in the bowl. Place the rock on top of the mixture and leave on counter or in refrigerator overnight. Seal in jars or serve.

Dough Charms

1 C each: salt, flour
½ c water (more or less depending on weather)
Additives according to your intent: for instance for love you may want to add rose oil, red food coloring, rose petals – see comprehensive herbal

Knead all ingredients together and form into a talisman, amulet, Celtic knot or beads to make a key chain, ornament, bracelet or doll. Let dry out for a week or cook on 250 for 20 minute to 1 hour depending on thickness. Carry or hang and use with intent and purpose – never reuse – bury instead.

Pickled Black Eyed Peas (Texas Caviar)

2 C Zesty Italian Dressing
3 bunches green onions with tops (sliced very thin)
2 C white onion-peeled, chopped
½ C Jalapeños-chopped
½ C fresh cilantro-chopped
14 oz hominy-drained
1 garlic clove-peeled, crushed
1 ½ C bell pepper-chopped
4 oz green olives-chopped
1 lb. dried black eyed peas

Soak dried peas overnight. Drain and put fresh water in them and cook for 40 minutes on medium low heat in a large pot. Drain and cool. Add remaining ingredients and salt to taste. Refrigerate.

Pickled Cabbage - One Penny Pickles

10 lbs cabbage-shredded
3 lbs onions-chopped
2 lbs sugar
1 Tbsp celery seed
1 C dry mustard
½ C each: salt, jalapeno peppers-seeded, chopped
4 large green sweet peppers-seeded and chopped
1 tsp turmeric
3/4 gallon cider vinegar

Combine all ingredients together in a large stock pot and cook on medium high heat for 20 minutes. Ladle into hot jars, leaving 1/2 inch head-space. Adjust lids and process in a boiling water bath for 10 minutes. Cool and store for up to 1 year.

Bread and Butter Pickles

6 cucumbers-sliced
4 onions- sliced
¼ C salt
1 pint white vinegar
¾ C sugar
1 tsp each: celery seed, mustard seed

Mix vegetables with salt and let stand 1 hour. Drain and rinse with 2 cups cold water. Combine vinegar, sugar, celery and mustard seeds and heat to boiling. Cook 3 minutes. Pack vegetables into jars; add hot vinegar mixture, leaving ¼ " headspace. Seal at once and process in boiling water bath for 10 minutes. Cool and store.

Pickled Green Tomatoes

5 lbs tomatoes	2 stalks celery
3 green peppers	2 onions-wedged
1 cauliflower-pieced	3 large carrots-sliced
2 C brown sugar	2 qt water
1 qt vinegar	1 C salt

½ tsp each: celery seed, mustard seed
1 Tbsp each: whole allspice, whole cloves
2-5 bulbs garlic-peeled

Put tomatoes, vegetables and garlic into a jar. Ina saucepan on medium heat combine water, vinegar, salt and bring to boil. Pour over vegetables in jar and seal. Refrigerate and use in two to three weeks.

Watermelon Rind Pickles

Rind (white only) from 1 large watermelon
1 C salt
2 gallons + 2 qrts + 2 qrts and then some water
4-6 tsp alum
4 inch piece of ginger-peeled, grated

Peel and cut watermelon rind into strips. Soak in a strong salt water solution (about 1 cup salt dissolved in 2 gallons water) for 24 hours. Drain and soak in 2 quarts of water in which 4-6 tablespoons of alum has been dissolved for 4 hours. Drain well and soak in water to cover, refrigerated, for 24 hours. Grate a 4 inch piece of fresh ginger and steep 2 quarts of hot water for 30 minutes to make a ginger tea. train the tea through a filter or cheesecloth to remove ginger. Boil the watermelon rind in the ginger tea for 2 hours at just above a simmer. Remove rind and allow to cool. Remove to jars, cover and use in 2-3 weeks.

Pickled Garlic

1 C sugar   ¼ C salt
1/3 C white vinegar   2/3 C water
½ galleon garlic cloves-peeled

Combine vinegar, sugar, salt and water in a large pot and bring to a full rolling boil. Drop in peeled garlic. Return solution to full boil and boil 2 minutes. Turn off fire and allow to cool. Put into glass mason jars, seal and store in cool place 3 months. Eat like peanuts. Bonus: The solution makes excellent salad dressing too.

Zucchini pickles

1 qrt distilled white vinegar   2 C sugar
¼ C salt   1 tsp dry mustard
2 tsp each: celery seed, turmeric-ground
5 lb zucchini-unpeeled, cut into 1/4-inch slices
1 qt thinly sliced onions (4-5 medium)

Combine first 6 ingredients in a large saucepan; bring to a boil then add zucchini and onions; remove from heat and let stand 1 hour, stirring occasionally. Bring mixture to a boil on medium heat once again, then lower heat and simmer 3 minutes. Continue simmering while quickly packing one clean, hot jar at a time. Fill to within 1/2 inch of top making sure vinegar solution covers vegetables. Cap each jar at once. Process 5 minutes in boiling-water bath; recipe makes 6-7 pints.

Pickled Green Beans

2 ½ C water   2 ½ C vinegar
¼ C salt
2 lbs stemmed tiny green beans

Pack lengthwise in each jar leaving ¼" headroom:
1/4 tsp. cayenne pepper
1 clove garlic
1 head of dill or 1 1/2 tbsp. dill seed

Bring to boil water, vinegar, salt and beans and pour over packed jars, leaving 1/4 inch headroom. Seal jars and process 15 minutes in boiling water bath. Makes 4 pints and cucumbers can be used for same recipe.

Invocation for a Wish

Hold the herbs you have chosen (always chose an odd number) and visualize in fine detail exactly what your wish is then breathe you wish onto the herbs and …
Turn to the North and say,
St. Uriel, Archangel of the North and of the Earth, I call on you to carry my wish to the northern hemisphere and by the Powers of GOD, I ask you to bring me success. Amen. Now blow ¼ of the herbs to the north.
Turn to the East and say,
St. Raphael, Archangel of the East and of the Air, I call on you to carry my wish to the eastern hemisphere and by the Powers of GOD, I ask you to bring me success. Amen. Now blow ¼ of the herbs to the east.
Turn to the South and say,
St. Michael, Archangel of the South and of Fire, I call on you to carry my wish to the southern hemisphere and by the Powers of GOD, I ask you to bring me success. Amen. Now blow ¼ of the herbs to the south.
Turn to the West and say,
St. Gabriel, Archangel of the West and of Water, I call on you to carry my wish to the western hemisphere and by the Powers of GOD, I ask you to bring me success. Amen. Now blow the rest of the herbs to the south.

Turn around in a circle three times and say – In the Name of the Father, and in the name of the Son and of the name of the Holy Ghost – Amen!
Now walk away knowing that you wish has been granted and give Thanks!

Wine, Mead and Beer

Important: It is essential to sanitize everything in bleach water before using (1 Tbsp bleach with every gallon of water) as 75% of the taste of your brew is due to proper or improper sanitation! Remember to also resanitize if reusing a bottle or equipment during the processing. Only use stainless steel or glass pots and pans for all brewing as aluminum and iron will ruin your mixtures!

Wine

18 lbs of fresh fruit or dandelion cleaned, bruised and double boiled into syrup and strained or 3 cans juice concentrate
½ cup sugar
1 pkg wine yeast (or 3 pkg of brewers works but not as well)
Soft water – not distilled! 2 times as much as the fruit syrup

1 gallon cleaned milk jug
Balloons
Measuring cups, rubber band, food grade tubing, funnel
2 X soft water than fruit syrup (tap water contains chlorine – distilled ruins the wine)
Pin to poke balloon (do not rip)

For Blackberry wine add: ½ oz each nutmeg and cloves

Pour juice and water into the milk jug and shake around without lid to aerate the mixture and make it ready for the yeast. Add ½ cup sugar and shake

vigorously with the cap on, don't let the sugar settle.
Separately, pour warm water in a cup and put in the yeast, but do not stir.
Add 2 Tbsp sugar and let it go to foam for 10 minutes and then add it to the juice mix and shake with the lid on for about 10 more minutes. Take off the lid and add the balloon that you have put 3-10 holes in with the pin. Put a rubber band around the balloon to keep it in place. Keep it in a warm dark place and leave it alone. Check in 24hrs to make sure the balloon is rising, if not add new yeast mixture. Check at 1 week, check at 2 weeks, the balloon should inflate and then deflate to be done. Strain with cheesecloth and transfer to bottles and cork. Let age at least two months.

Important information: if your wine needs settling, add egg whites to the mix. If you need to stop fermentation, add powdered vitamin C (not capsules).

Mulled Wine

2/3 C sugar
1 750 mo bottle wine
½ C Brandy
6-8 cloves
1 cinnamon stick
Zest from ½ orange (no white)

Cook in a enameled or glass pot on low heat until warmed then turn off and serve hot.

Spiced Wine

2 tsp, allspice, whole
¾ C lemon peel, grated
3 inch long cinnamon stick
3 C burgundy wine
¾ C raisins
½ C sugar

Tie the spices and raisins in a square of cheesecloth with kitchen string or tear a little piece of the cheesecloth to use as a tie. Mix all ingredients together and simmer and simmer in a glass pan until heated through and serve. Remove bag before serving.

Sangria

1 bottle of burgundy – cabernet sauvignon, zinfandel or merlot
1 bottle of dry or sparkling white wine
1 shot sweet vermouth
1 shot brandy or rum
1/2 C each: orange juice, cranberry juice, pineapple juice, raw honey
2 tsp grated lemon peel, nutmeg
1 cinnamon stick

Put lemon peel, nutmeg and cinnamon stick in a muslin bag and hang in a large bowl with remaining ingredients overnight. 1 hour before serving float your choice of fruit (any berries, bananas or kiwi) or just before serving add apple or pear slices.

Pan Wine

1 gal each: spring water, white grape juice
½ lb each: fairy sugar, honey
½ pkg active dry yeast

Suspend the yeast in a cup of warm water, then in a large brewing pot on low heat slightly – barely warm the rest of the ingredients until all sugars are dissolved and add the yeast, test sweetness and make sure it is to your liking. Cover and keep at room temperature over night. Set in bottles and cork loosely (as corks will pop off several times in the next 3-4 weeks). Then test sweetness of the wine (if not to your preference return to stove and brew again with more sugar and honey until sweetness is to your liking) and cork tightly and keep in cool darkness until used.

Protection Incantation

Get a number of old keys, one for each door and window in your home. With each key touch it to a corresponding door or window and say:

Lock out thieves in the night,
Lock out thieves in the light,
Lock out thieves out of sight!

Then tie all the keys together with a red ribbon and hang above your front door – and don't forget to count the pet door!

Mead

10 lbs raw honey
5 lbs sugar
5 gallons Soft water (19 liters)
2 ½ quarts apple juice
1 pkg champagne yeast
3 cups black or orange pekoe tea (tannic acid)
juice of 10 squeezed lemon, lime, orange etc (citric acid)
Optional: 1 ½ Tbsp of cloves, cinnamon, rose petals, apples, or grapes
Rubber stopper

Remove all juice from the citrus (unless using tea – then brew), pulp is okay but seeds and rind are not. Set aside 1-2 tbsp each of citrus, apple juices and tea, and then put the rest in the container. In a glass sauce pan add ½ Cup warmed water, 1 tsp each citrus, tea, apple juices, sugar and raw honey and mix then add yeast. Let mixture sit for 10 -15 minutes for foam to develop. Meanwhile add 1 gal of really hot water to the container and with the help of the funnel add the 5 lbs sugar and slosh it around really well to aerate and dissolve the sugar. Add 2 more liters of warm water and pour in the honey and add the spices. Add remainder of warm water. The temp should be about 90-95 degrees for you to add the yeast mix (too high will kill it – to low will not let it develop). Leave some space at the top for foam to develop. Add the rubber stopper to the top of the jug and keep at 70 degrees in the dark. Leave it alone for 2 months then remove the stopper and strain the mixture with a cheese cloth from one 5 gallon jug to the next without letting oxygen touch it. (continued next page)

Repeat monthly for 4-5 more months, on the last pass taste the mixture and sweeten as desired with more honey. The stronger the flavor the more it will need to age as aging helps to mellow the flavour of the mead. Average aging necessary is 6 months to 2 years before serving. Add Vitamin C powder to stop fermentation and bottle.

3 little Fishies Down by the Sea

3 little fishies down by the sea,
Swim out with the tide and take care of me
3 little fishies down by the sea,
All filled with good tidings and prosperity
3 little fishies down by the sea,
One to share, one to spare, and one just for me
3 little fishies down by the sea
Happily taking care of my every need

Sing as you are making and filling 3 sand fishes down by the ocean while the tide is coming in. Make sure you point the fishes as going out, fill each one with little tokens of your needs, written papers and instructions, gifts for the bearer of good tidings, encircle with salt, concentrate on your desire and light a candle as you watch them swim away!

Beer

1 ½ galleon Soft Water + 2 ½ galleons soft water + more water
1 pkg Wine yeast
Malt (made from barley that is soaked, sprouted, roasted and then crushed)
4 lbs corn sugar
Hops (are the flower portion of the vine)
1 ½ inch food grade plastic hose
5 galleon jug
Funnel
Lock assembly

In a large stainless steel stockpot brew 1½ galleons water and bring it to a boil. Add the malt, 1 ½ oz hop pellets and 4 lbs of corn sugar and boil for 1 hour, stirring regularly the last 10 minutes –strain - this is your Wort.
In a separate bowl stir yeast into 1 cup of very warm water and cover.
Fill your 5 galleon jug half way with water, funnel in your Wort and add more water until you are about 8 inches below the fill line. Slosh it around to aerate and leave until room temperature. Funnel in your yeast mixture, add your blow of tube (the other end of which you may want to put in a pail), seal and place in a dark place like a closet for 24 hours whereupon it should produce a lively foam. After 2 days remove the tube and place in the lock assembly and leave it alone for 6-14 days. Then boil 3 cups of water in a sauce pan with 1 cup corn sugar and add to mix to produce carbonation and mix thoroughly. Bottle and let set for at least one more week. Enjoy!

Beer Tricks and Treats

For darker more full bodied beer add: 2 cups of molasses to the malt while it is cooking and cut back a bit on the sugar.

For different flavours try you may try adding a few sticks of licorice or herbal tea bags to the Wort while it is brewing.

For more fun than a barrel of monkeys visit hbd.org/brewery/cm3/index.html – we didn't get any of our recipes there – but we are going to spend a lot of time on that site in the future!

Add Irish moss to help clarify the beer in the last 45 minutes of the boil.

Gypsum is a mild hardening agent that gives your beer a dry bitter edge and takes away the maltiness like pale British ale.

Burton water salts is a more severe hardening agent that adds much more hardness per teaspoon than Gypsum, emphasizing the bitter qualities of hops and reducing the sweet malt flavours

Calcium Chloride takes away bitterness and adds a sweet malty character found in most malts, ambers, browns and any other style that you want to suppress the bitter qualities.

Charm for Home Protection

Beneath thy guardianship I am safe against all tempests and all enemies, J. J. J. (J. = Jesus)

Herb Craft

"Come, sweetheart, come,
Dear as my heart to me,
Come to the room
I have made fine for thee.
Here there be couches spread,
    Tapestry tented,
Flowers for thee to tread,
Green herbs, sweet scented."

From Helen Waddell, Mediaeval Latin Lyrics

Since Mediaeval times sweet herbs and woods have been used to make life a little better. They were carried in pockets, strewn across floors, placed in the washing water and of course across several beds inducing romantic encounters. String them upside down in the corners of your house, tie them to your bedpost, make garlands, sachets and wreaths, they will induce sweet, gentle dreams, and joyous moments. The following list is a collection of my favorites with their common names - Live well.

Aromatic herbs, flowers and woods

Apple, Sweet Basil, Cedar, Cinnamon, Citrus, Clove, Chrysanthemum, Cypress, Frankincense, Freesia, Sweet Goldenrod, Honeysuckle, Iris, Jasmine, Lavender, Lilac, Day Lily, Magnolia, Maple, Oak, Pecan, Pine, Pinion Leaf, Sage, Sagebrush, Sandalwood, Sweet grass, Teakwood, Rosemary, Rose, Vanilla, Violet, Viola, and Sweet Woodruff.

Potpourri and Sachets
Basic Potpourri

In a large mason jar put 1 Tbsp orris root as a fixative (something to hold the scent) and add your herbs, woods and spices (e.g. Cinnamon, orange zest, cloves with cedar wood) Add 7-9 drops of essential oil cover tightly and shake to coat the orris root thoroughly. Keep in the container for 7-10 days (longer is stronger) then mix in your other ingredients (e.g. Rose petals, pine cone etc) and close jar again, mixing thoroughly and keep in a dark place for 4-6 weeks (from Harvest to Yule). Remove to a decorative container and give as gifts.

Sugar and Spice

Apple slices   orange peels
Cinnamon sticks   honeycomb
Cloves   rosehips
Scent with apple and cinnamon essential oils

Welcome Home

Lavender buds   rosebuds and petals
Angel wings flowers   straw flowers
Scent with lavender, rose and musk essential oils

Yuletide Greetings

White globe flowers   small pine cones
White angel wings   cedar tips
Cinnamon sticks   cloves
Scent with pine essential oil

I Dream of Thee Sachet

1 C mugwort
½ C each: rose petals, chamomile, sweet hops
1/3 C each: lavender buds, crushed catnip
¼ C peppermint leaves

For peaceful dreams add jasmine flowers
For dreams of peace and guidance add sage,
    mullein, sassafras, and pine needles
For knowledge add bay leaf
For vivid dreams add flowers of mugwort and mint
For physic dreams add dandelion seeds
To make a wish add marigold petals and say:
    I wish I want and wish I may
    Come to me through dreams do fair
    Come by night and come by day
    Come thou wish and ride thee here!
To stop nightmares add morning glories
To guard against nightmares add rosemary, valerian
    Frankincense and lemon balm
For dreams of love add rose petals, yarrow, violets,
    Crepe myrtle, dill and coriander
To make your dreams come true at 12pm on a
    Friday in silence gather 9 small holly leaves
    and add them to your sachet, make your
    wish and go to sleep.

Use 5 x 12 inch squares of linen, muslin or cheesecloth. Sew both ends so that a string can go through and then fold over and sew the sides inside out. Invert, stuff and tie tightly. Hang on your bed post or place inside your pillowcase.

Patchouli Passion Pillows

If you are making this for a man use a red material
If you are making this for a woman use lavender

Per Pillow:
8 oz buckwheat hulls
4 oz dried patchouli
10-20 drops of patchouli essential oil

Mix together in a mason jar and for at least 24 hours shaking from time to time to coat the buckwheat hulls then add to your pillow stuffing.

Cut your material into a 10 x 10 square, circle or heart shape (or larger as this will stay on their bed) then sew all but leave a 3-4 inch opening for stuffing. Stuff until soft but full and sew together the opening.

Sinus Headache Relief

½ tsp flax seeds
1 tsp each crushed leaves: spearmint, peppermint
1 tsp each whole leaves: eucalyptus, rosemary
1 tsp lavender buds

Keep in a tightly closed mason jar or sewn in sachets and breathe in as needed to aid in the relief of sinus headache symptoms.

Pet Pillow

2 C pennyroyal
1 C each: thyme, wormwood

Sew into a large pet pillow with cedar chips to aid in repelling fleas and odors.

Wintering Sachet

4 Tbsp each: tansy, patchouli
2 Tbsp lavender
2 tsp powdered orris root
Muslin or cheese cloth

Sew in 3 x 3 sachets and keep in closets or drawers where you are storing your winter clothes and *keep out of reach of children.

Kitchen Witch Sachet

1 Tbsp each: lavender, rosemary, crushed cloves,
            and lemon zest

Sew in muslin or cheesecloth squares and use in your cupboards and drawers to repel insects.

Lucky Purse

1 tsp each cinnamon, tea, salt and poppy seeds

Carry in a muslin bag in your purse for prosperity.

Essential Oils

½ cup carrier oil (sweet almond, grape seed, olive)
1 oz vitamin e oil (as a natural preservative)
4 C tightly packed flower petals OR 1 C packed fresh herbs OR 1 C chopped fruit peel– 1 cup a day for 4 days or ¼ a day for 4 days
Rubber mallet
2 wide mouth glass jars
Funnel
Amber, smoked or dark blue cobalt corked bottles
Cheese cloth or cotton gauze

Thoroughly rinse all flowers/herbs/rinds in cold water if organic – in 1 part apple cider vinegar to 10 parts water rinse if they are not. Each day for 4 days place 1 Cup of flower petals (or ¼ herbs or citrus peel) in a plastic bag and gently bruise them with a rubber mallet. Then place them with the oil into one of the glass jars, cover and shake gently until the oil completely covers the mixture. Leave the bottle in a warm place like you kitchen or out in the sun.

Each day go to your glass jar and fold the cheese cloth over the top and strain the oil into the other glass jar. Squeeze as much of the oil as possible out of the cheese cloth and toss away the old mixture. Begin again by bruising the materials and adding to the jar, gently shaking and covering with the oil. Do this for four days switching the oil back and forth between the two jars until the fourth day then strain it one last time and remove to smaller dark glass bottles with stoppers. You now have your own essential oil with a shelf life of 6-12 months.

Oils, Vinegars and Waters:

Making Herb infused oil

1 part herb by weight (e.g. 1 0z)
1 part alcohol by volume (e.g. 1 oz)
Wide mouth glass jar
5-6 parts (e.g. 5-6 oz) 1st cold pressed extra virgin olive oil
Cheese cloth

Put the herb in the cheesecloth and add to the alcohol in the glass jar and let it infuse for 24 hours, shaking every once in awhile to thoroughly coat. The next day add 5-6 parts 1st cold pressed extra virgin olive oil to the mixture and pour into a glass pot over low heat and warm until all the alcohol is evaporated then remove herbs and bottle.

Molybdomancy

A German tradition of melting tin or lead and dripping it into a pot of cold water on New Year's to divine the future. Done since the middle ages it is also used to learn the sickness of a person or to see if they have been bewitched. Done properly all aspects of the procedure are used – from the sound the metal makes when it enters the water, to the form or shape it takes as well as the direction it turns to properly divine the needed information. A great way to tune into your psychic abilities!

Raspberry Vinegar

2 lbs fresh raspberries, cleaned
1 pint malt vinegar

Put the mixture in a clean jug and set in a sunny window for 2 weeks and strain. Bottle and cork.

Rose Water
You may substitute any edible flower

1 C packed rose petals (the outside three of each rose are best)
2 C boiling spring water
1 Tbsp Alcohol (as a preservative)
Cheese cloth
Glass bowl

Put the petals in a glass bowl and pour the water gently over them. Steep for 20-30 minutes and strain with a cheese cloth. Allow to cool and then add the alcohol. Remove your rose water to a spray bottle and place in the refrigerator to refresh your skin daily. With the alcohol it will keep 4 weeks or longer without it 7-10 days.

Ceroscopy

In a small brass pot melt wax until it forms a liquid. Then pour by droplets into an Iron pot of cold water. Much like reading tea leaves or melted lead – these droplets are then read and divined – try it!

To Kiss Your Face

oh but to kiss your face
softly and slowly as we embrace
sweetly and gently to kiss each eye
your nose, your cheek, your ear, soft as a butterfly
and as I whisper within that this is only
where our love begins
down your neck and under your chin
treasuring each part slowly within
your goatee, your moustache, and finally your lips
slowly parting to give your tongue a flick
then ever so softly drinking you in
your head in my hands I would begin again
and this time I would hold your eyes
and show you a love with no good byes
where we were one where ever we may be
two hearts sailing fast and free
across the waters of eternity
fulfilling our every want and need
the same breath, the same touch, the same skin
glued to each other again and again
spouse, lover and friend, for you start where I end
as we set sail across an endless sea
hand in hand for eternity

Barbara Ann Daca

Soaps

General Information: Use Extreme Caution
Lye is a base known as an alkali and it is very caustic as it will burn anything it touches! If you do get lye on anything rinse with vinegar NOT water for at least 10 minutes! Lye can cause serious injury and even death if swallowed. Lye can cause blindness if splashed into the eyes. Wear long sleeves, safety goggles and plastic gloves. Keep away from all children and animals, never leave unattended. Do not splash or spill the lye solution. Call poison control prior to using lye at 1-800-222-1222 and visit www.poison.org.

To make your Great Grandmothers soap you will need:

To make your own lye, so you will need:

1 pair of thick latex gloves (the kind your use for your kitchen)
1 pair of goggles
Long sleeves and long pants
1 rain barrel (for catching rain –soft-water)
1 brewer's barrel for making the lye solution
1 cork about 3 inches long
1 drill to drill a hole in the brewer's barrel about 2 inches from bottom
Several Bricks to lay the brewers barrel on to raise it and steady it
Several river rocks to line the bottom of the brewer's barrel
Straw (hay or grass) to add about 6-7 inches on top of rocks

Hard wood ashes (oak, ash, fruit trees NOT evergreen or fir trees) from your fireplace or fire pit
A lock for your lye barrel

Wooden or glass crock or other container used only for lye making, make sure it is easy to pour from – you may use a funnel and an old clean dry wine jug or a jug from Mississippi mud black and tan beer works best just leave enough room at the top so it can get out easily

First go to your local brewer's and purchase two barrels – one for rain and one for lye – make sure that you NEVER mix them up! While you are there buy a cork as well or go to your local hardware for one.

Use your rain barrel to catch the soft water you will need throughout the year. For a batch of soap you will need at least 2-3 gallons.

For your lye barrel, drill a hole about 2 inches above the bottom making sure your cork will fit snugly into it. Place your lye barrel on top of some bricks and where it will not be disturbed by children or animals in any way.

Cover the bottom of your lye barrel with palm sized river rocks and then cover the river rocks with about 6-7 inches of hay – now this is your filter.

Take the burnt ashes from your branches and logs that you have collected throughout the year and put them in the lye barrel. (Remember these ashes should be cold – or you will burn down your barrel!)

Put a pot under the hole in the lye barrel and remove the cork. Put about 2-3 gallons of the soft water into the lye barrel until you see it start to drain out the hole and then cork the hole.

Let set for 3 days then leech every 24 hours. To leech, drain all the water in the barrel out and then put it back in.

You will know your lye is done when you can drop in a fist sized potato or a raw egg into it and you can see it floating with ¼ of it above the solution. Remember lye is caustic so do not remove the egg or potato by sticking your arm in it or you will be severely burned.

Catch your in a wooden crock or glass container that will be easy to pour from without splashing and use immediately or store briefly in a cool dark place.

Then to make it into soap you will need:

An outdoor kitchen (like a bbq) and a picnic table or a well ventilated kitchen with a fan

A double boiler or two stainless steel or enameled pans – one smaller than the other to use as a double boiler (one pot with water in it boiling and one pot sitting on the boiling water of the first pot)

2 large glass measuring cups (for lye only)
Spoons for mixing, wood, glass, stainless or plastic
Thick latex gloves

Goggles
Plenty of towels handy
Large glass microwave safe bowls
1 Sharp paring knife
1 large kitchen knife
Measuring spoons and cups for additions like essential oils and herbs
Molds like new litter boxes (without the litter)
Fragrances like essential oils or perfumes
Colorants
Herbs and flower petals of your choice (these will turn brown with the heat)

72 oz of Fat: e.g. tallow, bacon grease, lard

Pour12 oz of lye in a steady stream dissolving into 32 oz of soft water in a glass pot outside and stir constantly with a plastic or wooden spoon– put the lye into the water NOT the other way around or it WILL EXPLODE!
Set aside to cool. Next you need melt 64-72 oz of your choices of grease/shortening and any fragrance oils you want to use at this time in a double boiler and then cool. When both batches have cooled off to room temperature then grease your soap molds. Now slowly stir the lye into the fats/grease/oils stirring constantly, if you begin seeing bubbles then stir more slowly. From time to time drizzle the soap back into the pot, when it momentarily keeps it shape (tracing) before sinking back into the mix then its then it's almost ready. Separate 1 cup of the soap mixture and stir in any botanicals, grains or coloring you want into it and then add it back into the mixture. Pour the soap into a mold and wrap the mold in a towel and let set undisturbed for 18 hours – it should heat up and then cool down during this

time. Uncover and let set an additional 12 hours. To remove, loosen the sides by wiggling the mold a little and turn over onto a clean surface and cut the soaps into bars. Let the soap cure for an additional 3-4 weeks before use.

Additions:

For coloring use 1 tsp per lb of soap:
    Cocoa powder for brown
    Cayenne pepper or paprika for peach
    Liquid Chlorophyll for light green
    Turmeric for yellow
    Titanium dioxide for white

For every 4 lbs of soap:
1 oz of essential oil
8 oz of oatmeal for complexion
4 oz cornmeal for grit (handyman's soap)
½ oz geranium oil for dry skin
½ oz tea tree oil for problem skin

Note: you may use rose water for rose soap, lavender water for lavender soap etc.

Air Protection Spell

I weave this spell, through wind and air,
Protect me well, without a care,
Weave within, weave without,
Weave around me, all about,
Encircle me from up above,
Enclose me with Thy endless love!

Grandma's Soap

Use oil instead of fat: unfiltered olive oil or Crisco vegetable oil in the can
Use Water collected from your dehumidifier or distilled
Use Red devil brand 100% lye (available at home improvement centers, hardware stores and groceries for about $3 – NEVER use Drano)

Use the same instructions as printed on the previous pages.

Mama's Soap

1 Tbsp dried beaten herbs
¼ Cups soft water heated to boiling
5-6 drops of essential oil or your favorite perfume
2 cups of shredded Ivory soap (about 2-3 bars)
Mortar and pestle, small sauce pan, Cheese grater, medium glass mixing bowl, large glass plate, wooden spoon

With the mortar and pestle beat the herbs. In a small sauce pan bring to boil ¼ cup of water, turn off heat and steep the herbs. Add your scent to this mixture. Grate your soap in the bowl and then pour the mixture on top and mix thoroughly. Let stand for 20 minutes. Shape and let dry on a glass plate for 3-4 days before using or giving.

Wish upon a piece of paper,
    Keep it with you, watch it grow.
        Wish upon a piece of paper,
            Feel the magick ripple flow.

Your own Soap

3 cups of Glycerin or soap flakes
1 tsp Vitamin E (from oil or capsule)
2 Tbsp Raw Honey
3 oz beeswax
20 oz of Dry milk
5-6 drops of your favorite perfume or essential oil
Opt: ¼ C raw oats
Soap, candle or candy molds

Melt the glycerin or soap flakes in a double boiler or microwave. Spray molds lightly with alcohol to prevent bubbles. Add remaining ingredients and pour into molds. Spray the soap tops with alcohol lightly to make bubbles disappear. Let set undisturbed for 30 minutes then fit in the freezer for an additional 30 minutes. Remove from freezer and allow to sit for 10 minutes and your soap should pop right out.

Cucumber Lotion

2 large cucumbers peeled and sliced
¼ part white wine
¼ part aloe vera gel
¼ part elder flower water

Double boil the cucumber slices until soft and squeeze through a cheese cloth. Add ¼ part white wine and ½ part elder flower water (see rose water and substitute elder flowers), ¼ part fresh aloe vera gel (scraped from the inside of the leaf with a plastic knife) mix well and bottle.

Herbal Bathes and Salts

Do it yourself Bath Salts

Choose your Base

Epsom salt or Sea salt or Baking soda

Choose your Ingredients

Finely powdered herbs, powdered oatmeal, powdered milk, food coloring

Choose your Fragrance

Essential oils or flower petals

What to Do

All ingredients should be finely powdered and crushed with your mortar and pestle. Remove to a glass jar. To use place in a muslin bag and tie to the faucet so the bath water will run over it and then steep in the bath tub while you bathe.

Hives be Gone

Make the above recipe with 1 Cup German chamomile blossoms or 1 oz chamomile essential oil and 1 C oatmeal with ¼ C baking soda.

Ancient Relief from the Dead Sea

Muslin bag
Fill half way with Dead Sea salt
2 tsp lavender flowers
2 tsp lavender essential oil

Add to your bath and chant:
Pains and Aches and evil things,
Fly from me on rapid wings.
Leave my body and don't return,
For peace and quiet I do yearn.
Banish the forces of the night,
Send them off so they take flight!
And with Thy power, pure and white,
Fill me with Thy radiant light!

Herbal Rejuvenation Bath: sinus or colds

½ C each yarrow flowers, elder flowers, mint leaves, rose petals
Your choice of salts

Tie the herbs together in the cheese cloth and tie the cheese cloth with string. Steep in your bath for 10 minutes and then scrub the sickness away with it. Also works good as a tea.

Take me Away

½ C each comfrey leaves, mint leaves, chamomile flowers, and lavender flowers tied together in a cheese cloth with 1 C your choice of salts and steep in your tub for 10-20 minutes.

Magick for Muscles

2 parts each thyme, rosemary, lavender
1 part each cramp bark, Epson salt

Steep in your bath for 10-20 minutes in a cheese cloth bag.

Get Me Going

Equal parts in your choice of: basil, bay leaf, citronella, fennel, lavender, lemon, lemon verbena, peppermint, oregano, pine or rosemary with your choice of 1 C salts. Steep for 10-20 minutes in a muslin or cheese cloth bag.

Take my Blues Away

Equal parts of your choice of: rose petals, scented geranium leaves, lavender, mint, or patchouli with your choice of 1 C salts, steep for 10-20 minutes in a warm bath.

Aura Cleanse Bath

6 Tbsp ground nutmeg
1 tsp pineapple essential oil
1 tsp orange essential oil
1 tsp poppy seeds

Put in your coffee pot with a filter and brew. Then add to a warm bath and cleanse your aura and the negativity within that draws bad luck. Visualize accepting good luck and good things from others. Great bath to make others more accepting of you, for instance at a new job.

Bath of Pleasant Dreams

Muslin bag
1 tsp each lavender, chamomile, crushed rosemary
1 C bath salts
½ C lemon juice

Hang the sachet under the faucet/spigot and pour the lemon juice in the bath. Let Steep for 10 minutes while you relax in your tub while you breathe it in and slowly feel everything melting way.

Bath Oil

4 oz sweet almond oil
5 drops rosemary essential oil
15 drops sweet orange oil
5 drops lavender oil
1 Sprig rosemary with blossoms

Place all in a green mason jar and use as desired.

Invigoration

1 tsp each of 3-5 of the following: basil, bay leaf, Citronella, fennel, lavender, lemon, lemon Verbena, peppermint, oregano, pine or Rosemary
1 C either Epson salts

Steep with these in a muslin bag in a warm bath for 15-20 minutes and breathe deeply.

Abundance Bath

Steep in a bath a bag full of leaves
From 3 or 4 or 5 of these;
Marigold, mint. fennel, calendula, celery, grass
Menta si Larba, nasturtium, parsley, Telina, cress,
When the brew is green and the steam is sweet
Lie in the water and thrice repeat
I shall bathe and I shall be
As green and strong good herbs as thee
Draw me favor, draw me fame
Draw bright honor to my name
Rise from the water thrice empowered
Wear these virtues as a bower

Rejuvenation

1 tsp each: rose petals, scented geranium leaves,
    mint leaves
10 drops patchouli essential oil
1 Dead Sea salts

Sew in a muslin bag and steep in a warm bath for 20 minutes while breathing deeply

Relaxation

1 tsp each lavender, chamomile, rosemary
10 drops lemongrass essential oil
1 C Epsom salts

Tie in a cheesecloth bag and steep in a warm bath for 10-20 minutes and breathe deep and slow.

Golden Acceptance

6 Tbsp ground nutmeg
1 tsp each essential oil: pineapple, orange, poppy
1 C Epsom salts

Tie in a small cheesecloth and steep in your bath while visualizing the bad flowing away from you with every breath you let out and golden acceptance flowing in with every breath you breathe in. Great before starting a new job, beginning a new enterprise, meeting new people or when in charge of an important meeting.

Restful Evening

1 tsp calendula essential oil
7-10 drops lavender essential oil
5 drops of patchouli essential oil
1 C Dead sea salts

Steep in a muslin bag in a warm bath for 20 minutes before sleeping for best results.

Dandruff Shampoo

1 handful of nettle
3 regular aspirin
1 quart of soft water

Slow boil for 2 hours and bottle. Apply to the scalp every other night.

Raven Shampoo: for dark hair

1/3 rosemary
1/3 elder flowers
2 quarts soft water

Simmer on low heat for 1 hour, strain and bottle. Apply to scalp with a soft brush. Add ½ tsp of borax for dandruff prevention.

Hair Rinse

1 pt water
1 tsp each: burdock root
1 tsp each flowers: calendula, chamomile, lavender
1 tsp each: lemongrass, sage leaves
¼ C vinegar

Bring water to boil in a glass pan on medium heat. Remove and steep roots, flowers, and herbs for 30 minutes. Use as a final rinse on your hair after shampooing and do not rinse out for extra body and shine.

After Bath Powder

Equal parts of rice powder, ground orris root (keep from children) or ground calamus root

Mix with various ground spices and herbs of your own choosing, e.g. cloves, dried rose petals, lavender, magnolia, jasmine, violet, orange etc.

Body Powder

¼ tsp cinnamon, powdered
1/8 tsp cloves, crushed
¾ tsp lavender petals, crushed
1 C rice flour

Keep in a short mason jar with a natural sponge.

Mouthwash

2 tsp each: rosemary, sage, mint
2 C boiling water
Cheesecloth

Place herbs in the cheese cloth and crush. Tie into a bag and steep in the boiling water for 20 minutes. Cool and remove to a mason jar and use as needed.

Hand Washing Water

2 C water
5 drops rose oil
10 drops orange oil

Place together in a mason jar and set in the sun for one day then remove to the sink and use as needed.

Bedtime Massage

¼ C carrier oil (almond, grape seed, olive)
10 drops each essential oil: lavender, rosemary,
        bergamot

Keep in a closed jar beside your bed for use before restful sleep.

Fountain of Youth

2 Tbsp olive oil
2 Tbsp rape seed oil
10 drops each essential oil: palm rose, lavender, patchouli

For use on your skin just before bedtime.

Bounce Back

4 Tbsp walnut oil
10 drops spearmint essential oil
5 drops each essential oil: wintergreen, rosemary

For use midday to bounce back after a long night before or a difficult morning.

Sensual Pleasures

2 Tbsp Almond oil
2 Tbsp rape seed oil
10 drops each essential oil: patchouli, lemongrass, vanilla and rosehip

Great massage oil as part of a passionate evening.

Prosperity Sachet

Invite prosperity into your home by hanging a spring of basil, a magnet and 5 coins above your doorway.

Come to Me (Love Potion as Perfume)

9 drops each: jasmine, rose, bergamot, damiana
¼ C vodka

Combine in a small brown glass jar and keep in close reach for that moment when you see that which you desire, whisper Come to Me…

Be True to Me (Love Potion as Perfume)

½ C vodka
10 drops rose essential oil
15 drops lavender essential oil
10 drops musk oil

Place in a brown bottle and use around your intended to keep them faithful. Be True to Me…

Come Hither (Love Potion as Perfume)
Available from One Pot Witchery for $10.00 a dram
Used to make them all in your command

1 dram each: Lotus, Wishes, Success
3 drams each: High John, Dragon's Blood, Master
5 drams Bourbon Vanilla

Keep in a dark glass bottle in a cool place and use before going out. Take a small bottle with you to refresh periodically. Come Hither…

Love Potion #9   (limited quantities available)

9 oz sweet red wine, 1 ginseng root cut into 9 pieces
9 each: basil leaves, red rose petals, cloves, and
           apple seeds
9 drops each: vanilla extract, strawberry juice

On the 9th hour of the 9th day of the 9th month of the year stir this potion in your cauldron 9 times with a wooden spoon by the light of 9 pink votive candles.

"Let the one who drinks this wine, shower me with love divine-sweet love potion #9 make his/her love forever mine"

Bring to a boil on medium heat and then lower heat and simmer for 9 minutes. Remove from heat and cool off. Blow across the potion in cross 9 times reciting each goddess of love divine: Inanna, Ishatar, Astarte, Hathor, Nephthys, Aphrodite, Venus, Freya, and Arianrhod.

Sift through a cheesecloth and into a jar, seal and keep in the refrigerator. Serve to the man or woman of your affections – but do NOT let anyone else, see, touch, drink or even look at the potion!

WARNING: This potion is very potent – be absolutely sure of your feelings for your intended as it is near impossible to reverse, even more difficult to control, and is very intense and long lasting.

Note: According to the Jewish and Celtic Calendars the Ninth month is June! So take careful note what calendar you are using to realize your results!

Fresh Linen

15 drops spearmint essential oil
12 drops lavender essential oil

Put on a wash cloth and fold several times and insert in a muslin bag and toss in the dryer.

Privy Pleasure

4 oz purified water
30 drops each essential oil: sweet orange, cinnamon, clove

Place in a spray bottle and use as needed for removal of foul odor.

Summer Sunshine

4 oz purified water
50 drops lavender essential oil
30 drops lemon grass essential oil
20 drops gardenia essential oil

Keep in a spray bottle to freshen sheets.

Hot Summer Nights

4 oz purified water
30 drops patchouli essential oil
15 drops of lemon grass essential oil
10 drops of jasmine flower essential oil

Spray bed for a night of unbridled passion.

Ancient Invocation to Prepare Yourself

Touch the forehead and say: Atoh (Thou Art)
Touch the breast and say: Malkus (the Kingdom)
Touch the right shoulder and say: Ve-Gevurah
                                (and the Power)
Touch the left shoulder and say: Ve-Gedulah
                                (and the Glory)
Clasp the hands over the heart Le-Olahm, Amen
                                (Forever, Amen)
Note: In the ancient lands the cross is performed right to left – as was their writing and reading of ancient texts – you may change according to your present day order of left to right but keep the words in the same order.

Now draw a pentagram at each of the four cardinal quarters (North, East, South, West) and the name of the angel in that quarter (Raphael, Gabriel, Michael, and Uriel) with the four letter names of God (IHVH)

Extend your arms so that your body forms a cross and say:

Before me Raphael (east, IHVH)
Behind me Gabriel (west, VHIH)
On my right hand Michael (south, VIHH)
On my left hand Uriel (north, HVIH)
For before me flames the pentagram
And behind me shines the six pointed star

Repeat in each direction. See pages 129 and 197.

Salves and Ointments

General Information

Use 1 Tbsp beeswax per every C of oil. Collect all herbs and flowers after the dew and before the heat of the sun. Good carrier oils are 1st cold pressed extra virgin olive oil and grape seed oil. Other oils I have heard used included but are not limited to sesame, almond, shea butter and lanolin. A part is anything you make it – for instance if a part is 1 teaspoon, then ¼ part is ¼ teaspoon. If a part is a ¼ teaspoon than four parts and 1 teaspoon. Etc.

How to make Salve
Boiling Oil Method (Very effective)

Gather your chosen ingredients – fresh is best – and place your herbs at the bottom of a glass pot. Cover the herbs with water and simmer for 30 minutes on medium heat. Cool, strain and measure your resulting tea. Place your mixture back into the pot and place an equal amount of 1st cold pressed extra virgin olive oil into the pot and simmer on low until all the water bubbles have risen and the mixture is quiet. Stir occasionally to make sure the mixture is not sticking to the bottom. When making salve add 1 Tbsp beeswax per every cup of oil mixture, and keep adding until it doesn't run off a plate. Cool and set in jars.

Remove a Wart salve

Using above method use equal parts of comfrey and mint.

Black Salve
Drawing Salve (Salamanca Salve)

Using above method use equal parts of comfrey, plantain, slippery elm bark, chickweed, and pine tar.

Balm of Gilead
Burn Salve

Use the above method using rock rose buds and resin of one of the following: Cistus inconus creticus, Citus ladanifer maculates or Commiphora opobalsamum. Gather buds in spring and resin in midsummer when it flows naturally from the plant.

Baby's Salve
Diaper Rash

Use the above method adding 1 tsp Almond oil to the oil and equal parts: Calendula, comfrey, yellow dock, and mullein.

Grandma's Salve
Healing Salve

1 part each mullein, tansy, plantain and wormwood leaves, Slippery elm in a pine tar base.

5 Worts Salve:
Available from One Pot Witchery $30 for 2 oz

Equal parts dried mugwort, chamomile, nettle, chervil and fennel
With 2 parts aloe vera gel
Apple cider vinegar
Myrrh resin
Honeycomb (1 for ointment, 2 for salve and maybe one sheet of beeswax)

Gather all your dried herbs and beat them lightly to help express the oils. Place them all in a glass pan and cover with apple cider vinegar plus 1-2 inches and put on your stove's lowest setting and boil for at least 1 hour. Strain and add equal parts of oil to vinegar as well as the aloe gel and the myrrh resin and boil the vinegar out on the same low setting. You will know when the vinegar is out as it will boil in silence. Remove any leftover resins or mulch and dispose. Then add drained but not pressed honeycomb stirring constantly until it feels thicker about 1 Tbsp per cup of oil. Cool and place in glass jars. Instantly clots blood and seals any wound. Helps heal cuts and burns. If you prefer, you can steep all the ingredients (except oil) in a covered glass jar for 1-3 weeks. Put it in a sunny location and every time you walk by the jar give it a shake. When you feel it has set enough, strain it, measure it and add an equal amount of oil and slow boil until all the apple cider vinegar is gone – it will boil in silence when this happens. Add drained honeycomb, but do not press the honey out and stir constantly until it feels thicker than cool and jar.

9 Worts Galador Salve

Equal parts: Mugwort, Plantain, Watercress, Chamomile, Vipers Bugloss, Chervil, Fennel Crab Apple, Stinging Nettle

Per One Pot Witchery; use the standard method given for 5 worts salve and put in a beeswax or pine tar base. Keep refrigerated to extend life of product.

Per the Leech book of Bald, to make the salve: Mugwort, plantain that is open from the east, watercress and viper's bugloss, chamomile, nettle, crab-apple, chervil, fennel and old soap. Grind the herbs into a powder and mix them with soap and apple juice (Slippery elm, Pine Tar, Beeswax with Myrrh work as well). Make a paste of water and ashes (Warning: these are wood ashes and are caustic as they contain lye so you must wear goggles and plastic gloves and keep far away from children), take the fennel, boil it in the paste and bathe it with a beaten egg (you might want to skip the egg), when you apply the salve, both before and after. Sing the Nine Herbs Charm or 9 worts galador charm over each herb (see following page), three times before you prepare them and also on the apple; and sing it in the mouth and both ears of the patient and the same charm on the wound, before you apply the salve.

Note: A Wort is the ancient term for herb – as in mugwort, etc.

The Nine Herbs Charm (or 9 worts galador) from the Leech book of Bald. (924-946 AD)

Remember, Mugwort, what you revealed,
What you arranged at Regenmeld,
You were called Una, oldest of herbs,
Power against three and against thirty,
Power against poison and venom,
Power against the enemy who travels over the earth.

And you, Plantain, mother of herbs,
Opening from the eastward, inwardly mighty;
Over you carts creaked, over you queens rode,
Over you brides bridalled, over you bulls bellowed.
All these you weathered and withstood;
So may you withstand poison and venom,
And the enemy who travels over the earth.

This herb is called Stune; it grew on stone,
It withstands poison, withstands pain.
It is named 'Harsh', it withstands venom,
It exiles the enemy, works against venom.
This is the herb that fought with the serpent;
This power against poison, power against infection,
Power against the enemy who travels over the earth.

Cock's-spur grass, though minor, overcome mighty poisons, Mighty poisons conquer minor, till he is remedied of both.

Remember, Camomile, what you made known,
What you accomplished at Alorford;
That he never let up his life for infection,
After Camomile was cooked with his food.

This is the herb that is called crab-apple;
The seal sent this over the black of the sea,
As a nostrum for other noxious poisons.
These nine have power against nine poisons.

A worm came sneaking, it struck a man;
Then Woden took nine wonderous staves,
Smote the snake so it split into nine.
And there ended apple and poison,
So never again would she go in her house.

Chervil and Fennel, fearsome pair,
These herbs were wrought by the wise lord,
Holy in heaven, there did he hang;
He set and sent them in seven worlds,
To remedy all, the rich and the needy.

It stands against pain, stands against poison,
Has might against three and against thirty,
Against devil's hand and against deception,
Against the witchcraft of the wicked ones.

These nine herbs have power against nine horrors,
Against nine venoms and against nine poisons;
Against the red venom, against the running venom,
Against the white venom, against the purple venom,
Against the yellow venom, against the green venom,
Against the black venom, against the blue venom,
Against the brown venom, against the bay venom;
Against worm-blister, against water-blister,
Against thorn-blister, against thistle blister,
Against ice-blister, against poison-blister.
If any venom comes flying from the east,
Or any from the north, or from the south,
Or any from the west upon the tribe of men.

Christ stood over sickness of every sort.
Only I know the Running river,
Where the nine snakes behold it near.
May all the weeds now spring up worts,
The seas dissolve, all salt water,
When I blow this bane from you.

Do You Ever?

do you ever just awake
just to watch the mist take shape
do you ever stand there too
and peer inside like I do
do you ever see me there
on the lake with you near
have you ever once just come
out at 4 am like I've done
touched the mist and called my name
knowing I would be there again
and have you ever felt me too
in the mist waiting for you
crossing the bridges lost in time
in the recesses of our minds
could I be why you love the mist
can you stand there and feel my kiss
can you feel my hand there too
saying come on Jimmy I'll follow you
down the stair and across the docks
because now it's 4 O'clock
holding hands to keep you close
and not fall in as the mist rose
getting you to put on my worm

doing it for me so I won't squirm
smiling whispering listening to
the bird's songs as your whistle blew
catching our breaths as the sun rose
feeling its rays slowing cross our toes
looking at each other feeling sad
just heard the call from our Grandad
better put it all away
and come back out another day
down the docks across the bridge
back to where we both live
breakfast always toast and eggs
and who would get the last sausage
do as we're asked do as we're told
then out again no longer cold
listening to stories with Papa Ben
who always knew when we needed a friend
Grandma calls caught again
always in trouble have to stay in
but back out soon with a new plan
across the neighborhood exploring the land
hiding finding your biggest fan
and always willing to do it again
like the wind the days fly by
boiled dinner and fresh baked pie
home movies and popcorn too
how I always loved following you
tell me Jimmy can you feel my kiss
as you stand there in the mist
do you hear me calling your name
tell me isn't that why you came?

Barbara Ann Daca

Mini Magickal Wise Woman

Edible Play dough

We have included only those play doughs that a young child can make and eat with no cooking involved. Perfect for appetizers or desserts! Add any number of goodies to embellish with sweet savor or spread on veggies for a treat!

Chocolate Nutter Play dough

1 cup chocolate frostlings
1 cup Nutter butter
1 ½ cups dry milk

Mix all the ingredients in a bowl until easily pliable.

Chocolate frostlings

1 stick butter, softened
2/3 C cocoa powder – not mix (the darker the better)
3 ½ C sugar
1/3 + C milk
1 Tbsp vanilla extract
¼ tsp salt

In a large mixing bowl mix together the cocoa and the butter until soft. Add in the sugar and salt and mix again. Add in the vanilla and the milk slowly – like a Tablespoon at a time and mix thoroughly until it seems right.

Creamed Cheese Play dough

8 oz cream cheese softened
½ cup dry milk
1 Tablespoon Honey

Mix all the ingredients in a bowl until easily pliable.

Nutter butter Play dough

18 oz Nutter butter
6 Tablespoons raw honey
¾ dry milk

Mix all the ingredients in a bowl until easily pliable.

Nutter Butter

For smooth

2 C dry roasted peanuts or other dried nuts
1 Tbsp canola or nut oil

For chunky

1 1/3 C dry roasted peanuts or other dried nuts
1 Tbsp canola or nut oil
2/3 C chopped dry roasted nuts

Combine nuts and oil in a blender and blend until smooth. For chunky reserve 1/3 of the nuts and fold into the smooth mixture.

Nutter Butter and Oats Play dough

2 cups Nutter butter
2 cups instant oatmeal
2 cups dry milk
2/3 cups honey

Mix all the ingredients in a bowl until easily pliable.

Flour and Oats Play dough

1 cup flour
2 cups oatmeal
1 cup water

Mix all the ingredients in a bowl until easily pliable.

Fairy Sugar

1 small Mason jar with lid
1 vanilla bean, sliced
3 C white or turbinado sugar
3 drops each: yellow, blue, green, red food coloring
4 old cups
¼ C measuring cup

In each of the four cups, place ¼ cup sugar and 3 drops of the same food coloring in each cup. Stir with a spoon and dry overnight during the full moon. The next day, put 2 cups of regular sugar in the mason jar and then add the other sugars and stir – add the vanilla bean and cap. Leave until the new moon and remove the vanilla bean and use.

Little Sandwitches

Butterfly Butter Sandwitch

2 slices white bread
1 tablespoon softened butter

Spread butter on one slice and top with the other slice and eat.

Butterfly Butter

8 oz whipping cream
Quart size jar with lid
3 marbles
1 tsp salt – optional

Put the whipping cream and marbles in the jar and close the lid tightly. Leave the jar alone to get to room temperature (3 hours) and let the cream sour. Shake the jar for about 30 minutes (it is best to have helpers as your arms will get tired!). You should then have a lump of butter and buttermilk. Drain the butter milk and remove the marbles. Fill the jar with cold water and the salt and swirl it around.
Carefully drain the water from the butter and repeat until the water is not cloudy. Put the butter on a board and press out any remaining milk or it will sour. Wrap it and refrigerate.

Nutter Butter Sandwitch

2 slices white bread
1 tablespoon Nutter butter

Variations: 5 banana slices or 12 raisins or 1 Tbsp chocolate, hazelnut, jelly or marshmallow cream spread.

Pixie Jams and Jellies
Jam has fruit pieces – Jelly does not

2 ¼ C of fresh fruit of one or more kinds (jam)
or
1 C canned juice concentrate and 1 ¼ C water mixed (jelly)
4 ½ C sugar
¼ C lemon juice
1 packet pectin

If using fruit, clean, and stem or peel as necessary then mash, mash and mash again in a bowl. If using fruit juice concentrate, mix with the water in a bowl. Then add the sugar and thoroughly mix until completely dissolved. Add lemon juice and mix again. Add the pectin and thoroughly mix again. Put in quart jars leaving 1 ½ inches on top and tighten lid. Let stand at room temperature for 24 hours to set. If stored in freezer is good for 1 year. When removed to and stored in refrigerator is good for 3 weeks.

Pixie Sandwitch

Now take your homemade jam and spread it on a piece of your favorite bread and fold it over and eat!

Mermaid's Sandwitch

6 oz can albacore tuna (or salmon or crabmeat)
1 tsp yellow mustard
1 Tbsp salad dressing or mayonnaise
1 tsp dill relish or pickle chopped up
Pinch each: salt, pepper
4 slices of wheat bread

Open the can of tuna and drain the liquid from it. With a fork, remove the tuna from the can and put it in a small mixing bowl. Add the mustard, mayo, relish and seasonings and stir until it is well mixed. Divide in half and spread on two slices of bread. Top with another slice of bread and eat.

Selkie Sandwitch

6 oz pouch salmon
1 tsp chopped dill
4 oz soft creamed cheese
Pinch each: salt, pepper
2 bagels, sliced

Drain the liquid from the pouch and remove with a fork. Put it in a small mixing bowl with the dill, cream cheese and seasonings and stir. Divide mixture into two and spread on each bagel and eat.

Merlin's Mayonnaise

1 Tbsp vinegar
1 Tbsp lemon juice
1 large egg, room temperature
½ tsp salt Opt: 1 tsp sugar
1 C vegetable oil

With a wire whisk in a large bowl beat together; vinegar, lemon juice, egg and salt, fast and hard. Add the oil ¼ cup at a time and keep beating it together to blend thoroughly each time until well mixed. The mixture has to absorb the oil or it will separate. Store any unused portion in a tightly closed jar in the refrigerator.

Refrigerator Pickles

7 C cucumbers
1 C onion
1 C green pepper
1 Tbsp each: salt, celery seed, dry mustard
1 C sugar
2 C apple cider vinegar
1 galleon jug or jar

First wash and slice the cucumbers but do not peel them. The smaller cucumbers work best like Persian or gherkin. Put the cucumbers in the jar. Peel and cut the onions and put them in the jar. Cut the tops off of the pepper and take the seeds out. Cut into strips and put in the jar. Add the rest of the ingredients and stir. Fill the remaining parts with water to cover the rest. Eat on your sandwitches, stays good for several months.

Funny Jack Sandwitch

1 slice dark bread
1 Tbsp spread (mayonnaise, peanut butter or creamed cheese)
Face decorations: olive or banana slices or raisins for eyes, carrot curls or shredded cucumber or chocolate for hair, mandarin orange or apple slices for mouth etc.

With a butter knife, cover your bread with your favorite spread and decorate into funny or spooky face shapes and eat!

Cheese Sandwitch

1-2 Slices of white American cheese
2 slices of white bread
Squirt of yellow mustard

Put two slices of bread on a plate, on one squirt a smiley face of mustard, on the other put the cheese and fold together. Enjoy!

How to bring Faeries into your garden

Chose your special garden spot wisely – faeries don't like to be seen. Make sure they will have water and a place to go if it rains. Chose the plants you will put in your garden and plant them in a circle. As you plant your garden sing "Oh my magic faerie friends, I leave this spot for you to tend. May you live and laugh and play, and visit my garden everyday!" Keep repeating until your planting is done and surely the faeries will happily come!

Pixie Pizza Sandwitch

1 piece of toast
1 Tbsp pizza sauce
1 Tbsp shredded mozzarella
Optional: 4 slices turkey pepperoni, sliced black olives

Spread the pizza sauce evenly on your toast, then add the cheese and any toppings you enjoy and eat.

Sensational Salsa

1 clove garlic
½ onion
4oz can chopped green chilies or jalapeños
½ bunch cilantro
3 tsp lime juice
4 large tomatoes
½ tsp salt

First peel the garlic then crush it and put it in a large bowl. Next peel the onion and chop it up with a butter knife and put it in the bowl. Next use the can opener and open the peppers (chilies or jalapenos) and drain them then put them in the bowl. Clean the cilantro and chop the tops off and into little bits and then put those in the bowl, don't use the stems. Cut the brown top off the tomatoes and throw away. Then chop the tomatoes into little bits and put those in the bowl. Add the lime juice and salt and stir. Enjoy with tacos or burritos or chips!

Avocado Dip

3 Avocadoes
1 tomato
½ C cilantro
½ red onion
1 C sour cream
3 Tbsp lime juice
1 tsp salt

First peel the avocadoes and remove the seed. Then put them in a bowl and mash them down. Next cut the brown top out of the tomato and toss it away. Then cut the tomato into little bits and add it to the bowl. Next chop the tops off of the cilantro and into little bits and toss those into the bowl – but do not use the stems. Then peel the onion and cut it into bits and add it to the bowl. Now add the rest of the ingredients and stir a lot. Enjoy with vegetables or chips!

Fairy Guardians

Put some chamomile tea with fairy sugar in a cup
Put a small oatmeal cookie on a saucer

Light a tiny white votive candle on some dirt in your garden and place the cup and saucer next to it. Now say three times:

Precious Fairies of the night
Keep me safe 'til mornings light
Peaceful dreams to keep me warm
Watch me 'til the day is born

Hummus Dip

2 garlic cloves
1 C parsley or chervil or ½ C cilantro with 1 tsp cayenne pepper
16-19 oz can chick peas
1/3 cup lemon juice
1 Tbsp light olive or grape seed oil
1 C Nutter butter or Tahini (sesame seeds ground into a paste)
Pinch of each: salt, black pepper

Peel and crush garlic cloves and put in a bowl. Clean and chop the tops off the parsley (or chervil or cilantro) and toss the stems and put the tops in the bowl after you have chopped them. Drain the can of chick peas and add those to the bowl and mash everything together really well. Add the lemon juice and mash some more. Add the oil and mash some more. Add the peanut butter or tahini and mix around good. Add a pinch of salt and pepper to taste. Tastes great on crackers or with chips.

How to make Washing Water

In a glass jar put lots of rose petals and fill with water. Tighten the lid and set in the sun for 3 days. Pour the water out into another jar making sure that none of the rose petals get out. Use a little bit to do your dishes or to wash your hands after a party.

Three Things for a Hot Day

Make Chocolate Fondue

1 chocolate bar
1 pint strawberries

In a small pot, break up the chocolate bar and put in the sun. When it is melted, dip the berries in it and eat.

Make Sun Tea

1 galleon jug
1 galleon water
3 bags of either: chamomile, green or orange spice tea

Put the water in the jug and float the tea bags in it. Close the lid and set out in the sun for at least 1 hour or the whole day. Place in cups and drink as you want (with sugar or lemon) and enjoy!

Freeze your own Popsicles

You will need plastic molds, paper cups or ice cube trays as well as plastic spoons, Popsicle sticks, or plastic stirrers and a bowl. Decide what you want your popsicles to be. They can either be fruit juice, yoghurt, and pudding or mashed up fruit.
Pour your ingredients into the mold and fill half way. Freeze for 1 hour and then insert sticks and fill the rest of the way. Freeze until solid and share with your friends!

Friendship Fruit Salad

Have each friend bring their favorite fruit. Clean them; peel them and cut them into bite size pieces and mix with whipped cream.

Great Combinations

Kiwi, Strawberries, Banana slices
Banana slices, Pineapple pieces, Mandarin orange slices
Blueberries, Blackberries, Strawberries
Grapes, Peeled apple slices, walnuts
Cantaloupe, pineapple, strawberries
Pears, cherries, peaches
Watermelon, strawberries, kiwi

Whipped Cream

8 oz of whipping cream
Quart size jar with lid
3 marbles
1 tsp – 1 Tbsp sugar

Put the whip cream, sugar and marbles in the jar and keep refrigerated until you need some whip cream. Every time you need a little whip cream, take out the jar and shake it for 3-5 minutes. Always keep the whip cream cold.

Fairy Fruit Kabobs

Skewers
3 different kinds of your favorite fruit

Prepare your fruit by washing, peeling or slicing it into pieces with a butter knife. Alternate placing your fruit on a skewer, first one, then the other then the other, until each skewer is finished. Serve at a party with your friends.

Fairy Fruit Face Salad

1 Peach or Pear
2 Tbsp yoghurt or cream cheese
Face decorations: raisins, dried fruit, blueberries, banana slices

Peel and pit your fruit. Cover with your spread and decorate. Enjoy!

Fairy Fruit Soup

8 oz fruit or fruit and vegetable juice blend for broth
Cut up fruits like grapes, pineapple, apple slices or dried fruit pieces
Additional ingredients like carrot curls, crushed mint, melon balls

Arrange your ingredients into a bowl and pour your broth over top and enjoy!

Garden Soup

8 oz can tomato juice or V8 juice for broth
Cut up vegetables like zucchini, green peppers, green onions, carrots, Additional ingredients like tomatoes, dry roasted peanuts, sunflower seeds, shredded cheese or croutons

In a large soup bowl arrange your ingredients and pour your broth over it.

Wizard Soup

6 C watermelons
3 Tbsp sugar
2 Tbsp lime juice
1 tsp salt
Garni: ½ C cucumber, 2 Tbsp mint

Slice the watermelon and cut out the pink and take out any seeds. Chop the pink into pieces and put into a bowl and mash it really good. Add the sugar, lime juice and salt and mash it really good again and then put it in the refrigerator. Leave it in the refrigerator for at least 1 hour. Just before you are ready to eat it, peel, take out the seeds and grate a small cucumber and put it in a small bowl. Then wash and chop the leaves of mint and mix with the cucumber. Now take out the soup and put into bowls and add a little bit of the cucumber mint on top and eat. It's so good on a hot day!

Leprechaun Salad

Combine your favorite greens with your favorite vegetables and top with your favorite dressing. Remember to clean, peel and chop with a butter knife when necessary.

Herb salad mix, feta cheese, dried cranberries, walnuts
Spinach leaves, green onion, tomato, feta cheese
Lettuce, mandarin orange slices, black olives, sesame dressing
Romaine, carrots, apple slices, croutons
Lettuce, apple slices, berries and dried fruit pieces

Dancing Fairies Drink

1 pt ginger ale, or soft drink
1 pt blueberries

In each glass pour in the soft drink or ginger ale and IMMEDIATELY add the blue berries. The carbon dioxide will cling to the berries and make them dance.

Nu-nu Juice

1 galleon Hawaiian punch fruit juicy red
1 quart 7-up soft drink
1 quart no pulp orange juice
Optional: scoops of sherbet

Mix together in a bowl, float the sherbet on top and scoop into cups to serve.

Lemonade

2 Tbsp syrup (1 C sugar and 1 C very warm water to dissolve sugar)
1/8 C lemon juice
8 oz Water
2-3 ice cubes

Mix together the syrup and keep in the refrigerator in a jar until needed – it keeps indefinitely. For each glass of lemonade, add the syrup, lemon juice and stir. Fill the remainder of the glass with water and ice cubes and stir again. Enjoy!

Yoghurt Smoothie

1 banana, peeled
8 oz strawberry or vanilla yoghurt
8 oz orange juice

In a bowl, peel and mash banana. Mix in the yoghurt. Stir in the orange juice. Divide into two cups and drink!

Root beer Float

1 8 oz glass
2-3 scoops vanilla ice cream
4-6 oz root beer

Put the ice cream in the glass and pour the root beer over it. Enjoy!

Make your own Milkshake

1 C milk
½ tsp vanilla
½ C ice cream
Optional ingredients: ½ banana mashed, strawberries sliced, ½ C orange or pineapple juice, 2 Tbsp chocolate syrup, ¼ C chocolate chips, 2 Tbsp peanut butter, 1 Tbsp molasses with 1 pinch cinnamon and 1 pinch nutmeg, 1 Tbsp butter with ¼ C chopped pecans, 1/4 C miniature candies etc.

Combine ingredients in a bowl and mix together or put in a water bottle, close the lid tightly and shake.

Very Berry Sorbet

3 C berries
½ C water
2 Tbsp honey
1 tsp lemon zest
2 Tbsp lemon juice
1/8 tsp salt

Clean the berries and mash them in a bowl. Add the other ingredients and mash everything together really good. Put in a metal container in the freezer for 1 hour. Enjoy!

How to make your own Ice Cream

16 oz non dairy whip cream
1 tsp vanilla extract
6 egg whites
2 cans sweetened condensed milk
Additions: chocolate chips, caramel sauce, nuts, fruit pieces, crushed cookies, little bite size candies.

Whip the egg whites together until fluffy then whip in the other ingredients. Add what you want to make the ice cream your own and freeze in a metal container for 2 or more hours. Enjoy!

How to make a Pie

1 pie tin
½ box of graham crackers
½ stick butter
1 Tbsp sugar
1 C of yogurt or pudding
1 C of non dairy whip topping
Toppings: crushed cookies, chopped nuts, magic shell ice cream topping etc.

Leave the butter out until it is soft then put it in the pie tin. Crush the crackers with your hands or punch them in a baggie and add them to the pie tin and then add the sugar and stir until well mixed. Press the mixture up around the sides of the tin and all over the bottom. Now in a large bowl mix either your yogurt or pudding with the whip topping and pour into the pie tin. Top with something that is like what you put in, for instance if using strawberry yogurt, top with strawberries. If using chocolate pudding, top with crushed cookies etc.

Comprehensive Herbal

"... Then God said , "Let there the earth sprout vegetation, plants and herbs yielding seeds, and fruit trees bearing fruit after their kind, with seed in them, on the earth"; and it was so..." Genesis

The soul purpose of herbs is to heal all life. Herbs were so important and necessary that they actually preceded all other life. There are many herbs used in cooking for the purpose of healing and many more we have yet to discover. It is important to always try to get organic herbs or grow your own if possible – there is a lot to be said about knowing your source.

It is now being proven that there is a lot of knowledge in the old ways. We have found that many herbs and flowers that have magickal actions of healing and exorcism also have medicinal actions, and believe that medical science just hasn't caught up with the other ones. Coincidence? We think not. Healing women were often thought of as witches when they used herbs to cure when really they were our first doctors. In fact, many of today's medicines are derived from herbs – how much more don't we know that was lost and is now on the brink of new discovery? When we feed our families chicken soup we know it is healing and now medical science can tell us why. Perhaps there are many things we have always known that medical science is just catching up to – and therein lies the true magick in this book, let the power of sisterhood erupt!

Disclaimer

Please note that this herbal is in no way meant to take the place of a good physician or treatment. In fact if you are taking medications for the ailments here in listed DO NOT USE HERBS or HERBAL REMEDIES as well, as it will overdose you. If the conditions persists, worsens or you have and allergic reaction to any herb seek professional medical help immediately.

Dosing is the most important aspect of herbology. Doses must always be measured precisely and never guessed at. Standard doses follow:
Up to 1 year: 5 grains or 1/12 adult dosage
Up to 2 years: 8 grains or 1/8 adult dosage
Up to 3 years: 10 grains or 1/6 adult dosage
Up to 4 years: 15 grains or ¼ adult dosage
Up to 7 years: 1 scruples or 1/3 adult dosage
Up to 14 year: ½ drachms or ½ adult dosage
Up to 21: adult dosage of 1 drachms
Above 65: gradually decrease dosages in reverse of above

Remember when dosing the following:
Weight, height, sex, age and bone structure of individual: if an individual is smaller than average, lower dose by one step, if larger use regular dosage, and if working keep, if not up by one step.
Temperament of individual: a happy optimistic person can be more readily affected by a stimulant or purgative more than a sluggish or unemotional one and therefore may require a smaller dose.
Habits of individuals: those who smoke, drink alcohol or use stimulants will require larger doses.

Climate: The warmer the climate, the smaller dose is required as your blood flow is increased. Therefore, medicines may act differently on the same individuals in the summer as they do in the winter, as well, they make act differently for peoples in different climates or regions.

Liquid Measurements:
1 ml = 20 drops
5 ml = 1 teaspoon (tsp)
10 ml = 1 Tablespoon (Tbsp)
70 ml = 1 whiskey glass
125 ml = 4 oz = ½ cup
250 ml = 8 oz = 1 cup
500 ml = 16 oz = 2 cups = 1 pint
750 ml = 24 oz = 3 cups
1000ml = 32 oz = 4 cups = 2 pints = 1 quart
4 quarts = 1 gallon

Dry measurements:
1 grain (gr)
1 scruple (ei) = 20 gr
1 drachms (dr) = 3 ei or 60 gr
1 ounce (oz) = 8 dr or 480 gr
1 pound (lb) = 16 oz or 7,000 gr

Terminology:
ab lib: when needed

Note: always start with a small amount to check for an allergic reaction first, never consume any flower, vegetable, herb etc unless you are absolutely sure it has not been sprayed and is culinary safe.

Alliums/whole plant: (leeks, chives, garlic, onions, ramps and shallots) All parts and varieties of the plant are edible. Actions: Antibacterial, Antiviral, Antifungal. Medicinal: lowers blood pressure, blood sugar, cholesterol, and boasts the immune system – is a natural pesticide against mosquito larvae. Used to treat and purge intestinal parasites, treats fatigue and anemia, has anti-tumor effects, helps control excessive bleeding and is an antidote for ingested poisons. Flavours range from mild to strong. Culinary: leaves and flowers are great in salads, leaves and bulbs in soups etc. Magickal: guards against evil, repels thieves and vampires, turns away the envious, blesses the home, absorbs diseases, rub into your pots and pans before cooking to remove all evil (disease) and protect your cooking (kills all germs, worms etc).

Allspice/berry: (Pimenta dioica) Active ingredient is same as cloves, eugenol. Medicinal: Topical pain relief, tea, and mouthwash. Culinary: best used freshly ground in almost anything from salads to breads and desserts. Flavour: a mix between nutmeg, cloves and cinnamon. Substitutes for cinnamon, cassia, dash of nutmeg or mace or dash of cloves. Magickal: money, luck and healing.

Angelica/leaves/flowers/seeds/shoots/stems: Actions: Preservative. Medicinal: Crushed leaves in vehicles reduce travel nausea, as a tea (2 tsp root in 2 C water for 20 minutes and take 1 C twice a day) induces sweats, warms the body, aids digestion, as a salve for rheumatic pain. Culinary: used for candy, liqueurs, salads, fish or tea. Flavour: tastes like licorice or celery depending on variety. Magickal: exorcism, protection, healing, visions. Use as an incense as it creates a barrier against negative energy and fills you with positive energy. Removes hexes, curses or spells and enhances the aura.

Anise/seed: (Pimpinella anisum) Medicinal: cold remedy. Actions: diaphoretic, diuretic, expectorant, stimulant. Culinary: used as flavouring in cookies, hand fasting and wedding cakes, candies and pastries, also used in poultry dishes. Flavour: sweet and similar to licorice. Substitutes for fennel seed or a few drops anise extract. Magickal: used in dream pillow to prevent nightmares, protects one during astral travel.

Anise hyssop/flower: Medicinal: As a tea (1 tsp seeds steeped in 1-1 ½ C water for ten minutes and take no more than once a day) to quell nausea and colic, promotes estrogen, encourages breast milk, eases childbirth and stimulates libido. Essential oil is a natural insecticide used in pet pillows or as a dream sachet wards off nightmares. Culinary: delicate anise, licorice or root beer flavor, make attractive plate decorations and are often used in Chinese dishes. Flowers and leaves are used in fruit salads, stem and roots in sweet soups. Magickal: used in hand fasting cakes, averts evil, purification, entices spirits to aid in spells, divination and psychic awareness.

Apple/fruit/ blossoms: Actions: Aromatic; Culinary: used in fruit dishes, candied or as a garnish. Warning: flowers not for use with children. Eat in moderation as these flowers contain cyanide precursors, seeds of the apple and its relatives are poisonous. Magickal: love, healing, garden magic, immortality. Great for wands used in love magick, an apple branch will gain one admittance to the fairy world, split an apple in three pieces and rub on an injury or affliction during the waning moon and bury to help it disappear.

Apricot/fruit: Medicinal: expectorant, controls coughs, laxative. Inner stem bark and root are antidotes to kernel poisoning (never use kernel) Culinary: eaten fresh, fried, juiced, jams and jellies, brandies and liquors. Replace the juice for the water in pancakes, oatmeal, curried lamb and salted rice. Magickal: use juice in love spells or potions, leaves, flowers and pits can be used in love sachets or carried to attract love. Mashed as a paste and mixed with olive oil makes a good face for dry skin.
Arrowheads/tubers: other names: duck potatoes; Aquatic plant. Medicinal: clean and treat wounds, headaches and indigestion. Culinary uses: as a Native American food source. Magickal: cleansing.
Arrow root powder: Medicinal: 1 Tbsp in a cup of juice every few hours to relieve diarrhea. Can be used as a poultice to soothe skin inflammations. Culinary: used as a thickening agent for sauces, fruit pie fillings, glazes and puddings. (2 tsp arrow root = 1 tsp cornstarch or flour) Thickens at a cooler temperature making it good for cold soups.
Arugula/leaves/flowers: Other names; garden rocket, roquette, rocket-salad, Oruga, Rocket salad, rocket-gentle, Raukenkohl, rouquelle, rucola. Medicinal: stimulates digestion, calms nausea. Culinary: used in salads, sandwiches, stir fry dishes and potato salads. Flavors: tastes peppery.
Asparagus: Actions: Antibiotic, AnitSpasmodics, Cancer, cardiac, laxative, sedative, tonic. Medicinal: boil in water and drink the water for kidney problems. Dissolves uric acid deposits and promotes urination. Blood purifier, Gout , dropsy, rheumatism and nausea. Cooking: washed, ends cut and boiled for eight minutes, great with hollandaise sauce, in soups Magickal: Aphrodisiac, Love, passion, lust

Astragalus/root: (Astragalus membranaceua) Must be 4 years old before roots can be harvested. Action: stimulant; Medicinal: used to build up the immune system and balance the bodies system, for treating tumors of the eye, liver and throat, clear out spleen, as a tea to counteract the effects of chemotherapy, for puniness in small children, Chewed for chest, back pains and coughing and promotes milk production in lactating women., decreases blood sugar levels. Culinary: use as a tea or in broths with other herbs for best effects. Magickal: Exorcism

Avocado/fruit: Medicinal: oil is good for skin eruptions, seed can be pulverized and used in shampoo to treat dandwitch. Culinary: used at room temperature or cold in salads, on sandwitches and burgers. Seeds can be squeezed for ink. Magickal: love, lust, beauty. Wood makes great wands for any magickal purpose.

Banana /fruit/blossoms: Other names; banana hearts. Medicinal: the core of the stem is used as curry and good for stomach troubles, diabetes, dissolving stones in the kidney, and weight reduction (take before breakfast for 6 months)Culinary uses: remove tough coating to get to the tender white parts of the blossoms, then slice and sit in water until most of the sap is gone. Can be cooked or eaten raw. Used in many Southeast Asian dishes. Magickal: fertility, potency and posterity.

Balm of Gilead: Medicinal: as a salve for healing burns. Magickal: Love, manifestations, protection, healing. Carry buds to mend a broken heart, steep in red wine for a love potion, or use to as an oil to dress candles for healing.

Barley/grain: Medicinal: soothes digestive tract, controls cholesterol, and protects the immune system. Culinary: for use in soups and breads. Magickal: love, healing, protection.

Basil/herb/flower/leaf: (Octimum basilicum) Medicinal: used as a tea for colds, flu, cramps and bladder. Add fresh herbs or seeds to boiled water to make a tea for migraines and bed time restlessness. Douche for yeast infections, eliminates candida, gargle and mouthwash. Warning: Pregnant women should avoid medicinal use of basil. Culinary: best used fresh. Flowers are good for salads and pasta; herb is great in tomato dishes, with eggplant, for pesto, used in Thai, Vietnamese and Italian cookery, used as an addition to salads and many cooked vegetables. Flavour: pungent and somewhat sweet. Substitutes for oregano or thyme. Magickal: love, exorcism, wealth, flying, protection. Causes sympathy between two people and soothes tempers. Also attracts business and customers in put in a register, money box or windowsill.

Bay/leaf/stems: (Laurus nobilis) Medicinal: as a poultice on chest for bronchitis and chest colds. Warning: Do NOT take internally. Culinary: best used dried. Remove leaf before serving, used in soups, stews, tomato sauces and shellfish. Flavour: mild. Magickal: protection, psychic powers, healing, purification, strength.

Bay Laurel: Medicinal: cover leaves in olive oil and heat to make a salve for arthritis and aches. Beware internally as leaves, berries and oils have excitant and narcotic properties. Culinary: used as a flavouring in soups and stews. Magickal: attracts romance, divination (dream pillows), planted protects the home from lightening.

Beans: Magickal: Used in rattles to scare away evil spirits, rubbed on warts during the waning moon (as

this bean decays, so wart fall away) to remove them. Protection, exorcism, potency and love.
Bee Balm/flower/leaves: Other names: wild bergamot, wild Oswego tea, horsemint, and monarda. Actions: Antiseptic, antibacterial, antifungal, carminative, diuretic, stimulant. Medicinal: used as a tea in the treatment of cold s and flu to bring down fevers and as an expectorant. Culinary: tastes like oregano and mint, use in both fruit and green salads, curries, sausages and teas. Magickal: peace, happiness, contentment, leaves and flowers re used steeping in a warm bath for relaxation.
Bees wax: Used in cosmetics and embalming. Culinary: as a candy. Magickal candles.
Beet/root vegetable: Medicinal: beneficial to blood, heart and digestive systems. Cancer preventative, used in skin problems, lethargy, coughs and headaches. Culinary: best cooked, canned or pickled. Magickal: love, lust, aphrodisiac.
Bergamot rutaceae/flowers/peel: (citrus bergamia syn C.b. rutaceae syn C. aurantium var. bergamic) Other names: Bergamot Orange. Do NOT Confuse with Bergamot (Monarda didyma) as it is completely different. Medicinal: Orange blossom water is used for infant colic, dried flowers are used as a mild nervous stimulant, oil is used as a sedative and for healing. Actions: Aromatic (relieves stress, depression, anxiety and skin conditions) Bitter, relieves tension, antispasmodic, digestive aid. Warning: Not for use with children, those with stomach or intestinal ulcers, or ultraviolet light or sun therapy as it makes the skin photo sensitive. Culinary: used as an essential oil to make Earl Grey Tea, hard candy, tobacco, chewing gum, baked goods and desserts. Used as orange blossom water

in desserts and pastries. Magickal: rub fresh leaves on money before spending; keep young leaves in wallet or purse to attract fortunes.

Blackberry/fruit/leaves: Medicinal: root bark and leaves are used to treat dysentery, diarrhea, hemorrhoids, cystitis, thrush, mouth wash and cough remedy. Culinary: leaves are used in tea, fruit used in desserts, jams and jellies. Magickal: healing, money, protection.

Black pepper/berries: (Piper nigrum) Medicinal: for use at the first sign of any disease, pain relief from toothache, brings down a fever. Culinary: best used dried or freshly ground as a condiment or in any dish for a hot flavouring. Flavour: pungent, somewhat hot. Magickal: protection. Use as a wash before sunrise to scrub your house down and out the door (never in) and it will protect you from all curses and evil set against you.

Blueberry/fruit: Medicinal: to treat gout, coughs, diarrhea, rheumatism, scurvy, soothe mouth ulcers and calm the symptoms of typhoid fever. Improves night vision, water retention, varicose veins, arthritis and bruising. Culinary: used in jams, jellies and desserts. Magickal: protection, keep under your door mat to keep away undesired peoples and eat whenever under magickal attack.

Boneset/herb (Eupatorium perfoliatum): Actions: antispasmodic, diuretic. Medicinal: take warm with infusion for fevers and muscle aches of the flu. Culinary: Magickal: protection, exorcism.

Borage/flowers/herb: (Borago officinalis) Medicinal: anti-inflammatory, expectorant, emollient, diuretic. Used to treat depression, fevers, and bronchitis. Culinary: use fresh in punches, herbal tea, lemonade, gin and tonics, sorbets, chilled soups, cheese tortas and dips or candied. Flavour:

like mild cucumber. Magickal: courage, physic powers.

Brazil nut: Medicinal: used to treat stomach aches. Culinary: used alone or in desserts and breads. Magickal: love. High oil content, burns like a candle in the pod and wards off black flies.

Broccoli/flowers/stems: Medicinal: anti-cancer agents, eliminates carcinogens, lowers risk of cleft pallet and spinal cord defects in pregnancy. Inhibits thyroid production and should not be eaten by people taking thyroid medicine. Used as a a treatment for depression. Culinary: the top portion is actually flower buds (florets), delicious steamed, stir fried, soups, salads or casseroles.

Burdock Root: (arctium lappa) Medicinal: blood purifier, useful for any rash conditions such as psoriasis use both internally and externally; Useful for bites, stings, animal bites and boils. Internal uses include arthritic conditions, rheumatism and many types of infections. Primary ingredient: Essiac Tea (1tsp in 1 C water and simmered for 20 minutes then drank 3 times a day), a Native American cancer formula. Roots contain 45% insulin. Culinary: peeled is used in soups, salads, as a pot vegetable, and as a coffee additive or substitute. Magickal: protection, healing.

Burnet/flowers: Medicinal: made into an ointment and used to heal wounds. Flavour: resembles cucumber. Cabbage/leaf vegetable: Culinary: used in soups and salads, fried with carrots, potatoes and corned beef dishes. Magickal: luck.

Calendula/flowers: (Calendula officinalis): Other names: marigold; Medicinal: soothes inflamed tissues, reduces pain and aids in quick healing of cuts and abrasions. Culinary: add to soups, pasta, rice dishes, herb butters, salads, spreads and scrambled eggs. Actions: Makes a great yellow dye for foods and crafts. Flavour: spicy resembling saffron. Magickal: prophesy, clairvoyance, dreams, seeing magickal creatures, love; placed in your bath for beauty and under your mattress for prophetic dreams.

Capers/ flower buds: (Capparis spinosa) Medicinal: root bark is used as a tea to treat inflammation and rheumatism. Culinary: best used pickled in brine. For use in sauces, a flavouring for pickling, and many other dishes. Flavour: pungent. Magickal: potency, lust, love.

Caraway/seeds/root: (Carum carvi) Actions: antiviral. Medicinal: stimulates digestion, Bring 2 cups of water to boil and add 4 tsp lightly crushed seeds, simmer for 5 minutes then steep for 15 minutes and drink with meals to prevent gas or use for infant colic (breast feeding is best) Promotes menstruation and relieves uterine cramping. Culinary: best used whole. Used in goulash, cookies, cakes, apples sauce and herbal vinegars. Flavour: sweet and nutty. Magickal: protection, lust, health, anti-theft and mental powers. Any item that has caraway seeds in it is invisible to thieves.

Cardamom/seeds: (Elletaria cardamomum, a member of the ginger family) Medicinal: can be used in a decoction recipe for a cold, as a digestive aid, to ease gluten intolerance (celiac disease) sprinkle on cereal. Actions: carminative, stimulant, stomachic. Culinary: best used whole or ground. For use in stews and curries. Flavour: very strong and sweetly spicy. Substitutes for ginger. Magickal: lust, love. Add ground seeds to warmed wine or bake in an apple pie to induce desire.

Carnations/flowers: Medicinal: as a tea comforts the heart, expels the poison of sickness, and calms the fevers thereof. Culinary: cut away the bitter white base of the petal and steep in wine, use in candy, salads, aspics or cake decorations. Petals are especially sweet to the taste. Magickal: protection, strength, and healing.

Carob/bean: Medicinal: used to treat diarrhea and as chocolate for hyperactive children. Culinary: used as chocolate, in desserts. Magickal: protection and health.

Carrot/root vegetable: Medicinal: cleanses the intestines, grated it is effective against burns, a tea is made from the seeds (1 tsp per 1 C water) to aid digestion, help fluid retention and alleviate menstrual cramps. Culinary: used in salads, soups, stews, cakes and breads: Magickal: fertility, lust. Seeds are eaten to become pregnant or overcome impotency.

Cashew/nut: Medicinal: used against toothache, oil is anti-fungal, seeds are ground and used as a paste for snake bite. Culinary: used in breads, salads and trail mixes. Magickal: money.

Catnip/herb: (Nepeta catana): Medicinal: for use in feverish colds and flu's, thick nasal congestion, congested lungs, diarrhea and upset stomach. Actions: Diaphoretic, astringent (tones mucous membranes thereby creating discharge), sedative. Culinary: as a tea infused with chamomile and lemon balm. Warning: should not be used by pregnant woman. Magickal: cat magic, love, beauty, happiness.

Cattail/pollen/roots/shoots: Aquatic plant. Culinary: pollen is used in biscuits. Before the flower forms the shoots are peeled and eaten with an asparagus like flavour and can be added to salads, at the end of soup dishes, stir fry dishes (carrots, sesame oil, ginger). Magickal: lust.

Cayenne/fruit, seeds: (Capsicum frutescens) Medicinal: stimulates blood circulation promoting fast recovery for colds or flu's, stops internal and external bleeding, said to prevent heart attacks and also helps with digestion and headaches. Capsicum speeds metabolism. Capsicum cram and oils relieve the aches and pains of arthritis, not just by warming and stimulating the blood flow but also by blocking the pain transmission of the nerves (blocks substance P) Prevents blood clots, heals ulcers, drops blood sugar levels. Promotes excretion of cholesterol through the intestines, increases energy levels and aura brilliance. Has penicillin like qualities when added with garlic and is an effective antibiotic after the onset of colds or flu's Warning: should be avoided by Hypoglycemics. Culinary: Best used dried and ground, or fresh and finely chopped. Used in Mexican dishes, soups and stews. Flavour: fiery hot. Magickal: protection (hung in the corners of the house) strength, motivation, courage (as a tea) and increases the size of the aura.

Celery/ seed, stalk: (Apium graveolens) , Active ingredient: Thalide, Actions: Sedative. Medicinal: reduces hypertension, celery seed tea for use as a cleanser for your kidneys. Culinary: As dried whole seed use as a replacement for celery stalks in cooking, as a flavoring in tomato juice, sauces and soups. Flavour: Strong pungent celery flavour. Magickal: mental powers, lust and psychic powers.

*****Chamomile/flowers:** (Anthemic nobilis or Matricaria recutita) Actions: anodyne, antispasmodic, bitter tonic, diaphoretic. Medicinal: As a tea, used for fever and restlessness in children. Culinary: salads and sandwiches, has an apple like flavour. Warning: Drink in moderation as it contains thuaone; rag weed sufferers may be

allergic. Magickal: money, sleep, love and purification. Sprinkle around a new house or property to remove any spirits left behind.
Chaparral/leaf/berry: (Larrea divaricata) Actions: Antibiotic and antiseptic. Medicinal: as a tea is useful against bacteria, viruses, parasites, tuberculosis, venereal diseases and warts. As a salve it is useful for arthritis, cramping, wound healing, and relieves itching of eczema, scabies and dandruff. Note: Native Americans use for cancer treatment. Do not use if you have any history of liver disease or if nausea, fever, fatigue or jaundice occur. Culinary: White mulberries are good in syrups, sauces, pies, wines, jams and jellies. Magickal: protective, healing, clairvoyance.
Cherry(wild)/fruit/bark: (Prumus serotina) Medicinal: astringent, pectoral, sedative, is useful as a cough syrup as it soothes bronchial spasms Action: relaxing expectorant. Culinary: for use in desserts, syrups, sauces, jams and jellies. Magickal: love and divination, good for wands.
***Chervil/herb/flowers/stems: (Sweet Cicely) Medicinal: diuretic, expectorant, digestive aid, is a remedy for high blood pressure (as a tea) eyewash, relieves the symptoms of kidney stones and gout, roots were used to cure the bites of mad dogs and snakes. Culinary: best if used fresh or frozen, as a flavouring in soups, casseroles, salads and omelets. Best if used at the end of cooking or fresh on salads. Flavour: light tastes similar to parsley. Substitutes for tarragon or parsley. Magickal: comforts a broken heart, relieves depression, increases a love of life.
Chestnut: Medicinal: rheumatism, neuralgia, hemorrhoids. Culinary: used as a food source

cooked, in breads, and Asian cooking. Magickal: love.

Chicory/herb/flower: Medicinal: prepare like coffee for liver cleanser, fat cleanser, and to dissolve gallstones. Culinary: used in coffee, picked, or in salads and sandwiches; tastes like endive. Magickal: removes obstacles, invisibility, favours and frigidity.

Chickweed: (Stellaria media) Medicinal: cooling antiseptic herb used to treat inflammation, relieve itching, blisters, boils, and abscesses. Cooking: edible in salads or cooked greens. Magickal: fertility and love.

Chile Pepper/fruit/seeds: (Capsicum annum) Medicinal: can prevent or stop heart attack, thins the blood, reducing blot clot and stroke, internal disinfectant and detoxifier, lowers blood sugar levels, stops bleeding, guards against respiratory infections and strengthens the immune systems. Culinary: best if used dried and ground in chili or other spicy dishes. Flavour: spicy, hot (depending on the variety of chili peppers used. Substitutes for dash bottles hot pepper sauce plus a combination of oregano and cumin. Magickal: fidelity, hex breaking, love.

Chives/leaves: (Allium) Medicinal: see Allium. Culinary: best if fresh, or frozen if not available, used as a garnish, blended with soft cheeses and added to salads. Flavour: sharp, like onion or garlic. Substitutes for green onion, onion or leek. Magickal: see Allium.

Chrysanthemums/flower petals/leaves: Medicinal: whole petals can be used as a tea for influenza, pulverized flowers are used as an insect repellant and female mosquito bite inhibitor and is harmful to fishes and mosquito larvae. Reduces air pollution wherever it is planted. Culinary: remove bitter flower base and blanch first for salads, and teas; leaves are used to flavour vinegars. Magickal: protection.

Cilantro/flower/leaf/seed: (Coriandrum sativum) (coriander) Medicinal: as a food poisoning preventative. Culinary: best if used fresh in Middle Eastern, southeast Asian, Chinese, Latin American, and Spanish cuisines, common ingredient in Mexican salsa. Flavour: spicy, sweet or hot. Substitutes for parsley. Magickal: love, health and healing.

Cinnamon/ bark : (Cinnamomum zeylanicum) Medicinal: taken with milk offers a good balance after a heavy meal or dessert; also used for diarrhea, dysentery or general indigestion or upset stomach, as a mouthwash . Simmer sticks with cloves for 3 minutes and add 2 tsp lemon juice, 2 tsp honey, tbsp brandy as a cold medication for adults, great for yeast infections and athlete's foot in a 2% solution. Boil 8-10 sticks in 4 cups water, simmer 5 min, and steep 45 minutes then douche or apply to athlete's foot. Action: Cinnamon reduces the Cancer causing tendencies of many food additives. Culinary: best as dried sticks or ground powder for use in sweet dishes, curries and stews. Flavour: pungently sweet. Substitutes as nutmeg, or allspice (only use ¼ of the amount). Magickal: spirituality, success, healing, power, psychic powers, lust protection and love. Great in sachets and amulets.

Citrus/fruit/blossoms/rind: (orange, lemon, lime, grapefruit and kumquat) Medicinal: for use in thinning the mucus and draining the sinuses. Actions: Vitamin C, Aromatic. Culinary: rind may be grated for desserts, flowers are used in pastries and beverages. Citrus flavor. Magickal: purification, healing, love.

Clove/flower bud: (Syzygium aromaticum) Medicinal: chew for toothache, nausea and vomiting. Use the oil for pain relief for sore gums and toothache add clove oil to neutral oils for topical pain relief of arthritis, small amounts of clove in a tea for nausea, 3 cloves to two cups of boiled water, steeped for twenty minutes as a antiseptic and a mouthwash. Former alcoholics can suck on one or two cloves when the craving strikes to curb the desire. Actions: aromatic. Culinary: best as dried and ground, used in sweet dishes or as a contrast in stews and curries. Flavour: sweet or bittersweet. Substitutes as allspice, cinnamon or nutmeg. Magickal: protection, exorcism, love and money. Carry to attract the opposite sex.

Clover/flower petals: Medicinal: antispasmodic, expectorant, sedative, tonic and as a tea is effective anticancer herb against all womanly cancers. Culinary with a sweet anise-like licorice flavor that is prized in honey. It is also used a pot herb, salads, soups, and teas. Magickal: protection, money, love, fidelity, exorcism, success. 2 leaf: gives a maiden the power to see her future love, 3 leaf: ward off evil spirits and witches, 4 leaf: extreme power against all wizards and demons, 5 leaf: so powerful it is warn by witches to increase their powers.

Coconut/fruit/milk: Medicinal: milk is good for infants suffering from stomach and intestinal disorders and aids in growth, kills intestinal worms, urinary infections, cures malnourishment, can be substituted for blood plasma, and eliminates mineral poisons from the body. Applied to the body has a cooling effect and prevents prickly heat, summer boils, and subsides the rashes of poxes and measles,

Culinary: used in many desserts, frostings and beverages as well as flavouring for ice cream. Magickal: purification, protection and chastity.
Coffee: Medicinal: The caffeine in coffee can be used to alleviate some headaches and when sipped hot through a straw helps break up mucus congestion in the lungs. Coffee enemas with olive oil are used to thoroughly cleanse the bowel. Warning: Please use common sense and caution to avoid dependency. Actions: Decongestant, food dye. Cooking: often added to breads and cakes for flavour and colouring purposes. Magickal: breaking spells and bindings.
Comfrey/ root/ leaf: (Symphytum officinale) Medicinal: used both internally and externally and considered valuable in the treatment of all types of skin, bone and muscle injuries as well as burns, blisters, and inflammations as it helps wounds to heal quickly. Comfrey has a soothing effect on any organ it comes in contact with and therefore is also used for respiratory and digestive system disorders. Culinary: not recommended as long term use runs the risk of liver problems. Magickal: used as protection in traveling, root is used in money spells.
Coriander/leaves/flowers/seeds: Medicinal: as a tea can be drank to relive indigestion and flatulence, held in the mouth to relieve toothache pain or was used as a wash to remove unpleasant orders from the genital area for both men and women. Culinary: best if used fresh in Middle Eastern, southeast Asian, Chinese, Latin American, and Spanish cuisines, common ingredient in Mexican salsa and Hand fasting cakes. Flavour: spicy, sweet or hot. Substitutes for parsley. Magickal: love, health and healing. Used in love sachets and love spells. Added to warm wine produces lust. Gather at harvest and

hang in your house for protection. Promotes peace between people who are unable to get along.
Corn/vegetable: Medicinal: the hairs from the corn stalk are valuable in treating urinary, bladder, kidney, lowers blood pressure, strengthens the womb, purifies the blood and eliminates toxins. Culinary: used as a side dish, in soups and breads. High sugar content, cooked in lime water it nutritional values are released as in hominy, mesa and tortillas. Magickal: protection, luck, divination.
Corn flower/petal: (Bachelor's button) Medicinal: as an antiseptic for cuts, scrapes an bruising, remedy for conjunctivitis, eye swelling, puffiness and pain. Culinary: has a spicy sweet clove like flavor but is usually used as a garnish. Actions: Natural food dye. Magickal: clairvoyance, a decoction is used as an eye wash to increase clairvoyance filtered through 3 layers of linen, and consecrated beneath a full moon with a moonstone.
***Crab apple/fruit:** Medicinal: cleansing and diuretic, antiseptic and tonic, useful in the management of immunomediated diseases, antifungal, reduces skin inflammation and removes dead skin fragments. Is used instead of apple cider vinegar in herbal salves. Culinary: 3 whole eaten a day (and no more) contribute towards weight loss, Magickal: love, healing, garden magic and immortality. Used as fertility charms, image magic and seek and destroy spells.
Cucumber/fruit: Medicinal: Use a fresh peel on your head to ease a headache due to heat or sliced and put on eyes for inflammation. Culinary: used as a side dish, in tea sandwitches, in salads and cold soups. Magickal: chastity, healing and fertility.
Cumin/seed: (Cuminum cyminum) Medicinal: digestive illness, chest colds, coughs, as a pain

killer to treat rotten teeth, improves breast milk production, used to treat scorpion stings, insomnia and fever. Culinary: best if used whole or ground in soups, curries and pickles, stews, and sauces, use sparingly. Flavour: peppery. Substitutes as chili powder. Magickal: when given to a lover promotes fidelity, blended with salt and swept out of the house to clear evil, steeped in warm wine for a love potion. Protection, fidelity, antitheft, exorcism.
Curry Powder: combination of several ground spices. Culinary: use sparingly, taste the dish to gauge the heat level before adding to curries. Flavour: hot.
Dame's Rocket/flowers/leaves/sprouted seeds: (Hesperis matronalis) Other names: sweet rocket, dame's violet. Often mistaken for phlox – to differentiate – phlox has five petals, dames rocket has four. Medicinal: antiscorbutic – substitutes for ipecacuanha (syrup of ipecac) to induce vomiting. Culinary: part of the mustard family (radishes, broccoli, cabbage, cauliflower and mustard) a bitter used for salads. Note: leaves should be picked before flowering, not the same variety as the herb called rocket. Magickal: same as cornflower.
Dandelions/greens/flowers: Member of the Daisy family. Medicinal: the plan as a whole fights bacteria and heals wounds, inhibits the growth of staphococcus aureus, pneumococci, meningococci, bacillus dysenteriae, B. Typhi, C. diphtheriae, proteus, and the latex contained in the sap is good for removing corns and warts. Internally is used effectively to treat blood purifier, treatment of gall bladder, kidney, urinary tract, gallstones, jaundice, hypoglycemia, high blood pressure, heart weakness, hepatitis, chronic joint and skin complaints, gout, eczema and acne. A liquid plant food is made from

the roots and leaves, the base of the leave blades is used as a cosmetic lotion in water to clear the skin and fade freckles. Culinary: best when picked as buds or young as mature flowers are bitter. For use in wine, raw, steamed, tossed in salads or throw the petals over rice. Note: should be picked when they are close to the ground, tightly bunched in the center and about the size of a gumball. Magickal: lust, luck, divination, wishes, and calling spirits.

Day Lilies/flowers: Medicinal: caution: raw leaves are hallucinogenic. Flowers and tubers can be used in uterine bleeding, vaginal yeast infection, as a remedy for arsenic poisoning, and as a antibacterial agent. Culinary: to use, cut them away from the bitter white base of the flower, has a sweet with a mild vegetable flavour like sweet lettuce or melon, or more like a combination of asparagus and zucchini. Great with squash blossoms, in desserts, salad. Note: gather shoots 2-3 inches tall and use as a substitute for asparagus. Warning: there are many types of lilies – only day lilies are edible. Actions: Diuretic, laxative (eat in moderation). Magickal: protection and breaking love spells.

Dill/herb/flower/seed: (Anethum graveolens, Anethum sowa) Medicinal: For fresh breath: chew dill seeds; For pleasant sleep: bring one pint of white wine to a boil then remove from heat and steep (in a cheese cloth bag) 4 tsp dill seeds for 30 minutes and remove bag; To stimulate milk flow in nursing mothers: bring one pint of white wine to a boil and remove from heat, steep in a cheese cloth bag 1 tsp EACH of anise, caraway, coriander and dill for 30 minutes and remove bag. Culinary: best if leaves are fresh or seeds are used whole on good on hot or cold soups, fish, seafood, meats, salads, dressings, dips, potatoes, breads, sandwiches, for pickling and making dill flavoured vinegar. Seeds of sowa or Indian dill is used in curry. Flavour: mild, somewhat sour. Magickal: protection, money, lust and luck.

Echinacea/root: (Echinacea purpurea or E. angustifolia) also known as Purple Cornflower: Medicinal: beneficial in many topical applications to treat infected wounds, psoriasis and eczema as it stimulates the bodies defense at the sight of the wound and aids in the development of healthy tissue. As a wash with alcohol to remove poison ivy oils from the skin. For immune stimulation – avoid products with no root in them as this is the most efficient part of the plant. Best if home grown. Magickal: strengthening spells.

Elderberry/flower, berry: (Sambucus nigra or Canadensis): Medicinal: Remove the flower/berry from all other parts of the plant, used for colds, flu's, fevers, hay fever, sinusitis and upper respiratory tract infections. Warning: All other parts of the plant are poisonous; do not even eat the stems of the flowers. Actions: expectorant (decreases mucous accumulation), diaphoretic. Culinary: Check carefully for insects and use without washing as this takes away from the scent and flavor witch is sweet, uses jams, jellies, teas and wine. Magickal: exorcism, protection, healing, prosperity and sleep.

English daisy: Medicinal: has astringent properties. Culinary: most often used for its looks as a garnish and in salads as it has a bitter taste. Magickal: lust and luck.

Elecampane/root: (Inula Helena) Medicinal: used for coughs due to cold, flu, asthma or bronchitis and pulmonary diseases. Used to cure diseases of woman, sheep (scabwort) and horses (horseheal). Actions: Antibacterial, expectorant. Culinary: root is candied and used as a sweet meat (1 oz powdered root to 2 oz honey). Magickal: love, protection and psychic powers.

Eucalyptus: Medicinal: as a tea to soothe a sore throat. Magickal: healing and protection.

Fennel/herb/flower/seed/bulb: (Foeniculum vulgare var) Medicinal: As a tea to expel mucus with bronchitis, relief of colic in children, and sweeten breast milk. Chew the seed to relieve bad breath. Culinary: best if used raw or cooked in salads (raw), soups (cooked), entrees, and as a garnish. Flavour: like anise only lighter and sweeter. Magickal: protection, healing and purification.

***Fennel/leaves/bulbs/seeds**: (Foeniculum vulgare) Medicinal: soothes digestion, constipation, promotes lactation, used for gum disease, loose teeth, reduces the toxic effects of alcohol in the system. Culinary: for use with any kind of meat, salad, dessert, used in the preparation of absinthe. Magickal: used to lose weight, protective, wards of ticks and biting bugs (pet pillows, sachets), in charms against elves, sorcerers and insanity. Seven seeds are eaten for seeing spirits, discerning the creeping death, and finding the inner pain and disease in others.

Fenugreek/seeds: (Trigonella foenumgraecum) Medicinal: As a tea, 8 tsp of seed soaked in 4 cups of cold water for 4 hours then boil 2 minutes, strain and drink: to expel mucus, for relief of fever and colic in children, and to ease hay fever attacks. To reduce cholesterol takes 1 tsp daily. Culinary: best if used whole or ground seed in pastries, as flavouring for meat dishes and beverages and to make soups. Flavour: sweet, somewhat like burnt honey. Magickal: money.

Fig/Fruit: Medicinal: used in the treatment of parasites. Culinary: for use in desserts and sauces. Magickal: divination, fertility and love.

Flax/seed: Medicinal: partially ground seeds are called linseed (oil) and can be used as a poultice to treat infections and rheumatism. As a tea (2-3 tsp in 1 C water for 15 minutes and sweetened with honey) is useful for bronchial tubes, infections and coughs as well as breaking down cholesterol. Used in the inhibition and growth of breast cancer. Culinary: for use in all breads. As an oil used in cooking and salads. Magickal: money, protection, beauty, psychic powers and healing.

Forsythia/flowers: (Forsythia suspense) Medicinal: at the first sign of cold or flu. Unripe fruit and seeds are crushed to expel toxins from the body and used topically for burns, rashes, blemishes and carbuncles. Action: Antiviral. Culinary: tenderest young leaves can be useful in salads and soups, and flowers as a garnish though bitter. Magickal: exorcism, protection.

Frankincense/resin: for use as incense. Medicinal: once used as an antidote to hemlock poisoning, highly antiseptic externally used as a wash for cuts and bruises or added to salves. Magickal: protection, exorcism and spirituality. Used to anoint tools, sachets, or the body, used as an incense for spiritual endeavors.

French herb blend: combination of chives, parsley, marjoram, chervil and tarragon. Culinary: omelettes, grilled vegetables, pasta salad, and poultry.

Fuchsia/berries/flowers: Culinary: beautiful as a garnish, slight acidic flavor, fruit is best when picked 1-2 days after the petals have fallen, cut off them stem and blossom end and slice, for use in

salads and desserts. To eat the flower remove the stamen, pistils and all green and brown parts, good in salads, with fruit, pickled or crystallized.
Galangal/spice: (Catarrh root) a member of the ginger family. Other names: St. Hildegard's herb. Available in the frozen food section of Asian groceries, as a powder in the spice department and cut and sifted in bulk from herb suppliers. Hildegard firmly believed that metabolism is affected by the liver which has a direct relationship to the ears and hearing. Harsh sounds and harsh words disturb the body fluids and fluids contract the blood vessels and impact hearing. Hildegard believed that health is earned or forfeited by what we hear – sage advice. Medicinal: As a cure for deafness and a daily digestive aid: 1 C galangal, 1/3 C aloe powder, 2/3 C oregano and peach leaves, powdered and taken a few pinches daily after a meal. Formulae #1 for the Heart (also good for menopause – as heart disease is a leading cause of death amoung women due to the changes of estrogen during menopause): 1 C galangal, 1 C pellitory (a Mediterranean herb), ¼ white pepper – mix with fava beans and moisten with fenugreek juice. Take daily for at least 3 weeks or through out menopause. Formulae #2 for the Heart: ¼ C licorice, 1 ¼ C fennel, 1 ¼ sugar and a little honey and mix with water for a juice. Formulae #3: 1 C white pepper and galangal, 1/3 C cumin and fenugreek, powder and put on bread, reduces pain and fever that brings on heart attacks. Actions: a potent digestive aid, quick pain reliever for angina pectoris, heart attacks and gall bladder. German physicians have reported that galangal is as effective as nitroglycerin with no harmful side effects. Actions: stimulant, carminative, promotes

secretion of the gastric juices and neutralizes the gas of the gastrointestinal tract or by products of fermentation which circulate through the system causing spasms, hiccups and sharp cardiac pains. Properties: Antifungal, Antibacterial. For Rheumatism, arthritis, lumbago and sciatica – mix the powder with warm wine. The powder also relieves the dizziness and nausea of morning or motion sickness. It has been found effective as a douche in the treatment of candida albicans and the natural anthrax pathogen-like the red tide (no studies have been done on war grade). Known to improve circulation in the hands, feet and ears. You can not overdose and there is no known side effects however always consult a physician especially if you are already using heart medication.

Garden Sorrel/flowers: Medicinal: especially useful in scurvy, a syrup with the juice and mixed with vinegar is a cure for ringworms, a decoction of flowers with wine is good for ulcerated bowels. Culinary: uses include pizza, salad, seafood, sauces and cucumber dishes as it has a lemon flavour. Magickal: healing and health.

Garlic/bulbs/flowers/cloves: (Allium sativum) All parts are edible. Medicinal: used for acute colds and flu's, bronchitis, asthma, whooping cough, regulates blood pressure, removes intestinal parasites and infections, hypoglycemia, diabetes, reduces cholesterol, repels insects, and reduces sting of red ants. Actions: Antibiotic, antimicrobial, antifungal, expectorant and diaphoretic. Culinary: best if used fresh and crushed for most benefits, granulated is an acceptable substitute. Used in roasting or flavouring for pasta sauces, hot soups; beef, lamb or pork roasts, herb butter, stuffing and marinades. Flavour: pungent, onion-like, mildly hot to over hot.

Magickal: protection, healing, exorcism, lust and anti-theft.

Ginger/root: (Zingeber officinale) Medicinal: As a warm tea to break up congestion or cough, colds and flu, cramps and nausea. Works as a blood thinner DON'T USE IF USING COUMADIN. As a wash, boil 2/3 cup freshly chopped root wrapped in a cheese cloth and put in 1 gallon of water until the water is yellow. Then soak a washcloth and lay on the bruises and sprains while still hot to ease the pain. Warning: NOT for use with pregnant woman as it passes through the membrane. Actions: Antiviral, diaphoretic, cough suppressant Culinary: best if dried powder or freshly grated from root and used to detoxify meat – especially chicken, cakes, breads, cookies and Asian dishes. Substitutes as allspice, cinnamon, mace or nutmeg. Magickal: love, money, success and power.

Gladiolus/flower: Medicinal: cures constipation and severe dysentery. Note: remove anthers. Culinary: make lovely for sweet or savory spreads or mousses, or toss individual petals in salads. Flavour: like lettuce. Magickal: healing.

Goldenseal/root: (Hydrastis Canadensis): Medicinal: internally and externally for cuts, wounds, infection, bites, stings, sinus infections, inflammations of the mucus membrane. Best home grown and harvested at 5 years. Action: antiseptic and astringent. Magickal: healing and money.

Grape/fruit/leaf/seed: Medicinal: In the early spring when grape vines are trimmed a sap can be collected from early morning until noon (no later or it will spoil) and store in a dark room to be used as an ointment for ear ache and pinkeye (9/10 sap to 1/10 olive oil in a clean brown bottle) . Culinary: as a food source and in Mediterranean cooking, jams, jellies and wines. Seed is pressed into an oil used for cooking. Magickal: fertility, garden magick, mental powers, wealth.

Green Bean: Medicinal: slightly diuretic, anxiety, insomnia, hot symptoms. Culinary: as a vegetable, side dish, in salads and casseroles. Magickal: fertility, money.

Green peppercorn/unripe berries: (Piper nigrum) Culinary: best if preserved in brine or water packed for use in herbal vinegars and sauces. Flavour: mild, slightly sweet.

Herbs de Provence: a combination of lavender, chervil, garlic, marjoram, parsley, thyme, basil, savory, rosemary, and tarragon. Culinary: used on vegetables, in vinaigrettes, tomato or fruit salads and soups, stews, omelettes and sauces.

Hibiscus/flowers: Medicinal: as a tea (boil 15-30 grams in 1 C water and drink) for mumps, red flowers are purgative, entire plant as an emollient. Culinary: use sparingly in salads or as a garnish. Tastes like cranberry with citrus overtones. Magickal: lust, love and divination.

Hollyhock/flowers: Medicinal: used as a expectorant and in the treatment of genitor-urinary tract infections. Culinary: for use in sandwitches and salads, and for decorative purposes, as it has a bland taste. Actions: Aromatic, used in holy rituals to ward of evil. Magickal: protection, anti-lightning, luck and dream magic.

Honeysuckle/flowers: (Lonicera japonica) Medicinal: especially good at the onset of cold and flu symptoms Actions: antiviral. Warning: Berries are highly poisonous – do NOT eat them! Culinary: Used in Sandwitches, salads and teas, as it has a sweet honey flavour. Magickal: money, psychic powers and protection.

Hops/grain: Medicinal: have a mild sedative effect on the central nervous system, treatment for insomnia, stress and anxiety, has antibacterial qualities and estrogen precursors. Culinary: used in breads and beer. Magickal: healing and sleep.
Horseradish/root: (Armoracia lapathifolia) Medicinal: grated as a tea for pot nasal drip, and added to cold pressed oil as massage oil for muscle aches and pains or to break up chest congestion. Culinary: best used if fresh or jarred as a condiment or to flavour fish or beef, sausages and potato salad. Flavour: very sharp, with its own heat, similar to mustard. Magickal: purification and exorcism.
Huckleberry/berry: Medicinal: promotes circulation, lowers blood sugar and prevents diabetes, has laxative and digestive properties, strengthens the immune system and treats urinary tract infections, improves vision and increases glucose and urine. **Culinary**: jellies, jams, desserts and wine. Magickal: luck, protection, dream magic, hex breaking.
Hyacinth/bulb: Medicinal: diuretic and stimulant properties. Culinary: eaten raw or cooked it has a sweet nut like flavour. A favorite of the Nez Indians. Magickal: love, protection and happiness.
Impatiens/flowers: Medicinal: leaves are used as a poultice for piles. Juice is effective in Rhus poisoning. Culinary: salads or sandwitches as it has a very bland taste. Magickal: protective
Italian seasoning: a blend of basil, oregano, rosemary and ground red pepper OR marjoram, thyme, rosemary, savory, sage, oregano and basil.
Jasmine/flowers: Actions: Aromatic. Medicinal: Used in the treatment of intestinal worms, jaundice and vernal diseases, in the treatment of ulcers, boils and skin diseases. Cancer curative, calming and

relaxing. Culinary: used for scenting teas. Magickal: love, money and prophetic dreams.

Johnny Jump-ups/flowers: Medicinal: Used to treat skin diseases, asthma, and epilepsy; useful in heart disease, acne and impetigo. Culinary: They are a great addition to drinks, soups, desserts, salads, decorate cakes or served with soft cheese as it has a mild wintergreen flavour. Magickal: love magick and healing of broken hearts.

Lavender/flowers: Medicinal: stress, anxiety, depression, exhaustion, headaches, migraines, insomnia, colds and digestion. Culinary: used floating in champagne, with chocolate cake, as a garnish for sorbets, ice creams, white cheeses, tea cookies, jelly, savory dishes, hearty stews and wine reduced sauces. Magickal: love, protection, sleep, chastity, longevity, purification, happiness and peace.

Leek/root: (Allium) Medicinal: see Allium. Culinary: stronger than an onion, used in omelettes, soups, stews and casseroles. Magickal: love, protection and exorcism.

Lemon/fruit: Medicinal: in tea or as a juice or syrup for colds or flu. Action: Vitamin C. Culinary: used primarily for its juice and rind (zest) as flavouring in cooking, juices, teas liquors and baking, from desserts to chickens, Magickal: longevity, purification, love, friendship.

Lemon balm/herb: (Melissa officinalis) Medicinal: used for cold or flu that cause a fever or cause one to be depressed or tense, relives stomach and intestinal gas. Action: antispasmodic, diaphoretic. Culinary: primarily used in fruit dishes, custards, teas and salads. Magickal: love, success and healing. Steeped in wine for 3 hours can be used in love charms and spells to attract a partner, makes you more desirable to the opposite sex.

Lemon grass: Medicinal: to bring down a fever take ½ cup dried leaves in a cheese cloth to 1 quart of water and simmer for 10 minutes. Also relieves spasms, muscle cramps, headaches, rheumatism and digestion. Culinary: widely used in Thai and Vietnamese cooking, in curries, beef and seafood soups with garlic, chilies and cilantro. Magickal: repel snakes, lust and psychic powers.

Lemon Verbena/flower/leaves: Medicinal: relieves digestive tract spasms, reduces fever and strengthens the nervous systems, stress relief and expectorant. Culinary: used to flavour custards and flans, fruit jellies, punches and ice cream. Leaves and flowers can be steeped as a tea. Magickal: purification and love.

Lettuce/leaf: Medicinal: used as a diuretic, helpful in the digestive tract, improves circulation, appeases the sexual appetites, combats coughs, bronchial attacks and asthma spasms. Culinary: used in salads and sandwitches. Magickal: chastity, protection, love, divination and sleep.

Licorice/root: (glycyrrhiza glabra) Medicinal: for use with bronchial problems associated with colds or flu, as a tranquilizer, balances nervous system and stimulates liver function. Warning: long term usage could cause liver damage. Actions: Antiviral, expectorant, demulcent, laxative. Culinary: used mostly as a confectionary flavouring, in candy, fruit juices, liquors, beers and syrups. Magickal: love, lust and fidelity.

Lilac/flower: Medicinal: as a substitute for aloe in the treatment of malaria. Culinary: great in salads, slightly bitter with distinct lemony flavour. Actions: Aromatic. Magickal:

Linden/flower: Culinary: for use in teas and cakes as it has a honey like flavour. Warning: Frequent use has been linked to heart attacks. Magickal: protection (hang over the door or grow in the garden), immortality, good fortune, sleep and love.
Linseed (Flax): (Linum usitatissimum) Medicinal: Takes out the pain and heat of burns. 3 Tbsp linseeds boiled in 2 C water and cook until the water turns slimy, like jelly. Then strain and soak a clean linen cloth in it and use as a warm compress and replace as soon as it begins to dry out or become cold. When the burn is out then use a regular burn salve. As a tea it fights cough, cold, asthma, hay fever, stomach and intestinal problems, throat problems, PMS, bladder and urinary problems and constipation. Care must be taken as immature seeds are poisonous and you can overdose on mature ones. Signs of an overdose include: increased respiratory rate, gasping, staggering, weakness, paralysis, convulsion. Warning: do not use if you have a bowel obstruction, inflammation or narrowing of the stomach or digestive tract. Culinary: as an oil, as a flavoring in baked goods and breads. Magical: Flowers are carried as protection against black sorcery. Put some in your shoe for prosperity. A child who dances in it will become beautiful. Fibers are used for weaving (linen)
Lime/fruit: (Citrus Limata) Medicinal: acne, brittle nails, boils, greasy skin, herpes, insect bites, high blood pressure nose bleeds, obesity, asthma, arthritis. Culinary: primarily used as a flavouring and preservative in juices, liquors, salsa, avocado dip, and Mexican cooking. Magickal: purification, protection, love spells and incense.

Lovage/leaves: (Levisticum officinale) Medicinal: A tea is made from the dried leaves has diuretic and carminative actions that are good for stomach disorders, feverish attacks and jaundice. As a poultice is good for breaking boils. . Culinary: leaf stalks can be blanched and used like celery in soups, stews, sauces, meat or fish dishes and salads or for confectionary purposes like angelica. Flavour: similar to celery only stronger. Magickal: love.
Mace/nut: (outer covering of the nutmeg seed) Medicinal: used for gas, indigestion, nausea, vomiting and kidney problems; make a paste of 1tsp powder with cold water and then add to a cup of boiled water and drink. Caution: watch dosing as 1 Tbsp can cause a floating euphoria for 6 to 24 hours, constant erections, and overdose; side effects include bone and muscle aches, burning eyes, sinus drainage and limited diarrhea. Culinary: best if used dried or ground in custards, spice cakes and fruit desserts. Flavour: similar to nutmeg, but stronger. Substitutes as allspice, cinnamon, ginger or nutmeg. Magickal: psychic powers and mental powers.
Marjoram/flower/herb/leaf: (Origanum majorana) Medicinal: Used as a tea to break up bronchitis and help reduce fevers, relieve cramps, irregular menstruation, as well as eases suffering from childhood diseases like mumps and measles. Culinary: best if used fresh or dried in soups, stews, and marinades. Add to the end of cooking to preserve flavour. Flavour: delicate, like parsley. Substitutes for basil, thyme or savory. Magickal: protection, love, happiness, health and money.
Marigold: Medicinal: see Calendula. Culinary: for use in salads and desserts as decorations. Magickal: Wish magick, antitheft, protection, consecration and divination. Aids in locating stolen property by

giving visions of the thief and location of stolen property. As an incense to consecrate divination tools, or with sunflower oil to make consecration oil.

Marshmallow/root: (Althaea officinalis) Medicinal: for use with coughs associated with colds or flu. Actions: Expectorant, demulcent, antiseptic. Culinary: use the powdered root thickened with water and heated with sugar to create the confection. Seeds and young leaves may be sprinkled on salads or cheese, and roots may be boiled soft and fried. Magickal: love, protection and exorcism.

Mint/flowers/leaves: (Menthe spp.) Medicinal: used as a tea excellent for stomach aches and disorders, to buffer the action of other herbs, migraines, nervousness, and ease the symptoms of the herpes virus. Culinary: for use in teas, cold soups and Middle Eastern dishes. Culinary: best if used fresh in salads, with vegetables and in teas. Flavour: varies as there are more than 30 species. Substitutes for basil, marjoram or rosemary. Magickal: money, love, lust, healing, exorcism, travel and protection.

***Mugwort/leaves/roots:** Medicinal: leaves should be gathered in August and root in autumn and then dried. In a tea 1 oz of herb to 1 pt water and taken in ½ tsp doses for cold three times daily. 1 drachm up to four times daily is given for epilepsy, Parkinson's, hysteria and palsy. Magickal: strength, psychic powers, protection, prophetic dream, healing and astral projection. Used as a wash or an oil to consecrate divination tools such as crystal balls, keeps one safe from dark forces, protects children, used in sachets for visionary dreams, burned with sandalwood during scrying sessions, as a tea with honey to enhance divinations powers.

Mulberry/ berry: Medicinal: used to flavour cough syrup. Culinary: wine (1 gal of berries to 1 gal of boiling water then to set for two days- sieve and add 3 lb sugar then cask. In 4 months add 1 clove and 1 lump sugar to each bottle and cap for 1 year.), mixed with hard cider, jams (make sure the berries are very ripe to avoid a bitter taste), jellies, syrups and desserts. Magickal: protection and strength.

Mullein/flowers, leaves: (Verbascum thapsus) Medicinal: used in olive oil is used for ear aches (one to two drops with head tilted and cotton inserted), and as a tea with coughs or as a spray is very soothing and as a massage oil to treat inflamed skin.. Actions: Antiviral, relaxing expectorant. Magickal: courage, protection, health, love, divination and exorcism.

Mustard/leaves/seeds: (Brassica juncea - yellow, Brassica hirta- brown)Medicinal: for a sprained back, or other sprains use 1 ½ cups of dry yellow mustard in a tub full of water and soak. For rattling coughs use as a plaster mixing 1 tsp each powdered mustard and ginger with 2 ½ tsp of olive oil, rub over the chest and back and cover with an old shirt. Culinary: best if used as a whole seed or powdered, young leaves can be steamed, used as an herb, and eaten raw or cooked like spinach. Either is great in lamb and beef dishes. Used for pickling, as a seasoning boiled with cabbage or corned beef. Brown is used for preparing Oriental mustard sauces. Yellow is used ground it is primary ingredient in prepared mustard. Flavour: pungent, hot and tangy. Magickal: fertility, protection and mental powers.

Myrrh/resin: (Commiphora myrrha) Medicinal: internally for used to treat fungal infections, congestion, ulcers, and as a wash for sore gums. Externally is best used as a salve, combined with goldenseal is good for wounds, bedsores, abscesses and hemorrhoids. Actions: Antiseptic, astringent. Magickal: protection, exorcism, healing and spirituality.

Nasturtiums/flowers/leaves/seeds: Actions: Antimicrobial Medicinal: eaten or as a tea is used in treating respiratory infections, viral infections and as a poultice for wound infections. Culinary: used with savory mousse, salads, cheese tortas, sandwitches, and savory appetizers. Pickle the seed pods and use as an alternative for capers. Tastes peppery.

***Stinging Nettle:** Medicinal: stops bleeding, and soothes the skin making it good for internal and external bleeding and eczema - for use in teas and salves (Caution: use gloves and cut and let air dry for two weeks or boil) Culinary: steam or boil and serve with butter and lemon or add to soups, stews and broths. Magickal: exorcism, protection, healing and lust.

Nutmeg/seed: (Myristica fragans) Medicinal: used for gas, indigestion, nausea, vomiting and kidney problems; make a paste of 1tsp powder with cold water and then add to a cup of boiled water and drink. Caution: watch dosing as 1 Tbsp can cause a floating euphoria for 6 to 24 hours, constant erections, and overdose; side effects include bone and muscle aches, burning eyes, sinus drainage and limited diarrhea. Culinary: best if used freshly ground in cakes, cookies, sweet pastry dishes, white cheeses and potatoes. Flavour: warm, spicy and sweet. Substitutes as cinnamon, ginger or mace. Magickal: money and prosperity charms.

Oats/grain: Medicinal: used to prevent heart disease, cancers, enhance the immune system, stabilize blood sugars, in the treatment of rheumatism, weakness, stress, insomnia, depression and cannibalism. Green oats are used to treat withdrawal from opiates and tobacco (period of 30-45 days required). Cosmetically oats are used for it restorative properties and for dryness in soaps, baths and shampoos. Culinary: used for cereals, breads and desserts, making whiskey, beer, coffee substitute. Magickal: money.

Okra/flower/seed pod/vegetable: also known as Ochro, Okoro, Quimgombo, quingumbo, Ladies fingers and Gumbo. Medicinal: Demulcent, emollient, carminative, stimulant, cordial, antispasmodic. Culinary: When pickled tender produces a vegetable dish when stewed or fried. When cooked it resembles asparagus and is used extensively in Cajun and southern cooking. May be left raw for a salad or dried and powdered for storage and future use. The ripe seeds have also been used as a coffee substitute. Magickal: for use in healing and exorcism.

Olive/fruit/leaves: Medicinal: (oil) cleanse wounds, good in the treatment of gout, lowering blood sugars and blood pressure levels, leaves are antimicrobial and are useful in fighting fungi, yeasts, viruses and bacteria. Olive leaf extract is effective in fighting HIV, herpes, candida, lupus or any chronic infection. Also used in treating chronic fatigue, fibromyalgia, coughs, psoriasis, malaria, prostate difficulties, and parasites. It also treats things such as athlete's foot, botulism, encephalitis, lice, hepatitis, pneumonia, bladder infections, warts,

Caution: olive leaf extract is considered to strong for internal use in pregnancy and nursing. Culinary: used as an oil, as a fruit in salads, pizzas, and Italian cooking and as a condiment. Magickal: healing, peace, fertility, potency, protection and lust.

Onion/bulb: (Allium cepa officinalis) Medicinal: for burn dressing, bee or wasp sting, crush sliced onion with a little bit of salt and apply. For adult asthma; puree an onion, cover it in brandy and let it set overnight, strain it, filter it through a coffee filter and refrigerate. Take 2 Tbsp 20 minutes before expected onset or just prior to bed. Used before and during a cold and for longevity. Actions: Antimicrobial, expectorant. Culinary: for use alone, as a condiment, in soups, salads, sandwitches, pickled etc. Magickal: protection, exorcism, healing, money, prophetic dreams and lust.

Orange/fruit/peel: Medicinal: used as a flavoring in syrups or as an aromatic in bath salts. Culinary: candied, used in breads, as desserts, salads and as a food. Magickal: love, divination, luck and money.

Oregano/flower/herb: (Ariganum vulgare) Medicinal: Used as a tea to break up bronchitis and help reduce fevers, relieve cramps, irregular menstruation, as well as eases suffering from childhood diseases like mumps and measles. Culinary: best if used fresh or dried in Italian dishes and sauces, chili, with vegetables and soups, stewed beef, poultry, game meats, shellfish, potatoes, cheeses and combination dishes. Flavour: similar to marjoram, but not as sweet. Substitutes for thyme or basil. Magickal: repelling snakes and evil, fortune telling, banishing sadness.

Orris root: Medicinal: very small amounts used as a strong purgative, chewed root is used for water retention, foul breath, coughs and congestion, dropsy and edema. Culinary: used as a bitter for certain liquors. Magickal: used as a love drawing powder, roots are used to keep love, leaves are added to bath for protection. Dry shampoos, bath salts, talcum powder, as a fixative in potpourri and sachets.

Osha/root: (Ligusticum porteri) Medicinal: for use during colds or flu to relieve congestion (1 part root to 2 parts honey and extract after 1 hour over a low heat). Actions: antiviral, antibacterial, expectorant. Use as root tea to cleanse the digestive system or as an ointment to repel bodily parasites. Culinary: Seeds are used in breads. Caution: can be confused with deadly hemlock – however the roots are hairy and smell like celery. Magickal: purifications, protection against rattle snakes and evil, attracts bears (like catnip for cats), for bringing people out of trances, and for healing spells.

Pansy/flower: Medicinal: as a treatment against epilepsy, asthma and skin disease. Culinary: used in garnishes, fruit salads, green salad, deserts and cold soups. Flavour: wintergreen. Magickal: love, rain magic and divination.

Papaya/fruit: other names Paw Paw. Action: Vitamin C. Medicinal: the juice is used to reduce enlarged tonsils, warts, cancers, tumors, corns, and skin defects. Culinary: used in salsas, beverages and as a food source. Magickal: love, protection, and fertility.

Paprika/fruit: (Capsicum annum) Medicinal: high in vitamin C, see red pepper. Culinary: best if dried and ground for use in Hungarian. Turkish, Spanish and Portuguese dishes including goulash, soups, eggs, salads, cheeses, chicken, soups, stews, casseroles, and salad dressing as it temporarily holds vinegar and oil together.. Flavour: Sweet to hot and somewhat bitter.

Parsley/leaves: (Petroselinum crispum) Medicinal: used as a tea; 1 cup of parsley to 1 quart of water to purify the blood, inhibit tumors, kidney stones and problems, as well as painful urination. As an aphrodisiac: 2 cups of tea in 1 quart of water, steep one hour and drink warm (stimulates ovulation). Actions: Vitamin C (a few springs will provide 2/3 the vitamin C of an orange), Vitamin A, and the important amino acid histidine. Culinary: best if used fresh as dried is a very poor substitute. Use in sauces, potatoes, tomatoes, soups and salads or as a garnish. Flavour: mildly peppery. Substitutes for chervil or cilantro. Magickal: love, protection and purification.

Pea/vegetable/flower/shoots/vines: Medicinal: prevents heart attack, stroke, benefits the immune system and is high in iron and vitamin C. Culinary: use as you would peas, in salads, sandwitches, and soups or cooked etc. Tastes like peas. Warning: All sweet pea blossoms (regular and ornamental) are poisonous – do not confuse with other varieties. Magickal: money and love.

Peach/fruit/flowers: Medicinal: anti-cancerous, protects against stomach ulcers, protects the arteries, keeps us young, helps teeth, skin, gums, vision and acne. Culinary: used in desserts, salads and sandwitches. Magickal: love, exorcism, longevity, fertility, beauty and wishes.

Pear/fruit/blossoms: Medicinal: stimulates urine elimination, for use against obesity, arterial hypertension, kidney, bladder, urinary and prostrate issues. Culinary: used in desserts, salads and sandwitches. Magickal: lust and love.

Pecan/nut: Medicinal: contain a high level (70%) of monounsaturated and polyunsaturated fats which help in the lowering of cholesterol, heart disease, blood pressure and breast cancer. Eating walnuts and pecans actually decreases body fat. Essential oil is used as an inhalant, bath or as massage oil to stimulate antibodies, endorphins, and build a strong immune system. Culinary: as a food source, in desserts, salads and breads. Magickal: healing, money and employment.

Peony/flowers/roots/bark/seeds: Medicinal: soothes teething pain, gall stones, jaundice, seizures, and soothes coughs. Actions: Antibacterial Culinary: parboiled and sweetened as tea time treat, peony water is used for drinking, also goes well in summer salads, floating in punches, teas, lemonades or sugared on desserts. Magickal: nightmares, protection and exorcism.

Pepper/vegetable: Medicinal: aids digestion, as a tonic, corrects gas and nausea. Culinary: served in many dishes, in salads, casseroles, and stews. Magickal: protection and exorcism.

Peppermint/leaf: Medicinal: pains, cramps, nausea, colic, fevers, and heart palpations. Tea for colds or flu: equal parts peppermint, elderflower, boneset, yarrow. Tea for nervous disorders: equal parts of peppermint, wood betony and a few drops of caraway tincture. Action: antispasmodic, stimulant, carminative. Culinary: teas, salads and desserts also as a flavouring. Magickal: purification, sleep, love, healing and psychic powers.

Pineapple guava/fruit/flowers: Culinary: used in cold soups, summer salads, and desserts. Tastes tropical like papaya or melon.

Pimento: Culinary: used to stuff green olives and for... Magickal: love.
Pine/nuts/tar: Medicinal: pine tar is used as a base in many salves. Culinary: nuts are used as a food source and in cooking and salads. Magickal: healing, fertility, protection, exorcism and money.
Pineapple/fruit: Medicinal: lessens inflammation, speeds tissue repair, eases digestion and improves circulation and reduces plaque from arterial walls. Actions: diuretic, purgative. Culinary: as a food source, juice, in salads, on pizzas, in Hawaiian cooking and desserts. Magickal: luck, money and chastity.
Pistachio/nut: Medicinal: decreases bad cholesterol, prevents heart disease, reduces blood pressure. A diet which includes 35% of nut fats and oils reduces weight gain (47 nuts 5 times a week). Culinary: Mediterranean cooking, fruit composts, puddings, stuffing, ice cream, sauce (grind and use as a thickener), stir fry, soups, casseroles and desserts (Baklava, Nougat, Turkish delight). Magickal: breaking love spells.
***Plantain:** (Plantago Major - Anasazi) Medicinal: relieves the pain of bites, stings, cuts and infections of the skin as it draws the poison out. Also the source of psyllium seeds for use as a bulk laxative so don't use if you are taking an over the counter bulk laxative. Actions: Astringent, antiseptic, emollient and laxative. Culinary: as a bitter for soups, stews and salads. Magickal: healing, protection, strength, snake repelling.
Plum/fruit: Medicinal: mildly laxative. Culinary: picked as a food source, or dried (prunes) in jams, jellies, the making of brandy and culinary sauces (Asian cooking). Magickal: healing.

Pomegranate/fruit/seed: Medicinal: as a gargle I sore throat, a powder for intermittent fever, Actions: astringent, demulcent, refrigerant. Culinary: as a food source, juice, in grenadine as a syrup and flavoring, Greek and Iranian cooking, sauce – with walnuts (poultry, wild duck), salad dressing, meat marinade, salads, relish, dips. Magickal: divination, luck, wishes, wealth, fertility.
Poppy/seed: (Papaver somniferum) Medicinal: as a pain killer (codeine, morphine) Actions: sedative, euphoriant. Culinary: best if used dried and whole in muffins, cakes and salad dressings. Warning: will cause you to fail a drug test because of the opium's within. Flavour: nutty. Magickal: fertility, love, sleep, money, luck, invisibility.
Potato/root vegetable: Medicinal: protects the body against degenerative diseases, juiced can soothe peptic ulcers and stomach acidity (juice of one potato a day), raw as a poultice for rheumatic joints, or as a plaster for scalds, burns, hemorrhoids and wounds, Culinary: as a food staple, in casseroles, as a side dish, in soups, and as a salad. Magickal: fertility, abundance, and regeneration, used in image magic and healing.
Poultry seasoning: usually sage plus a blend of thyme, marjoram, savory, black pepper and rosemary.
Provencal Salt: mixture of kosher salt, thyme, basil, fennel, savory and lavender. Culinary: seafood and vegetables.
Pumpkin/fruit/flower: Medicinal: used to treat irritable bladder and prostate problems, to treat boils, carbuncles, fever, measles, pregnancy, skin ailments, smallpox, sprains, tumor, urinary ailments, warts, and women's ailments; seeds relieve dizziness. Actions: antirheumatic,

demulcent, diuretic, nervine. Culinary: wash and remove stems, stamens and cook in everything from desserts to soups.

Radish/flowers/vegetable: Medicinal: promotes digestion, blood circulation and relieves gall stones (1/2 - 2 C juice daily for 3 weeks and the continued at ½ C three times a week for 3-4 more weeks). Culinary: as a food source, used in salads and as a condiment to beer as they have a spicy bite. Magickal: protection and lust.

Raspberry/berry/leaves: Medicinal: as a tea (1 oz dried leaves to 1 pt water boiled) used as a gargle for mouth sores and a wash for wounds. Cures diarrhea. Actions: astringent and stimulant. Culinary: in jams, jellies, syrups, salads and desserts. Magickal: protection and love.

Red Pepper: Medicinal: see green pepper. Culinary: use same as cayenne pepper. Flavour: hot. Substitutes as a of dash bottled hot pepper sauce or black pepper.

Rhubarb/stalk/root: Medicinal: as a root powder is a safe and effective purgative (30 grains of powder every 2-3 hours until it appears in the stools for adults – in children 5 gains every two hours for 3 doses only), Actions: astringent, tonic. Culinary: for use in pies and jams. Magickal: protection and fidelity.

Rose/flowers/hips: (Rosa species) Medicinal: used as a preventative and to thin mucus during cold an flu season. Action: Vitamin C. Culinary: remove the bitter white portion of the petals and then use in jams, jellies, syrups, perfumed butters, sweet spreads, atop ice cream, desserts, and salads. Freeze in ice cubes and float in punches. Flavour ranges from fruity to minty. Magickal: love, psychic powers, healing, divination, luck and protection.

Rosemary/herb/ flower: (Rosmarinus officinalis) Medicinal: boil water with rosemary to make a tea for treating headaches and body aches, increases bile flow of the liver. As a mouthwash take 2 handfuls of flowering tips and soak in 2 cups of brandy for 10 days, strain and seal, use twice daily. As an oil to relieve stress and headaches. As a muscle liniment chop 2 handfuls of twigs and put in a pint of olive oil for one week. Actions: Antioxidant, diuretic, Aromatic. Culinary: best if used fresh or dried for use with lamb or fowl (chicken, turkey, quail, peacock, etc.). Also used in fish dishes and sauces. Flavour: faintly lemony and piney. Substitutes: thyme, tarragon or savory. Magickal: protection, love, lust, mental powers, exorcism, purification, healing, sleep and youth.

Rye/grain: Culinary: used in breads and beer. Magickal: love, fidelity.

Saffron/stigma and upper stiles: (Crocus cativus) Actions: Aromatic. Culinary: best if used dried as a flavouring and coloring in rice, stews, curries, fish dishes. Flavour: pungent. Substitutes as dash turmeric as a food coloring. Magickal: love, visions, healing, happiness, wind raising, lust, strength, psychic powers.

Safflower/flower: Medicinal: Diuretic, sedative, nervine, laxative, purgative, antirheumatic, helps digestion, increases appetite, relieves renal colic and reduces tension. In small quantities it regulates menstruation and helps conception. Culinary: oil is widely used in cooking and salads, margarines, candles, liquors, tender young shoots are eaten as a potherb, seeds are roasted and used in chutney, flowers are uses as red and yellow dye. Action: food dye. Magickal: healing, exorcism, fertility.

Sage/flower/herb: (Salvia officinalis): Medicinal: As a tea, prevents blood clots, to soothe the throat during colds and flu, 2 cups a day will dry up mother's milk. As a topical aid chew a fresh leaf to reduce swelling and take the sting out of insect bites, for itching skin steep a handful of freshly crushed leaves in a pint of boiling water for one hour and bathe the area, then sprinkle whole wheat flour on it. Culinary: best if used fresh or dried in salads, with beans, corn, sautéed or stuffed mushrooms, or pesto sauce. Also used with beef, fish dishes, stews, stuffing's and common sausage flavouring. Flavour: musty, slightly bitter. Substitutes as poultry seasoning, savory, marjoram or rosemary. Magickal: immortality, longevity, wisdom, protection and wishes.

Saint John's Wort/flower: (Hypericum perforatum) Medicinal: As a salve is good for burns, wounds, bruises, sores, insect bites, fungal infections such as eczema and itching. Internally for the treatment of depression. Warning: photosensitivity may develop with use. Do not use if using other antidepressants. Action: Antidepressant, Astringent. Magickal: health, power, protection, strength, love, divination and happiness.

Salt: (salt mines and sea water) Culinary: best used if granular in baking, preserving, curing, or as a condiment. Flavour: salty. Magickal: protection and blessing (use in each corner of a room and cast in a circle around you, as holy salt used at exorcisms and baptisms). May be combined with saltpeter and black pepper for extra protection. As a bath has many uses: 9 tsp salt, 1 dime saltpeter and 8 quarts of water and bather nine times with it in downward strokes, them when finished throw the water out

towards the sunrise and it will be finished by morning. Throw a handful of salt after an evil or jealous. person after they leave your house.
Saltpeter: Culinary: used in curing (corned beef) and pickling foods. Magickal: keeping husbands at home (by ingestion).
Sarsaparilla: Medicinal: used in chronic disease of the skin. Culinary: flavouring. Magickal: love and money.
Sassafras/bark: Culinary: flavouring for root beer and tea, powdered is file a herb in gumbo. Magickal: health and money.
Savory/herb/flower: Medicinal: As an aphrodisiac, one quart boiled water, 3 ½ Tbsp fenugreek seed and steep 5 minutes. Remove fenugreek and add 2 handfuls of savory leaves and steep 50 minutes, drink 2 cups. Culinary: for use in salsas, hot soups and meat salads. Magickal: mental powers.
Scarlet runner beans/ flower/vegetable: Culinary: use flowers and young beans in any place beans would go. Magickal: protection, exorcism, wart charming, reconciliations, potency and love.
Scented geraniums/flowers: Medicinal: for and effective flu/heart powder take geranium anglicum or robertianum, a little less of pellitory (anacyclus pyrethrum and nutmeg and mix the powder then take 2-3 pinches a day for 1 month. Culinary: for use summer drinks, frozen in ice cube or sprinkled on summer deserts. Taste depends on variety and can be citrus to spicy to fruity. Warning: Citronelle variety is NOT edible. Magickal: fertility, health, love and protection.
Schisandra/berries: (Schisandra chinensis) Medicinal: to build up the immune system. Actions: Tonic, astringent.

Sesame/seed: (Sesamum indicum) Medicinal: laxative, tonic, skin softener, stimulate menstruation. Culinary: best if used whole in breads, cookies and salad dressings or as an oil in dressings and cooking, widely used in Asian cooking. Flavour: nutty. Magickal: money and lust.
Shallot/bulb: (Allium) Medicinal: see Allium. Culinary: use same as onion. Magickal: purification.
Slippery Elm/bark: Medicinal: as a drink will induce sleep, is good for internal bleeding, for cough and typhoid fever. Actions: emollient, expectorant, nutrient. Culinary: ancient food source used like oatmeal (1 tsp powder to 1 pt boiling water and flavoured with cinnamon, nutmeg or lemon). Magickal: love.
Spearmint/herb: Medicinal: see peppermint but less powerful. Culinary: in teas and beverages. Magickal: healing, love and mental powers.
Star Anise/fruit: (Illicium verum) Medicinal: used for colic and rheumatism. Culinary: best if used whole in herbal teas, chicken, casseroles or as a substitute for anise. Flavour: very similar to anise. Magickal: psychic powers and luck.
Squash/fruit/flower: Culinary: wash and remove stems and stamens then cook and use in every thing from a side dish to a main dish. Flowers can be deep fried or used in salads. Magickal: see pumpkin
Sugar cane/cane: Culinary: as a sweetener. Magickal: love and lust.
Summer savory/leaves: (Satureja hortensis) Medicinal: good for use in cough syrups. Actions: carminative. Culinary: best if fresh or dried in pates, soups, meat, fish, butters, vinegars, poultry, stuffing, and bean dishes. Flavour: strong, so use sparingly, is a cross between thyme and mint, a bit milder than winter savory.

Sunflower/flower/seed: Medicinal: can be used to treat coughs due to infections. Actions: expectorant, diuretic. Culinary: when the flower is picked in the bud stage it is a substitute for artichokes and is steamed, once opened it can be used like chrysanthemums. The seed has a variety of uses in trail mix, salads, breads and cold soups. The oil is used in salads and cooking. Magickal: fertility, wishes, health and wisdom.
Sweet woodruff: Medicinal: used to thin blood clots in the legs. Actions: blood thinner. Culinary: used in desserts and breads and on sandwitches, has a sweet nutty flavour with a hint of vanilla. Magickal: carried to attract money and prosperity, promote victory, and guard against all harm.
Tamarind/bean: Medicinal: cools fevers, helps digestion, and is astringent. . Culinary: used in condiments, brown sauce, chutneys, as a flavouring in beverages, as a souring agent in curries, glazes and marinades for seafood, grilled fish or chicken. Magickal: love.
Tarragon/leaves: (Artemisia dracunculus cv. Sativa) Medicinal: As a tea 1 ½ tsp cut dried herb in a 1 ¾ cup boiled water, steep for 40 minutes and drink warm for insomnia, hyperactivity, depression or nervousness. To aid digestion, steep a handful of dried leaves in a jar with apple cider vinegar and let stand 7 hours, strain and seal. Take 1 Tbsp before each meal. Culinary: best if used fresh or frozen (Russian tarragon is not considered to be of culinary value). Is great in tartar sauce, as flavouring for cream sauces, egg dishes and seafood salads. Flavour: anise-like. Substitutes as chervil, dash fennel seed or dash anise seed. Magickal: peace
Tea/leaves: Medicinal: relieves migraines, relaxes the blood vessels, kills dental plaque. Actions:

Antioxidant. Culinary: as a tea or agent for other herbs. Magickal: riches, courage, strength.

Thyme/flower/herb: (Thymus vulgaris) Medicinal: As a tea, 1 tsp to ½ boiled water, to rid intestinal worms, mouthwash, bad breath, tooth decay, cold, flu or allergy symptoms, migraine headaches and stomach cramps. As a bath for nail fungus and athletes foot. As a douche. As a compress for bumps and bruises. As a adult health tonic, 6 sprigs of thyme in 1 ½ cups of brandy for 5 days, shaking daily, take 1 tsp every 3-4 hours when you feel a cold coming on. Action: Antibacterial, Antispasmodic (muscle relaxant) Antimicrobial. Culinary: best if used fresh or dried in omelettes, stews, bland soups, stuffing for chicken, flavouring in green salads and cooked vegetables. Flavour: minty and lemony. Substitute: basil, marjoram, oregano or savory. Magickal: health, healing, sleep, psychic powers, love, purification and courage.

Tuberous Begonia/flowers/stems: Medicinal: flower tea is used to promote blood circulation and eliminate toxins from the body. Culinary: petals are used in beverages, and summer salads due to their fruity, citrus flavour. Stems are used as a substitute for rhubarb. Warning: do NOT use if you suffer from gout, kidney stones or rheumatism as these contain oxalic acid. Magickal: protective charm.

Tulip/flowers: Culinary: great in green salads and sandwitches as they have a lettuce or cucumber like flavour. Magickal: Love

Turnip/root vegetables: Culinary: in soups and stews and sometimes mixed with potatoes. Magickal: protection and ending relationships.

Turmeric/root: (Curcuma domestica – related to ginger) Medicinal: As a tea with warm milk regulates menstrual cycle, As a paste out of powder and lime juice for any ulcerated skin condition (mumps, chicken pox, herpes, scabies etc) As a wash for discharges of conjunctivitis and opthamalia. For arthritis and rheumatism for inflamed joints. Added ½ tsp to daily morning juice can remove the fat around the liver. To enhance insulin production and metabolize blood glucose, take a pinch of cinnamon, 2 cloves, ½ bay leaf and 1 tsp turmeric. Warning: do not take if you are already taking insulin products. Actions: Antioxidant, Anti-inflammatory, insulin enhancer and regulator, food dye. Culinary: best if used dried and ground in curries, East Indian recipes and ballpark mustard. Magickal: purification, protection.

Vanilla/bean: (Vanilla planifolia – orchid) Medicinal: to quickly calm hysteria, soak a cotton ball, squeeze it out and place under the tongue (make sure it isn't made with alcohol if tending a child) Actions: Ant hysteria, sexual stimulant, Aromatic. Culinary: best if seeds are removed from whole bean, as a dried bean or in an extract. Great in coffee, desserts, ice cream, puddings and cakes. Flavour: sweet. Magickal: love, lust, and mental powers.

Vinegar/apple cider: Medicinal: 1 Tbsp of equal parts vinegar, honey and water is useful to reduce inflammation due to arthritis and cleanse the blood. Culinary: To wash fruits and vegetables: 1 part vinegar to 3 parts water removes traces of surface wax, pesticide residue, and 98 % of surface bacteria.

***Viper's bugloss:** (Echium Vulgare) Medicinal: breaks fevers, diuretic, expectorant, for use with inflammation, snake bites and to drive away melancholy and depression, to expel poisons or poisonous herbs from the body. Culinary: flowers can be added to cordials, crystallized, or added to salads. Magickal: exorcism, protection.

Violets/flowers/leaves: other names include Johnny jump-ups, violas and pansies. Medicinal: Violet salve brings a harmless cyst to a head- to make press out the juice of the violets and measure, and an equal measure of goat fat and one third as much olive oil as violet juice and boil down softly. Rub into the affected part and all around it – also good for headaches (rub onto forehead) and other sores. Culinary: for use in summer salads, iced drinks, desserts, frosted cakes, and sorbets. May be crystallized as well. Leaves taste like spinach and are great in salads and soups. Magickal: protection, luck, love, lust, wishes, peace and healing.

Black walnut/hulls: (juglans nigray) Medicinal: relieves athletes foot, and other fungal infections, parasites, abscesses and boils. Actions: Antifungal. Culinary: desserts, breads, pesto, soup, relish and sauces, meats, poultry, soups and stews. Magickal: abundance (hang a bag in your kitchen), health, mental powers, infertility and wishes, for love sneak a leaf of the tree in the shoe of those you desire, longevity.

***Watercress/herb: (Nasturtium officinale) Medicinal: used before or during cold an flu. Used in salves against bites, stings and to stop bleeding and reduce inflammation. Purifies the blood and is a tonic for the whole system. Valued for weight loss. Actions: antiviral, antibacterial, detoxifier, pain reliever. Vitamin C, and B17, minerals, expectorant. Culinary: used in sandwitches, salads, soups, stews and stir fry's. Can be used with pineapple and paw paw, pesto, omelettes, quiche, dips, stuffing,

casseroles and rice dishes. Magickal: divination, exorcism, protection, healing.
Wheat/grain: Culinary: used in crackers, breads, pies and cakes. Magickal: fertility and money.
White pepper/unripe seeds: (Piper nigrum – peeled and dried unripe peppercorns) Culinary: best if fresh ground and used as a condiment. Flavour: similar to black peppercorn but milder.
Winter Savory/leaves: (Satureja Montana) Medicinal: see Summer Savory – the winter variety is stronger. Culinary: best if used dried or fresh in pates, soups, meat, wild game, stews, fish and bean dishes. Flavour: strong, use sparingly, combination of thyme and mint. Magickal: see summer savory.
Wintergreen/herb: (Mint family) Medicinal: beneficial in acute rheumatism (must be taken internally in capsules 10 minims one daily) or steep berries in brandy and taken in very small quantities. Can be brewed as a tea and used as a wash for muscle ache and pains Caution: oils may cause is able to give rise to eruption on skin or in stomach. Actions: tonic, astringent, stimulant, aromatic. Culinary: in cold soups, teas and beverages and summer salads. Magickal: protection, healing and hex breaking.
Yarrow/flowers: (achillea millefolium) Medicinal: for use with fevers associated with colds and flu's, to fight infections due to surgery and cancers. 3 days before and operation take one pinch of yarrow daily- the first day in fennel tea – the next two in warmed wine, Then continue for 8 days after the operation as it protects against radiation damage and wound infection. Actions: Diaphoretic. Culinary: to make beer more intoxicating, brew with the hops. Magickal: courage, love, psychic powers and exorcism.

Yucca/flowers: Medicinal: Leaves soaked and used as a shampoo to strengthen hair; as a salve for sunburns and dry skin and creates a blue dye out of the ashes. As a salve it is beneficiary for inflammation and joint pain, as a tea it is beneficial cleanser for kidneys and toxins. Culinary: use just opened blossoms in the springtime for salads, they are mildly sweet and taste a bit like artichoke. Magickal: transmutation, protection and purification.

*** Nine Sacred Herbs

US/European Conversion table

1 teaspoon (tsp) = 1/3 Tablespoon (Tbsp) = 1/6 fluid ounce (oz) = 5 milliliters = .005 liters

1 Tablespoon (Tbsp) = 3 teaspoons (tsp) = ½ fluid ounce (oz) = 1/16 Cup (C) = 15 milliliters = .015 liters

1 fluid ounce (oz) = 6 teaspoons = 2 Tablespoons= 1/8 Cup = 1/32 fluid quart = 29.56 milliliters =.030 liters

1 Cup = 16 Tablespoons = 8 fluid ounces = 236 milliliters = .236 liters

1 fluid quart (qrt) = 64 Tablespoons = 32 fluid ounces = 4 Cups = 946 milliliters = .946 liters

1 milliliter (ml) = .203 or 1/5 tsp
1 liter (l) = 203.04 tsp = 67.68 Tbsp = 33.814 fl oz = 4.227 C = 1.057 qrt = 1000 milliliter

Tasseomancy - Reading Tea Leaves

To read tea leaves simply steep a heavy pinch of your loose leaf tea into your cup. It should fall to the bottom so you may drink it – make sure not to leave too many tears behind! But as always a few are needed in life. Then turn over your cup on your saucer and turn in a clockwise motion three times. Now look into your cup (like looking into the clouds) and see what figures come up and what they mean! Those closest to the handle are those closest to being, as the handle represents you and your question. All things need to be read together to understand the fullness of the meaning as many things have multiple meanings and must be deciphered through the abilities of the reader and how they adhere to the life of the readee-Have fun!

FIGURES

Angels – Hope, good news, good fortune, love, Radiance, happiness and peace

Artist – Happy nature, joy & beauty in life

Baby alone – Sadness and disappointment caused By those you love, money worries
Baby in arms- Reconciliation

Barber- New interests emerging

Bishop-Benevolence, authority, progress
  w/Cope & Miter-Preferment & honor

Bride-Wedding, coming joy, a rival for your Affections

Carpenter- You must work at getting things
  in order

Child-New plans and projects in the near future
  Running-bad news, warning of danger lurking
  Playing-tranquility, contentment and pleasure
  Blowing bubbles-sadness and joy
  Dancing with a doll-wish granted through
    unexpected means
  With Tambourine-good news, pleasure,
    light heart

Clergyman-A long standing feud will be reconciled

Clown-Your folly is apparent to everyone

Cobbler-A hard life, ill paid for your work, poor
  Health and constant struggle

Dancers-fulfillment of hopes and dreams, many
  Changes about to occur all necessary for
  Your success and happiness

Devil-Warning to reform your life, you must work
  to rip yourself from the grip of a bad
  influence before it's to late

Dwarf-Calamity, accident and disgrace

Elf-Be on guard or you will be the victim of an
  unpleasant practical joke

Faces-Invitations, social events
  Ugly-domestic disturbances, bad news
  Pretty-pleasure and love
  Two on one head-deception and falseness
  Bearded-health and strength with indolence and
      Vexation

Figures-Good omens, love and marriage
  Dancing- good news, happiness in love,
        friendship, unexpected invitations
  Flute player-Fertility, joy, music
  Jumping -Change will be to your advantage
  Kneeling-Take great care in to think over a
        new project well and seek advice
  Running-You will need to have all your wits
        about you in an emergency
  Twisted-Grievances, disturbance and
        Vexation

Giant-Serious obstacle is in your path

King on his throne-Security, peace, a high position
        may be attained through influential friends

Knight in Armor-Good fortune, success in love,
        loyalty of friends

Man-Expect a visitor
  Carrying a burden-Unhappy marriage or affair
  Carrying a mace-personal promotion or
        advancement for you are someone close
  Speaking from a platform-Public developments
        which concern you.

Mermaid-Warning of misfortune

Nun-You will be unjustly implied and undue Suspicion will loom over your head

Pedestrian-Good news, important appointment, Urgent business

Policeman-Beware of theft, underhanded practices, And trouble from those close to you

Pope-Gain, fortune and unexpected happiness

Queen-Security, peace, honor and attainment

Sailor-Interesting news from overseas

Shepherd-do not take any unnecessary risks

Skeleton-Secret information will disgust you

Soldier-Your friends are loyal and affectionate, Expect news quickly

Twins-perfection of happiness, sympathy turned Towards you, birth expected

Vampire-Sorrow and gloom, news of a death

Witch on a broom-You will prove yourself to Family and friends

Woman-Happiness and pleasure
  With dots-Wealth or children
  Carrying a burden-Unhappy marriage, affair
  Carrying a child-distress, illness, separation, Sadness
  Holding a mirror-Clairvoyance, predictions

AMPHIBIANS AND REPTILES

Alligator-Personal danger, distress, worries; Mental disturbance, possible catastrophe

Dragon-Great, sudden and dangers and changes

Frog – Change in residence, success in love and Business, new work or profession

Lizard – False friends who plot against you

Reptile-Misfortune, treachery, illness, quarrels

Serpent/Snake-Caution to avoid misfortune – Spiteful enemies, bad luck, illness and possible grave danger to you and yours

Toad-Deceit and unexpected enemies, malicious Talk from friends

Turtle/Tortoise - self - contained creative source, Attempting that which you have no Prior knowledge, possible wealth

Worms- Misfortune, treachery and evil plots by Secret foes

SPIDERS AND INSECTS

Ant-team player, worker

Bee-Success comes from your own abilities,
Many friends, enjoyment, full life
Hive-Eloquence, creative endeavors, attainment,
Forming and carrying through, power,
Honor

Beetle-Unrest, domestic tribulation, slander,
Abuse by friends, disagreements

Caterpillar-Be on your guard as unpleasant gossip
Has been spread about you by those you
Consider friendly through their own
Jealousy and envy

Dragonfly-Unexpected occurrences and events,
Advantageous opportunities, new
Belongings

Fly-Small vexations and annoyances which bother
you greatly, your success will bring about
Jealousy and unpleasantness in others

Grasshoppers-Poor harvest, severe illness, Call to
serve your nation

Scorpion-Be on your defense, self-protection

Spider-You will receive an inheritance or will
triumph in a money settlement

Spiders-Profitable transactions, much wealth

LAND CREATURES

Apes-Secret enemies, malicious, slander, anxiety, Dangerous person, despondency

Ass- Misfortune overcome

Badger- Single life of freedom, health, success

Bat- Fruitless endeavors, trouble at home, sickness, Possible death

Bear – Prolonged travel, power, adaptability

Beasts- Misfortune

Beaver – You are called to gather and build

Buffalo – Unexpected unusual happening

Bull – Slander, misfortune, pain, personal danger, Illness

Calf- Gentleness and kindness are needed

Camel – Burdens, responsibility, frustrated plans, Unexpected monies

Cat – Difficulties caused by treachery, trickery, meanness, and quarrels amoung relations
  Jumping – worries and difficulties
  Coming towards you-bringing wealth
  Turning from you-taking your wealth with it

Cow – prosperity and prosperous transactions

Deer – Warning that new ventures will fail
  Running-Failure at undoing past mistakes
  Dead-You will cause distress to a loved one,
      Although you won't have meant to

Dog – Adverse conditions approaching; misfortune,
      Money troubles, broken heart, missed
      Chances and opportunities
  Large-Protection of good friends
  Small-You will be vexed and impatient

Elephant – Power, travel, promotion, happiness,
      Good health and stability in love

Ferret-Your enemies are plotting your distress
      Through their jealousy

Fox-Theft, trickery and treachery by a trusted friend
      Or dependant

Goat-A new enterprise is risky and will wield
      Misfortune

Hare-Reunion with a long lost friend
  Running-A pleasant journey with friends
  Dead-Money shall be acquired through business

Hedgehog-A confirmed bachelor marries

Horse-Comforts, loyal friends, pleasure
  Galloping-A rushing in of events and changes in
      Your life of which you have no control

Kangaroo-A rival in business or love or you will be
      Surprised by interesting news

Lamb-A doubtful undertaking will be successful
 Prancing-Trouble will lead to contentment and
   happiness and other beneficial results

Lion-High hopes, excellent prospects, you will
   attain greatness through powerful friends

Lynx-Treachery, episodes of a painful nature,
   Divorce, estrangement, separation

Monkey-Unpleasant rumors and scandals will be
   Publicly spread about you or yours, grief
   And pain
 On a Organ-Difficult circumstances and hard
   Struggles are ahead

Mouse-Danger of poverty through theft or
   Swindling so be on guard

Otter-Those you regard as loyal and affectionate
   Will be spiteful towards you

Pig-Gain and success in agriculture, a present of
   Money of legacy, faithful over and
   Envious friends

Ox in his stall-Domestic peace and abundance

Panther-An honorable friend will prove
   To be treacherous

Rabbit- Illness of a child, quick medical attention
 Dead-Boring domestic duties, money worries
 Standing up-New plans bring success
 Rabbits-You must be contented with simple
   Amusements of your own

Rhinoceros-Heed the warnings of friends and
  Family as a risky endeavor will prove
  Fruitless and devastating

Tiger-Those who should be protecting you will
  Place you in peril through their own folly

Unicorn – Secrets kept, a secret wedding

Weasel- Sly and cunning behavior from someone
  You associate with but don't suspect

Wolf-Beware of heard-hearted neighbors, friend
  And their jealousies

Zebra – Something you have long awaited is in
  Sight but it proves not worth the wait

FLYING CREATURES

Albatross-Distress, sadness, sorrow, possible death

Bat - guardian of the night, cleaner

Bird- lucky sign, good news, fortunate journey
   Feeding young- Desires fulfilled after waiting
   Of Paradise- Difficulties vanishing, future of
       Comfort and pleasure
   On Perch- Incoming pleasant news
   Caged- Wish prevented
   Cage door opened- Obstacles have been removed
   Nest-Happy discovery, fortunate enterprise, love,
       Good omen, friends, increase of fortune

Butterfly – Passing pleasures and success,
       Flirtations and admirers

Chicken- New interests and pleasures to come
   Roosting-Domestic trials and disturbances
   Flying-Troublesome matters will come a head

Doves-Personal happiness, assurance of love,
       Peaceful circumstances, high ideals and
       Progress, reconciliation, comfort and
       Hope, successful business

Dragonfly-Unexpected circumstances and events
       With advantageous opportunities, new
       Possessions

Eagle-Beneficial changes, realization of dreams,
  Possibility of inheritance
Flying-Coming of wealth and change of residence
On its nest-A life of wealth and ease though
  Associations with those of wealth and
  Honor
Dead-Public loss and mourning
With a Vulture-Death of a Monarch

Falcon-Be on your guard as you have a persistent
  Enemy who stops at nothing

Goose-Proceed with caution or an otherwise
  Successful venture will be a bad mistake
Geese-Arrival of troublesome visitors

Hawk-There are those working against you to place
  You in awkward and embarrassing
  Situations and promote themselves

Hen-Increase of wealth or and family addition
  Roosting-Domestic annoyances and lack of
    Money
  Hens-Comfort and domestic peace

Magpie- One for sorrow, two for mirth, three for a
  Wedding, four for a birth

Ostrich-Achievement in creative endeavors
  Running-Public upheavals and rumors

Owl – Warning of sickness, poverty, disgrace,
  Deception in love, warn against new
  Endeavors, unpleasant rumors
  Flying- News of grief

Parrot-Foreign travel and new friends, mental Energy, inclination to spread slander

Peacock-Property acquired, prosperous and happy Marriage

Pegasus – Storms and lightning

Pelican-Loneliness, separation, yearning
   Flying- News from those far away

Pheasant/Quail-Good fortune and new friends
   Flying- Good news

Pigeons-Reconciliation with someone dear
   Flying-Important news
   Resting-Domestic bliss, wealth in business

Raven- Gloom and despondency, disappointment in Love, separation, failure in work, possible Death looming

Robin-Much good fortune, good fortune and Happiness in love

Rooster/Cock: Forthcoming good news and Triumph

Seagull-Storms
   Flying-News from overseas

Thunderbird – Rain

Vulture-Warning of impeding evil and unrest, Powerful enemies, possible death
   Flying-tragedy, sorrow and tears

SEA CREATURES

Crab-Strife and family disagreements, an enemy

Dolphin – Pleasurable journey on water

Eels-Malicious tongues and treacherous friends

Fish- Good news from far away
  With dots-emigration

Limpets-Good luck and big haul, also you will not
  Possess a valuable secret which you desire

Oysters- Enjoyment of expensive things,
  Appreciation of things comes later in life
  Not in your youth

Penguin-Interesting news, expeditions, discoveries

Prawns/Shrimp-Pleasures, presents and
  Satisfactory arrangements

Salmon–Persistence is called for to reach your
  Dreams

Seahorse- Show confidence and graces will follow

Shark – Danger is lurking be attentive

Starfish- Good luck

Whale – You will acquire great wisdom

SYMBOLS

Anchor-Luck, success in love or business
    If blurred then reverse

Arch- Journey, desired wish developing,
    Ambitions triumph

Balloon-Little success after much effort

Barrel-Festivity outdoors, prosperity

Basket-An addition to the family

Bath-Grief and dismay with comfort

Bear Paw - strength, mobility

Bell-Amazing news

Besoms-Warning to stay out of the
    Business of others

Bones-Misfortune overcome with courage

Bonnet- The best of life is yet to come

Book open-desire for information, alert mind
  Book closed-expectancy

Bookcase-Pleasing success through study and
    Perseverance

Boomerang-Unexpected developments, travel

Boots-Fortunate business, good income, Gratification

Bottle-Happy days

Bow-Reunion after absence

Bower-Happiness in love

Box open- troubled love affair
   Box closed-You will find something you lost

Bracelet-A discovery made too late

Bricks-New plans, enterprises, prosperity

Bridge- favorable journey

Broom-Be careful with your choice of friends, Avoid rushing in or regret

Building-Removal

Buoy-Hope, friends that will stand by you

Bush-Invitation, special enjoyments

Buttons-Arrangements, plans without definition

Buffalo Skull - sacredness, reverence for life

Cabinet-Unexpected fortune and discovery, much Pleasure and satisfaction, possible wealth And prosperity

Candle-Trials, worries, illness, look at the situation differently for better perception

Cap-Be cautious of your dealings for that which You seek to hide will become known

Car-Approaching wealth or visits from friends

Canoe-New friendship will lead to love

Castle-Unexpected fortune and legacy

Cathedral-Great prosperity, contentment, and happiness with those you love

Cauldron- Carefully consider any new Opportunities

Cave-Call to come out of hiding and give yourself a push to attain greater rewards

Celtic Knot - long life, eternity, peace

Chain-Engagement, wedding, union or partnership
  Entangled-Dilemma will tax your ingenuity
  Long and Thick-A union you wish undone
  Broken-Troubles await

Cherries- Love, happiness and health

Church-Courage, honor and legacy

Circle-Money or presents, social engagements, loyal friends

Clouds-Disappointment, failure, dismay, trouble

Coat-Sadness in parting, distress, failure

Coffee Pot-Dependence on comfort and inability to succeed on your own

Coffin-Long sickness, impending death of a someone you are close to

Comb-Misplaced confidence in a friend or Associate

Comet-Separation, misfortune and trouble

Compass-A life spent in interesting activities and travel

Corn-Wealth and success

Cornucopia-Great happiness and success

Cross-Hindrances and obstacles and in the way of your desires, sorrow and misfortune may follow

Crown-Advancement, success, honor and attainment of position

Curtain-Someone is hiding a matter from you that you need to learn

Dish-anxiety and loss in household matters

Dustpan and Brush-Domestic tribulation

Ear (large)-shocking scandal or abuse
Ear (normal)-pleasant news, valuable information

Easel-Union and increase

Egg-New ideas, plans or birth
   Cups-Escape from natural disaster

Eye-Difficulties solved, depth of character, love
   Glasses-Beneficial discovery

Feathers-Achievement, prosperity, success, Courage

Fireplace-Home interests, small duties, simple Pleasures

Flag-Danger, rebellion, war and wounds inflicted by an enemy

Flowers-Good fortune, success, happy union

Foot-journey
   Swollen-injury or accident
   Feet-Decisiveness required for change

Fork-Flattery leads to harm

Fountain-Happiness, Success in love and marriage, prosperity in business, good fortune in all undertakings, unexpected legacy

Four Leaf Clover - good luck

Fruit-Forthcoming prosperity and advancement

Garters-Contempt for feminine weakness

Gate-Excellent opportunity awaits
  Massive, high-Restriction and imprisonment

Grindstone-Indiscretion and its aftermath

Guitar-Strong power of attraction, pleasant adventures and a happy love affair

Gun/Pistol-Grave danger, sudden calamity, Possible violent death

Hammer-Troublesome tasks that need be done

Hammock-A mournful ending to something you looked forward to

Hand-Good fellowship, loyalty, affection, conclusion of a meeting
  Bell-Your ambition is gratified, it is time to startle the world by your great discovery or amazing theory
  Cuffs-Disgrace, imprisonment, misfortune
  Hopi Hand-Creation and life

Harp-Success in love and marriage

Harvest- You will sow that which you have reaped

Hat- Luck and success in new enterprises or business, arrival of a visitor

Head (large)-Family trouble and serious illness
Head (small)-Waning abilities and power
Heads-Mental distress or derangement

Heart - Lover, fondness
   w/Dots-Money
   w/ Ring- Marriage
   Blurred- Your lover is fickle

Hoe- Good health, cheerfulness and many things occurring that will need your attention

Honeycomb-Prosperous undertakings, honor, renown and many delights

Horns-Powerful enemy and unpleasantness

Horseshoe-A successful journey and union, achievement of a wish, good luck in all undertakings,
   Double-Arrival of desires hastened
   Reversed-Upset, disappointment, vexation
   Broken-Dilemma, trails, discomforts

Hourglass- Do not delay your plans or Arrangements as illness or accident could Easily follow

House-Success in business transactions

Initials-Indicates places and people to come

Ivy-Honor and happiness through faithful friends

Kettle-Illness, trouble and possible death

Key-Circumstances will improve, path is smooth, hoped for success is realized
  At a distance-Need for assistance of good and influential friends in difficulty
  Crossed -Authority, power, honor, assurance of comfort, help in difficult times
  Hole-Need for caution as someone you would not suspect is untrustworthy
  Lock and Key-Warned against losses of value

Kite-Vanishing pleasures and benefits due to slander and scandal

Knife-Quarrels, broken friendships, tears

Lines-Journeys and direction
  Wavy-troublesome journey with losses
  Dotted-Journey with many stops or destinations

Looking glass/Mirror-Desire to know the truth Prophetic dreams

Magnet-Irresistible attraction to someone in which you will immensely dislike

Magnifying glass-Your exaggeration amounts to untruthfulness

Mallet-Wise conclusion after difficulty

Maypole- Little satisfaction will come from your small amusements as you crave more

Medal-Rewards for past industry come by future prosperity

Medicine bottle- Illness where a doctor is required

Moon-Good news, prosperity, romance, public recognition and honor

Mortar-Illness where herbs are the answer

Mountain-Great ambitions realized by the Influence of powerful friends
Mountains-Powerful enemies and obstructions

Mug/Cup- Merry meeting

Mushroom-Great success achieved through small risks, quarrels and broken engagements

Nail-Toothache and dentistry needed

Necklace-A good present or money
  Broken-Broken bond that became unendurable

Needles-Mischief, deceit, and disappointment

Nose (large)-Useless and profitless activity
Nose (crooked)-Wayward and untrustworthy person
Nose(long, thin)-You change you ideas and alter your life accordingly

Numbers-Amounts of money, days or weeks for news or journeys, or lucky or unlucky circumstances.

Oak Tree-Good omen of wealth, strength. attainment, happiness and prosperity

Onions-Treacherous friends will unveil your secrets

Palm Tree- Good luck, success in any undertaking, marriage or children to come, increase in wealth, honor and fame

Pears-Improves social condition, new plans and birth, success and riches

Pestle-Decisive measure, remedy for illness to come

Piano-Advancement because of gained opportunities

Pin cushion- A well regulated household due to thrift and order

Pine Tree- Happiness followed by regret

Pitcher-Desire to relieve an dull and monotonous life by throwing your life into unnecessary work

Pitchfork-Stirring up a feud may be the only path to a peaceful conclusion

Plate-Everything will remain ordinary

Potato-Your daily life requires patience money difficulties

Purse-Caution to take measures to avoid carelessness as it will lead to theft

Pyramids-Attainment of honor, fame and wealth

Rake-Your persevering nature will bring you a good amount of success in whatever you undertake, also luck in speculation

Razor-Disagreement, separation, quarrels and the need to stay out of others affairs

Ring-Marriage
  w/Initial- indicates future spouse
  w/clouds-Unhappy marriage
  w/dots-Business contract
  w/Figures-Wedding forthcoming
  at the bottom of the cup- Will be called off

River-Trouble, perplexity, illness and bereavement

Rocket-Joy and gladness to come

Rolling pin-You will smooth out your difficulties

Rose-Good fortune, joy and love

Sack- Most fortunate event coming

Saddle-Success I solving a troublesome matter

Scepter-Distinction and honor to follow

Scissors-Friction, disputes, quarrels, and trouble

Screw-Troublesome affairs and vexations

Ship-Successful journey, voyage, news

Shoes-Unconventional pleasure and amusements

Star of David – Incoming favorable union

Telephone- Considerable inconvenience through forgetfulness

Thumb-You prove yourself to those who were once apposed to you

Toadstool-You are warned against rash and unguarded statements, slander, and gossip

Tongue-You are called to make amends for your indiscreet unkind words and mischief

Torch- Undiscovered talent and good fortune

Tower-An opportunity rises you to a good position

Trees-Good health, prosperity, happiness
  w/Dots-Inheritance of property

Triangles- Fortunate meeting, good luck, unexpected legacy

Trident-Success, honor and promotion

Trowel-Good weather and mildness

Trunk- Arrivals and departures, travel

Tub-Evil is lurking

Tunnel-Caution to avoid making the wrong decision in a matter of importance

Umbrella-Bad luck, annoyance and trouble

Urn-A sign of illness

Vampire-Gloom, sadness, news of a death

Vase-Promise of good health

Vegetables-Times of hard work followed by leisure and monetary ease

Violin-Coming success and pleasure

Wagon-Approaching poverty, take measures

Walking Stick-The arrival of a male visitor

Wedding cake-Speedy and prosperous union

Wheel-Prosperous career or inheritance
  Broken-Disappointments due to loss of expected funds

Windmill-Success in a doubtful enterprise

Wreath-Union and happiness

Yacht-Increased wealth, pleasure and happiness

Wolf Paw – Freedom and success attained with guidance

Stone Soup:
The Grimoire of the Kitchen Hedge Witch

The name "Grimoire" is derived from the word "Grammar". A grammar is a description of a set of symbols and how to combine them to create well-formed sentences. A Grimoire is, appropriately enough, a description of a set of magickal symbols and how to combine them properly. Most of the texts linked below are descriptions of traditional European ritual magick, which is based on Judeo-Christianity. Even though this must not be confused with neo-Paganism, many of the neo-Pagan traditions use similar rituals and techniques, albeit with a different (usually Celtic) vocabulary and have their references and workings herein as well.

To Remove an Unwanted Visitor
Go out the front door (or the door they came in) and sweep from inside the house out the door and down the walk or steps. Place your broom by that door and this should speed you visitors on their way and give you peace of mind. Try to do this without being seen if possible.

Charm to Gain an Advantage over a Man of superior Strength

I [name] breathe upon thee. Three drops of blood I take from thee: the first out of thy heart, the other out of thy liver, and the third out of thy vital powers; and in this I deprive thee of thy strength and manliness:

Hbbi Massa danti Lantien. I. I. I.

Lost and Found Spell To find whatsoever is lost – chant this spell:
Guiding Angels, I ask your charity
Lend me your focus and your clarity
Bring to me (name what is lost) at this time
Restoring me that and my peace of mind
With harm to none, this spell is done
Let it not be reversed
Or placed unto me as any curse
Let no evil come near
Or other wise be lurking
May all astrological correspondences
Be correct for this working
And so by the law of three
As I will it so mote it be

Charm Against Fire Arms I
Three holy drops of blood have passed down the holy cheeks of the Lord God, and these three holy drops of blood are placed before the touchhole. As surely as our dear lady was pure from all men, as surely shall no fire or smoke pass out of this barrel. Barrel, do thou give neither fire, nor flame, nor heat. Now I will walk out, because the Lord God goeth before me; God the Son is with me, and God the Holy Ghost is about me forever.

To Make a Wick which is Never Consumed
Take an ounce of asbestos and boil it in a quart of strong lye for two hours; then pour off the lye and clarify what remains by pouring rain-water on it three or four times, after which you can form a wick from it which will never be consumed by the fire.

To Make a Wand for searching for Water or Ore
On the first night of Christmas, between 11 and 12 o'clock, break off from any tree a young twig of one year's growth, in the three highest names (Father. Son. and Holy Ghost), at the same time facing toward sunrise. Whenever you apply this wand in searching for anything apply it three times. The twig must be forked, and each end of the fork must be held in one hand, so that the third and thickest part of it stands up, but do not hold it too tight. Strike the ground with the thickest end, and that which you desire will appear immediately, if there is any in the ground where you strike. The words to be spoken when the wand is thus applied are as follows: Archangel Gabriel, I conjure thee in the name of God, the Almighty, to tell me, is there any water here or not? do tell me! + + +

If you are searching for Iron or Ore, you have to say the same, only mention the name of what you are searching for.

Charm against Fire Arms II
Blessed is the hour in which Jesus Christ was born; blessed is the hour in which Jesus Christ was born; blessed is the hour in which Jesus Christ was born; blessed is the hour in which Jesus Christ has arisen from the dead; blessed are these three hours over thy gun, that no shot or ball shall fly toward me, and neither my skin, nor my hair, nor my blood, nor my flesh be injured by them, and that no kind of weapon or metal shall do me any harm, so surely as the Mother of God shall not bring forth another son. + + +. Amen.

A Charm against Misfortune
The heavenly and holy trumpet blow every ball and misfortune away from me. I seek refuge beneath the tree of life which bears twelve fold fruits. I stand behind the holy altar of the Christian Church. I commend myself to the Holy Trinity. I [name] hide myself beneath the holy corpse of Jesus Christ. I commend myself unto the wounds of Jesus Christ, that the hand of no man might be able to seize me, or to bind me, or to cut me, or to throw me, or to beat me, or to overcome me in any way whatever, so help me. [N.]

To Charm Enemies, Robbers and Murderers
God be with you, brethren; stop, ye thieves, robbers, murderers, horsemen, and soldiers, in all humility, for we have tasted the rosy blood of Jesus. Your rifles and guns will be stopped up with the holy blood of Jesus; all swords and arms are made harmless by the five holy wounds of Jesus. There are three roses upon the heart of God; the first in beneficent, the other is omnipotent; the third is his holy will. You thieves must therefore stand under it, standing still as long as I will, In the name of God the Father, Son and Holy Ghost; you are conjured and made to stand.

Charm Against Fire Arms III
I (name) conjure ye guns, swords and knives, as well as all other kinds of arms, by the spear that pierced the side of God, and opened it so that blood and water could flow out, that ye do not injure me, a servant of God, in the + + +. I conjure ye, by Saint Stephen, who was stoned by the Virgin, that ye cannot injure me who am a servant of God, in the name of + + +. Amen.

Protection Against all Weapondry
Jesus, God and man, do thou protect me against all manner of guns, fire-arms, long or short, of any kind of metal. Keep thou thy fire, like the Virgin Mary, who kept her fire both before and after her birth. May Christ bind up all fire-arms after the manner of his having bound up himself in humility while in the flesh. Jesus, do thou render harmless all arms and weapons, like unto the husband of Mary the mother of God, he having been harmless likewise. Furthermore, do thou guard the three holy drops of blood which Christ sweated on the Mount of Olives. Jesus Christ! do thou protect me against being killed and against burning fires. Jesus, do thou not suffer me to be killed, much less to be damned, without having received the Lord's Supper. May God the Father, Son, and Holy Ghost, assist me in this. Amen.

A Charm Against Ball or Blade
In the name of J. J. J. Amen. I (*name*); Jesus Christ is the true salvation; Jesus Christ governs, reigns, defeats and conquers every enemy, visible or invisible; Jesus, be thou with me at all times, forever and ever, upon all roads and ways, upon the water and the land, on the mountain and in the valley, in the house and in the yard, in the whole world wherever I am, stand, run, ride or drive; whether I sleep or wake, eat or drink, there be thou also, Lord Jesus Christ, at all times, late and early, every hour, every moment; and in all my goings in or goings out. Those five holy red wounds, oh, Lord Jesus Christ, may they guard me against all fire-arms, be they secret or public, that they cannot injure me or do me any harm whatever, in the name of + + +. May Jesus, with his guardianship and

protection, shield me (*name*) always from daily commission of sins, worldly injuries and injustice, from contempt, from pestilence and other diseases, from fear, torture, and great suffering, from all evil intentions, from false tongues and old clatter-brains; and that no kind of fire-arms can inflict any injury to my body, do thou take care of me. + + +. And that no band of thieves nor Gypsies, highway robbers, incendiaries, witches and other evil spirits may secretly enter my house or premises, nor break in; may the dear Virgin Mary, and all children who are in heaven with God, in eternal joys, protect and guard me against them; and the glory of God the Father shall strengthen me, the. wisdom of God the Son shall enlighten me, and the grace of God the Holy Ghost shall empower me from this hour unto all eternity. Amen.

To Charm Fire Arms IV
The blessing which came from heaven at the birth of Christ be with me (*name*). The blessing of God at the creation of the first man be with me; the blessing of Christ on being imprisoned, bound, lashed, crowned so dreadfully, and beaten, and dying on the cross, be with me; the blessing which the Priest spoke over the tender, joyful corpse of our Lord Jesus Christ, be with me; the constancy of the Holy Mary and all the saints of God. of the three holy kings, Caspar, Melchior and Balthasar, be with me; the holy four Evangelists, Matthew, Mark, Luke and John, be with me; the Archangels St. Michael, St. Gabriel, St. Raphael and St. Uriel, be with me; the twelve holy messengers of the Patriarchs and all the Hosts of Heaven, be with me; and the inexpressible number of all the Saints be with me. Amen.

**Papa, R. tarn, Tetregammate Angen.
Jesus Nazarenus, Rex Judeorum.**

A Charm to be carried About a Person
Carry these words about you, and nothing can hit you: Ananiah, Azariah, and Missel, blessed be the Lord, for he has redeemed us from hell, and has saved us from death, and he has redeemed us out of the fiery furnace and has preserved us even in the midst of the fire; in the same manner may it please him the Lord that there be no fire.

```
            I
    N       I       R
            I
```

To Spell Bind a Thief so they Cannot Stir
This benediction must be spoken on a Thursday morning, before sunrise and in the open air:
"Thus shall rule it, God the Father, the Son, and the Holy Ghost. Amen. Thirty-three Angels speak to each other coming to administer in company with Mary. Then spoke dear Daniel, the holy one: Trust, my dear woman, I see some thieves coming who intend stealing your dear babe; this I cannot conceal from you. Then spake our dear Lady to Saint Peter: I have bound with a band, through Christ's hand; therefore, my thieves are bound even by the hand of Christ, if they wish to steal mine own, in the house, in the chest, upon the meadow or fields, in the woods, in the orchard, in the vineyard, or in the

garden, or wherever they intend to steal. Our dear Lady said: Whoever chooses may steal; yet if anyone does steal, he shall stand like a buck, he shall stand like a stake, and shall count all the stones upon the earth, and all the stars in the heavens. Thus I give thee leave, and command every spirit to be master over every thief, by the guardianship of Saint Daniel,

p. 46

and by the burden of this world's goods. And the countenance shall be unto thee, that thou canst not move from the spot, as long as my tongue in the flesh shall not give thee leave. This I command thee by the Holy Virgin Mary, the Mother of God, by the power and might by which he has created heaven and earth, by the host of all the angels, and by all the saints of God the Father, the Son, and the Holy Ghost. Amen." If you wish to set the thief free, you must tell him to leave in the name of St. John.

Charm Against Weapons

I (*name*) conjure thee, sword or knife, as well as all other weapons, by that spear which pierced Jesus' side, and opened it to the gushing out of blood and water, that he keep me from injury as one of the servants of God. + + + Amen.

Charm Against Murderers

The peace of our Lord Jesus Christ be with me [*name*]. Oh shot, stand still! in the name of the mighty prophets Agtion and Elias, and do not kill me! oh shot, stop short. I conjure you by heaven and earth, and by the last judgment, that you do no harm unto me, a child of God. + + + Amen.

Charm Against Thieves
There are three lilies standing upon the grave of the Lord our God; the first one is the courage of God, the other is the blood of God, and the third one is the will of God. Stand still, thief! No more than Jesus Christ stepped down from the cross, no more shalt thou move from this spot; this I command thee by the four evangelists and elements of heaven, there in the river, or in the shot, or in the judgment, or in the sight. Thus I conjure you by the last judgment to stand still and not to move, until I see all the stars in heaven and the sun rises again. Thus I stop by running and jumping and command it in the name of + + +. Amen.
This must be repeated three times.

Charm for making Divinatory Wands
In making divinatory wands, they must be broken as before directed, and while breaking and before using them, the following words must be spoken:
Divining rod, do thou keep that power,
Which God gave unto thee at the very first hour.

Charm for the Liberation of prisoners
Once sat women, They sat here, then there.
Some fastened bonds, Some impeded an army,
Some unraveled fetters: Escape the bonds,
flee the enemy!

To Attach a Dog to a Person
Try to draw some of your blood, and let the dog eat it along with his food, and he will stay with you. Or scrape the four corners of your table while you are eating, and continue to eat with the same knife after having scraped the corners of the table. Let the dog eat those scrapings, and he will stay with you.

Charm for Horse Healing
Phol and Wodan rode to the woods,
Then, Balder's foal wrenched his foot.
Then did Sinthgunt enchant it,
(so did) Sunna her sister,
then did Freya enchant it.
(so did) Fulla her sister,
then did Wodan enchant it,
as he well could:
If a bone-wrenching,
if a blood-wrenching,
if a limb-wrenching:
Bone to bone,
blood to blood,
Limb to limb,
As if bonded.

Charm against Thieves and Enemies
There walk out during this day and night, that thou mayest not let any of my enemies,, or thieves, approach me, if they do not intend to bring me what was spent from the holy altar. Because God the Lord Jews is ascended into heaven in his living body. O Lord, this is good for me this day and night. + + + Amen.

Charm of Protection
In the name of God I walk out. God the Father be with me, and God the Holy Ghost be by my side. Who ever is stronger than these three persons may approach my body and my life; yet whoso is not stronger than these three would much better let me be. J. J. J. (J. denotes Jesus)

A Benediction to Prevent Fire
"The bitter sorrows and the death of our dear Lord Jesus Christ shall prevail. Fire and wind and great heat and all that is within the power of these elements, I command thee, through the Lord Jesus Christ, who has spoken to the winds and the waters, and they obeyed him. By these powerful words spoken by Jesus, I command, threaten, and inform thee, fire, flame, and heat, and your powers as elements, to flee forthwith, The holy, rosy blood of our dear Lord Jesus Christ may rule it. Thou, fire, and wind, and great beat, I command thee, as the Lord did, by his holy angels, command the great heat in the fiery oven to leave those three holy men, Shadrach and his companions, Meshach and Abednego, untouched, which was done accordingly. Thus thou shalt abate, thou fire, flame, and great heat, the Almighty God having spoken in creating. the four elements, together with heaven and earth; Fiat! Fiat! Fiat! that is: It shall be in the name of God the Father, the Son, and the Holy Ghost, Amen.

Charm to Prevent being Cheated, Charmed or Bewitched and to be all times Blessed
Like unto the cup and the wine, and the holy supper, which our dear Lord Jesus Christ gave unto his dear disciples on Maunday Thursday, may the Lord Jesus guard me in daytime, and at night, that no dog may bite me, no wild beast tear me to pieces, no tree fall on me, no water rise against me, no fire-arms injure me, no weapons, no steel, no iron, cut me, no fire burn me, no false sentence fall upon me, no false tongue injure me, no rogue enrage me, and that no fiends, no witchcraft and enchantment can harm me. Amen.

Charm of Protection against Blades
I conjure thee, sword, sabre or knife, that mightest injure or harm me, by the priest of all prayers, who had gone into the temple at Jerusalem, and said: An edged sword shall pierce your soul that you may not injure me, who am a child of God.

The Great Charm of Protection

Dullix, ix, ux. Yea, you can't come over Pontio; Pontio is above Pilato. + + +

Charm for Binding Wounds
Speak the following: "This wound I tie up in three names, in order that thou mayest take from it heat, water, falling off of the flesh, swelling, and all that may be injurious about the swelling, in the name of the Holy Trinity." This must be spoken three times; then draw a string three times around the wound, and put it under the corner of the house toward the East, and say: "I put thee there, + + + in order that thou mayest take unto thyself the gathered water, the swelling, and the running, and all that may be injurious about the wound. Amen." Then repeat the Lord's Prayer and some good hymn.

Salve to Heal Wounds I
Take tobacco, green or dry; if green a good handful, if dry, two ounces; together with this take a good handful of elder leaves, fry them well in butter, press it through a cloth, and you may. use it in a salve. This will heal up a wound in a short time. Or go to a white oak tree that stands pretty well isolated, and scrape off the rough bark from the eastern side of the tree; then cut off the inner bark, break it into small pieces, and boil it until all the

strength is drawn out; strain it through a piece of linen, and boil it again, until it becomes as thick as tar; then take out as much as you need, and put to it an equal proportion of sheep-tallow, rosin and wax, and work them together until they form a salve. This salve you put on a piece of linen, very thinly spread, and lay it on the wound, renewing it occasionally till the wound is healed up.

Or take a handful of parsley, pound it fine, and work it to a salve with an equal proportion of fresh butter. This salve prevents mortification and heals very fast.

Salve to Heal Wounds II
Take tobacco, green or dry; if green a good handful, if dry, two ounces; together with this take a good handful of elder leaves, fry them well in butter, press it through a cloth, and you may. use it in a salve. This will heal up a wound in a short time.

Or go to a white oak tree that stands pretty well isolated, and scrape off the rough bark from the eastern side of the tree; then cut off the inner bark, break it into small pieces, and boil it until all the strength is drawn out; strain it through a piece of linen, and boil it again, until it becomes as thick as tar; then take out as much as you need, and put to it an equal proportion of sheep-tallow, rosin and wax, and work them together until they form a salve. This salve you put on a piece of linen, very thinly spread, and lay it on the wound, renewing it occasionally till the wound is healed up.

Or take a handful of parsley, pound it fine, and work it to a salve with an equal proportion of fresh butter. This salve prevents mortification and heals very fast.

Ointment of Albertus Magnus

It says: If you burn a large frog to ashes, and mix the ashes with water, you will obtain an ointment that will, if put on any place covered with hair, destroy the hair and prevent it from growing again.

Peace Stone of Albertus Magnus

If you find the stone which a vulture has in his knees, and which you may find by looking sharp, and put it in the victuals of two persons who hate each other, it causes them to make up and be good friends.

Amulet Against Evil

```
                   I
          N        I        R
                   I
    Sanctus                 Spiritus
                   I
          N        I        R
                   I
```

All this be guarded here in time, and there in eternity. Amen. You must write all the above on a piece of white paper and carry it about you. The characters or letters above signify: "God bless me here in time, and there eternally."

Charm to Protection for People and Animals

To be written and placed in the stable, or placed on the bed stead. "Trotter Head, I forbid thee my house and premises; I forbid thee my horse and cow-stable; I forbid thee my bedstead, that thou mayest not breathe upon me; breathe into some other house, until thou hast ascended every hill, until thou hast counted every fence-post, and until thou hast crossed every water. And thus dear day may come again into my house, in the name of God the Father, the Son, and the Holy Ghost. Amen."
This will certainly protect and free all persons and animals from all evil set against them.

Charm Against Mishaps and Dangers I the Home

Sanct Matheus, Sanct Marcus, Sanct Lucas, Sanct Johannis

Charm of Protection Against Sickness and Theft

**Ito, alto Massa Dandi Bando, III. Ament
J. R. N. R. J.** Our Lord Jesus Christ stepped into the hall, and the Jews searched him everywhere. Thus shalt those who now speak evil of me with their false tongues, and contend against me, one day bear sorrows, be silenced, dumbstruck, intimidated, and abused, forever and ever, by the glory of God. The glory of God shall assist me in this. Do thou aid me J. J. J. forever and ever. Amen

Gypsy Charm of Protection
Like unto the prophet Jonas, as a type of Christ, who was guarded for three days and three nights in the belly of a whale, thus shall the Almighty God, as a Father, guard and protect me from all evil. J.J.J.

Charm to Banish Fear, Fancies and Collect Fish
Whenever you hold stinging nettle in your hand together with Millefolium, you are safe from all fears and fancies that frequently deceive men. If you mix it with a decoction of the hemlock, and rub your hands with it, and put the rest in water that contains fish, you will find the fish to collect around your hands. Whenever you pull your hands out of the water, the fish disappear by returning to their former places.

Red Dye
For each pound of cloth, soak half a pound of madder in a brass kettle over night, with sufficient warm water to cover the cloth you intend to dye. Next morning put in two ounces of madder compound for every pound of madder. Wet your cloth and wring it out in clean water, then put it into the dye. Place the kettle over the fire, and bring it slowly to a scalding heat, which will take about half an hour; keep at this heat half an hour, if a light red is wanted, and longer if a dark one, the color depending on the time it remains in the dye.
When you have obtained the color, rinse the cloth immediately in cold water.

Scarlet Dye
Bring to a boiling heat, in a brass kettle, sufficient soft water to cover the cloth you wish to dye; then add 1 1/2 oz. cream of tartar for every pound of cloth. Boil a minute or two, add two oz. lilac dye and one oz. madder compound (both previously mixed in an earthen bowl), boil five minutes; now wet the cloth in warm water and wring it out and put it into the dye; boil the whole nearly an hour, take the cloth out and rinse it in clear cold water.

Blue Dye
Boil the cloth in a brass kettle for an hour, in a solution containing five parts of alum and three of tartar for every 32 parts of cloth. It is then to be thrown into warm water, previously mixed with a greater or less proportion of chemic blue, according to the shade the cloth is intended to receive. In this water it must be boiled until it has acquired the desired color.

Green Dye
For every pound of cloth add 3 1/2 oz. of alum and one pound of fustic. Steep (not boil) till the strength is out; soak the cloth till it acquires a good yellow, then remove the chips, and add the chemic blue by degrees till you have the desired color.

Charm to Stop Bleeding
I walk through a green forest;
There I find three wells, cool and cold;
The first is called courage
The second is called good,
And the third is called stop the blood. +++

Salve to heal burns

Pound or press the juice of male fern, and put it on the burnt spots and they will heal very fast. Better yet, however, if you smear the above juice upon a rag, and put it on like a plaster.

Charm to Banish Convulsive Fevers

Write the following letters on a piece of white paper, sew it on a piece of linen or muslin, and bang it around the neck until the fever leaves you:

   A b a x a C a t a b a x
   A b a x a C a t a b a x
   A b a x a C a t a b a
   A b a x a C a t a b
   A b a x a C a t a
   A b a x a C a t
   A b a x a C a
   A b a x a C
   A b a x a
   A b a x
   A b a
   A b
   A

Charm to Extinguish Fire without Fire

Write the following words on each side of a round plate, and throw it into the fire, and it will be extinguished forthwith:

   S A T O R
   A R E P O
   T E N E T
   O P E R A
   R O T A S

Remedy when someone is cursed
Let the person in perfect soberness and without having conversed with anyone, catch rain in a pot, before sunrise; boil on egg in this; bore three small holes in this egg with a needle, and carry it to an ant-hill made by big ants; and that person will feel relieved as soon as the egg is devoured.

The Hunter's Talisman
It is said that anyone going out hunting and carrying it in his game-bag, cannot but shoot something worth while and bring it home.
An old hermit once found an old, lame huntsman in a forest, lying beside the road and weeping. The hermit asked him the cause of his dejection. "Ah me, thou man of God, I am a poor, unfortunate being; I must annually furnish my lord with as many deer, and hares, and partridges, as a young and healthy huntsman could hunt up, or else I will be discharged from my office; now I am old and lame; besides game is getting scarce, and I cannot follow it up as I ought to; and I know not whit will become of me." Here the old man's feelings overcame him, and he could not utter another word. The hermit, upon this, took out a small piece of paper, upon which he wrote some words with a pencil, and handing it to the huntsman, he said: "there, old friend, put this in your game-bag whenever you go out hunting, and you shall certainly shoot something worth while, and bring it home, too; yet be careful to shoot no more than you necessarily need, nor to communicate it to anyone that might misuse it, on account of the high meaning contained in these words." The hermit then went on his journey, and after a little the huntsman

also arose, and without thinking of anything in particular he went into the woods, and had scarcely advanced a hundred yards when he shot as fine a roebuck as he ever saw in his life.

This huntsman was afterward and during his whole lifetime lucky in his hunting, so much so that he was considered one of the best hunters in that whole country. The following is what the hermit wrote on the paper:

Ut nemo in sense tentat, descendre nemo.

* *

*

At precedenti spectatur mantica tergo.

The best argument is to try it.

Charm for a Hunter
Pronounce the name of the hunter, (___), shoot whatever you please; shoot but hair and feathers with and what you give to poor people. + + +
Amen.

Charm to Fasten or Spell Bind Anything
You say, "Christ's cross and Christ's crown, Christ Jesus' colored blood, be thou every hour good. God, the Father, is before me; God, the Son, is beside me; God, the Holy Ghost, is behind me. Whoever now is stronger than these three persons may come, by day or night, to attack me." + + +
Then say the Lord's prayer three times.

Charm to further Spell Bind for Protection

After repeating the above, You speak, "At every step may Jesus walk with (*name*). He is my head; I am his limb; therefore, Jesus, be with (*name*)."

Charm to Release a Spell Bound Person

You horseman and footman, whom I here conjured at this time, you may pass on in the name of Jesus Christ, through the word of God and the will of Christ; ride ye on now and pass.

Solomon's Charm of Protection for People and Animals

In adversity and to repress the pride of Spirits

```
S A T O R
A R E P O
T E N E T
O P E R A
R O T A S
```

"His Domination shall be also from the one sea, unto the other, and from the flood unto the world's end"

This must be written on paper and surrounded by two circles then carried, hung or put in the animals feed.

NOTE:
Double Acrostics are that they read in every direction the same: horizontal, perpendicular, backwards and forwards. And must be read and printed with each letter in an individual square

and all letters in one big square secured by two circles lest one be set upon by a great vexing. It may be written on parchment, linen or muslin and secured by cords or for less permanent in chalk surrounded by holy salt and candles.

To know all things-Past-Present-Future

M I L O N
I R A G O
L A M A L
O G A R I
N O L I M

Place in a square in two circles.

To know things in the Past forgotten

N V D E T O N
V S I L A R O
D I R E M A T
E L E M E L E
T A M R R I D
O R A L I S V
N O T E D V N

Place in a square in two circles.

To know the signs of Tempests

        R O T H E R
        O R O R I E
        T O A R A H
        H O R A O T
        E I R O R O
        R E H T O R

Place in a square within two circles.

To know True and False Friends

        M E B H A E R
        E LI AI LE
        B I K O S I A
        H A O R O A H
        A I S O K I B
        E LI AI LE
        R E A H B E M

Place in a square within two circles.

To obtain Information and Enlightenment

        A L L U P
        L E I R U
        L I G I L
        U RI E L
        P U L L A

Place in a square within two circles.

To make Visions Appear in the Air

```
A P P A R E T
P
P
A
R
E
T
```

In a square with in two circles draw in the air and wait for the visions to appear.

To make Visions Appear in a glass or crystal Mirror

```
G I L I O N I N
I
L
I
O
N
I
N
```

In a square with in two circles and the mirror placed with in.

To make Visions Appear in the Water

A D M O N
D
M
O
N

Make into a square with in two circles and place with in your scrying bowl.

To make Visions Appear in your Hand

L E L E H
E
L
E
H

Make into a square within two circles and place in your hand.

To excite Tempests to cause Rain

S A G R I R
A
G
R
I
R

Make into a square with in two circles outside in the dust of a field.

To undo any Magick whatsoever

```
C   O   D   S   E   LI  M
O
H
A
B
I                       O
M                     O   C
```

Draw in a square – be concerned about placement – within three circles bound.

To heal the Bewitched

```
L  A  C  H  A  T
A              A
C              H
H              C
A              A
T  A  H  C  A  L
```

Draw in a square – be concerned about placement – with each letter in the square and all encompassed within three circles bound.

To Heal Malignant Fevers

    B E T E M
    E M E R E
    T E N E T
    E R E M E
    M E T E B

Draw in a square with each letter in a square and all within a circle and place on the person or hang on their bed post.

To Heal all kinds of Wounds

    H A P P I R
    A MA OS I
    P A RA O P
    P O A RA P
    I S OA M A
    R I P PA H

Draw in a square with each letter in a square and all within a circle and place on the wound (or write on a piece of muslin and wrap the wound with it).

Evening Hymn of St. Patrick

MAY thy holy angels,
O Christ, son of the living God,
tend our sleep, our rest,
our bright bed.
Let them reveal true visions
to us in our sleep,
O High prince of the universe,
O great mysterious King.
May no demons, no ill,
no injury or terrifying dreams
disturb our rest,
our prompt and swift repose.
May our waking,
our work and our activity be holy;
our sleep, our rest,
unhindered and untroubled.

Blessing

Whoever carries this book with him is safe from all his enemies, visible or invisible; and whoever has this book with him cannot die without the holy corpse of Jesus Christ, nor drown in any water, nor burn up in any fire, nor can any unjust sentence be passed upon him. So help me.

Sources:
My Generations:

For all culinary recipes, herbal, and magickal knowledge, charms, spells, how-to's, teas, brews, crafts, poetry, and fortune telling techniques not otherwise referenced I thank my Generations.

Contributing to 20% of the book in the area of Culinary Recipes: I wish to thank...

5% - Brenda Paulson – Gladys, VA
15% - Kara Vonovich - Huntington Beach, CA

The Leech book of Bald: also called the Lacnunga written by a monk named Bald and penned between 924-946 by a scribe named Cild. This is the oldest surviving medical book showing herbs as medicine. Anglo Saxon medical practices were truly holistic and sought to heal both body and spirit. Charms, amulets were used in conjunction with songs. Truly skilled leeches (herbalists, those skilled in Wort cunning) were highly prized individuals as healing women, monks and nuns. The latter having the education and therefore the ability to write it down.

St. Hildegard of Bingen (1098-1179)
Described the building stones of life and pointed out the natural healing powers found in trees, fruits, grains, spices, herbs, animals, birds, fish precious stones and metals and connected this healing power to the health of the whole person.
Abbess of the Benedictine order at Rupertsberg convent in the German Rhineland. Suffered severe migraines in which she claimed God commanded her to heal the sick and compile her herbal

fourmulas. Her books combine Catholicism and folk medicine. She is highly regarded as the only medieval woman to leave a written account of "wise woman healing practices".

She used the 4 elements of fire, air, water and earth for heat, dryness, moisture and cold and sought to balance them from within.

She introduced the four humours still used today of Choler (yellow bile) Choleric; blood – sanguine, phlegm-phlegmatic; melancholy (black bile) melancholy for use in healing.

She also put together several hymns and plays for the peace of body and spirit. See – Seqentia, canticles of Ecstasy for Hildegard's music.

Pow Wows; Or Long Lost Friend
By John George Hohman 1820
A Grimoire in the Pow Wow Tradition of the Pennsylvania Dutch. It is a rural European healing and hexing system which was imported across the pond into the States in the 18th and 19th century by German immigrants. Within it is the ways of the old Magick systems brought forth to new traditions. The Charms and spells are short and easily understood without loss of power.

Botanical.com a modern herbal by Maud Grievt
This site was used this to check any information I had about all herbs, flowers and seasonings.

Cunningham's Encyclopedia of Magical herbs
by Scott Cunningham. I consider this THE leading resource in all magical herbology and used it as a reference and to check all my materials.

Culpeper's Complete Herbal
By Nicholas Culpeper (1616-1654) During his lifetime he devoted much study to astrology and medicine. He left a legacy of a vast collection of herbal remedies which are still valuable today. Nicholas Culpeper was married with 7 children and was always willing to give free advice and help to the many poor who sought his aide.

3CatsMeow at hbd.org/brewery/cm3/index.html
Visit this site for an extensive list of great beers you can home brew, although I didn't include any in this book – I am sure going to try some!

The Grimoires and Magickal Writings of:
Whether used or not are given as a historical references to you the reader for further exploration.

Sefer Raziel Ha-Malakh
Enoch
Moses
Levi
Solomon
Dogma ET Ritual
Sanctum Regnum
Arthur Edward Waite
Eliphias Levi
W. Wynn Westcott
Rev. Doctor Johannes Faust
S. L. MacGregor Mathers
John Dee
Peter de Abano
Henry Cornelius
John G. White
Stephen J. Zietz
Franz Bardon

Marius Malchus
A.O. Spare
Phil Hine
Robert Blosh
Simon
Ray Sherwin
Saint John of the Cross
Karl von Eckhartshausen
Dr. Micheal De Molinos
Herbert Stanley Redgrove
John Yarker
Isreal Regardie
Francis Barrett
Dion Fortune
Zoroaster
G.R.S. Mead
Phillipus Theophrastus Paracelsus
Christian Rosenkreutz
Hermes Trismeqistus
J. S. M. Ward
Gerald Massey
Anton Josef Kirchwager
Phil Hansford
Paul Foster Case
Sephariel
Roger Bacon
Raymond and Susan Drewry
Pashcal Beverly Randolph
Dr. Georg Lomer
M. A. Atwood
W. B. Yeats
Charles G. Leland
K. Amber
E.A. Wallis Budge
Donald Mackenzie
Richard Payne Knight

Thomas Wright
Margaret Alice Murray
Sir James George Frazer
F.L. Griffith
Herbert Thompson
Heinrich Kramer
James Sprenger

Love is the Law – Love under Will
Under Love, Under Will – do as Thou wilt!

Made in the USA
San Bernardino, CA
22 May 2013